THE BAUM PLAN
for
FINANCIAL INDEPENDENCE

AND OTHER STORIES

THE BAUM PLAN
for
FINANCIAL INDEPENDENCE
AND OTHER STORIES

JOHN KESSEL

Small Beer Press
Easthampton, MA

Those portions of the story "Powerless" dealing with behavioral
effects of brain damage draw from "Law, Responsibility, and the Brain"
by Dean Mobbs, Hakwan C. Lau, Owen D. Jones, and Christopher D.
Frith, published in *PloS Biology*, Creative Commons ℗ 2007, Mobbs, et al.

Small Beer Press
150 Pleasant Street #306
Easthampton, MA 01027
www.smallbeerpress.com
info@smallbeerpress.com

Distributed to the trade by Consortium.

Library of Congress Cataloging-in-Publication Data

Kessel, John.
  The Baum plan for financial independence and other stories / John Kessel.
    p. cm.
  ISBN 978-1-931520-51-5 (hardcover : alk. paper) -- ISBN 978-1-931520-50-8 (pbk. : alk. paper)
  I. Title.
  PS3561.E6675B38 2008
  813'.54--dc22
                                2007052319

First edition 1 2 3 4 5 6 7 8 9

Printed on 50# Natures Natural 50% post consumer recycled paper by Thomson-Shore of Dexter, MI.
Text set in Centaur MT 11.5. Titles set in ITC Slimbach 18.

Cover art © Nathan Huang 2007.

CONTENTS

For Emma Hall Kessel
Tell me a story, Dad.

The Baum Plan for Financial Independence

—for Wilton Barnhardt

When I picked her up at the Stop 'n Shop on Route 28, Dot was wearing a short black skirt and red sneakers just like the ones she had taken from the bargain rack the night we broke into the Sears in Hendersonville five years earlier. I couldn't help but notice the curve of her hip as she slid into the front seat of my old T-Bird. She leaned over and gave me a kiss, bright red lipstick and breath smelling of cigarettes. "Just like old times," she said.

The Sears had been my idea, but after we got into the store that night all the other ideas had been Dot's, including the game on the bed in the furniture department and me clocking the night watchman with the anodized aluminum flashlight I took from Hardware, sending him to the hospital with a concussion and me to three years in Central. When the cops showed up, Dot was nowhere to be found. That was all right. A man has to take responsibility for his own actions; at least that's what they told me in the group therapy sessions that the prison shrink ran on Thursday nights. But I never knew a woman who could make me do the things that Dot could make me do.

One of the guys at those sessions was Radioactive Roy Dunbar, who had a theory about how we were all living in a computer and none of this was real. Well if this isn't real, I told him, I don't know what real is. The softness of Dot's breast or the shit smell of the crapper in the Highway 28 Texaco, how can there be anything more real than that? Radioactive Roy and the people like him are just looking for an exit door. I can understand that. Everybody dreams of an exit door sometimes.

I slipped the car into gear and pulled out of the station onto the highway. The sky was red above the Blue Ridge, the air blowing in the

I

windows smoky with the ash of the forest fires burning a hundred miles to the northwest.

"Cat got your tongue, darlin'?" Dot said.

I pushed the cassette into the deck and Willie Nelson was singing "Hello Walls." "Where are we going, Dot?"

"Just point this thing west for twenty or so. When you come to a sign that says Potters Glen, make a right on the next dirt road."

Dot pulled a pack of Kools out of her purse, stuck one in her mouth, and punched the car's cigarette lighter.

"Doesn't work," I said.

She pawed through her purse for thirty seconds, then clipped it shut. "Shit," she said. "You got a match, Sid?" Out of the corner of my eye I watched the cigarette bobble up and down as she spoke.

"Sorry, sweetheart, no."

She took the cigarette from her mouth, stared at it for a moment, and flipped it out her opened window.

Hello window. I actually had a box of Ohio Blue Tips in the glove compartment, but I didn't want Dot to smoke because it was going to kill her someday. My mother smoked, and I remember her wet cough and the skin stretched tight over her cheekbones as she lay in the upstairs bedroom of the big house in Lynchburg, puffing on a Winston. Whenever my old man came in to clear her untouched lunch he asked her if he could have one, and mother would smile at him, eyes big, and pull two more coffin nails out of the red-and-white pack with her nicotine-stained fingers.

One time after I saw this happen, I followed my father down to the kitchen. As he bent over to put the tray on the counter, I snatched the cigarettes from his shirt pocket and crushed them into bits over the plate of pears and cottage cheese. I glared at him, daring him to get mad. After a few seconds he just pushed past me to the living room and turned on the TV.

That's the story of my life: me trying to save the rest of you—and the rest of you ignoring me.

On the other side of Almond it was all mountains. The road twisted, the headlights flashing against the tops of trees on the downhill side and the cut earth on the uphill. I kept drifting over the double yellow line as we came in and out of turns, but the road was deserted. Occasionally we'd pass some broken-down house with a battered pickup in the driveway and a rust-spotted propane tank outside in the yard.

The sign for Potters Glen surged out of the darkness, and we turned off onto a rutted gravel track that was even more twisted than the paved road. The track rose steeply; the T-Bird's suspension was shot, and my rotten muffler scraped more than once when we bottomed out. If Dot's plan required us sneaking up on anybody, it was not going to work. But she had assured me that the house on the ridge was empty and she knew where the money was hidden.

Occasionally the branch of a tree would scrape across the windshield or side mirror. The forest here was dry as tinder after the summer's drought, the worst on record, and in my rearview mirror I could see the dust we were raising in the taillights. We had been ten minutes on this road when Dot said, "Okay, stop now."

The cloud of dust that had been following us caught up and billowed, settling slowly in the headlight beams. "Kill the lights," Dot said.

In the silence and darkness that came, the whine of cicadas moved closer. Dot fumbled with her purse, and when she opened the car door to get out, in the dome light I saw she had a map written on a piece of notebook paper. I opened the trunk and got out a pry bar and pair of bolt cutters. When I came around to her side of the car, she was shining a flashlight on the map.

"It shouldn't be more than a quarter of a mile farther up this road," she said.

"Why can't we just drive right up there?"

"Someone might hear."

"But you said the place was deserted."

"It is. But there's no sense taking chances."

I laughed. Dot not taking chances? That was funny. She didn't think so, and punched me in the arm. "Stop it," she said, but then she giggled. I swept the arm holding the tools around her waist and kissed her. She pushed me away, but not roughly. "Let's go," she said.

We walked up the dirt road. When Dot shut off the flashlight, there was only the faint moon coming through the trees, but after our eyes adjusted it was enough. The dark forest loomed over us. Walking through the woods at night always made me feel like I was in some teen horror movie. I expected a guy in a hockey mask to come shrieking from between the trees to cut us to ribbons with fingernails like straight razors.

Dot had heard about this summer cabin that was owned by the rich people she had worked for in Charlotte. They were Broyhills or related to the Broyhills, old money from the furniture business. Or maybe it was Dukes and tobacco. Anyway, they didn't use this house but a month or so out of the year. Some caretaker came by every so often, but he didn't live on the premises. Dot heard the daughter telling her friend that the family kept ten thousand dollars in cash up there in case another draft riot made it necessary for them to skip town for a while.

So we would just break in and take the money. That was the plan. It seemed a little dicey to me; I had grown up with money—my old man owned a car dealership, before he went bust. Leaving piles of cash lying around their vacation home did not seem like regular rich people behavior to me. But Dot could be very convincing even when she wasn't convincing, and my father claimed I never had a lick of sense anyway. It took us twenty minutes to come up on the clearing, and there was the house. It was bigger than I imagined it. Rustic, flagstone chimney and entranceway, timbered walls and wood shingles. Moonlight glinted off the windows in the three dormers that faced front, but all the downstairs windows were shuttered.

I took the pry bar to the hinges on one of the shuttered windows, and after some struggle they gave. The window was dead-bolted from the inside, but we knocked out one of the panes and unlatched it. I boosted Dot through the window and followed her in.

Dot used the flashlight to find the light switch. The furniture was large and heavy; a big oak coffee table that we had to move in order to take up the rug to see whether there was a safe underneath must have weighed two hundred pounds. We pulled down all the pictures from the walls. One of them was a woodcut print of Mary and Jesus, but instead of Jesus the woman was holding a fish; in the background of the picture, outside a window, a funnel cloud tore up a dirt road. The picture gave me the creeps. Behind it was nothing but plaster wall.

I heard the clink of glass behind me. Dot was pulling bottles out of the liquor cabinet to see if there was a compartment hidden behind them.

I went over, took down a glass, and poured myself a couple of fingers of Glenfiddich. I sat in a leather armchair and drank it, watching Dot search. She was getting frantic. When she came by the chair I grabbed her around the hips and pulled her into my lap.

"Hey! Lay off!" she squawked.

"Let's try the bedroom," I said.

She bounced off my lap. "Good idea." She left the room.

This was turning into a typical Dot odyssey, all tease and no tickle. I put down my glass and followed her.

I found her in the bedroom rifling through a chest of drawers, throwing clothes on the bed. I opened the closet. Inside hung a bunch of jackets and flannel shirts and blue jeans, with a pair of riding boots and some sandals lined up neatly on the floor. I pushed the hanging clothes apart, and there, set into the back wall, was a door. "Dot, bring that flashlight over here."

She came over and shined the flashlight into the closet. I ran my hand over the seam of the door. It was about three feet high, flush with the wall, the same off-white color but cool to the touch, made of metal. No visible hinges and no lock, just a flip-up handle like on a tackle box.

"That's not a safe," Dot said.

"No shit, Sherlock."

She shouldered past me, crouched down, and flipped up the handle. The door pushed open onto darkness. She shined the flashlight ahead of her; I could not see past her. "Jesus Christ Almighty," she said.

"What?"

"Stairs." Dot moved forward, then stepped down. I pushed the clothes aside and followed her.

The carpet on the floor stopped at the doorjamb; inside was a concrete floor and then a narrow flight of stairs leading down. A black metal handrail ran down the right side. The walls were of roughed concrete, unpainted. Dot moved ahead of me down to the bottom, where she stopped.

When I got there I saw why. The stairs let out into a large, dark room. The floor ended halfway across it, and beyond that, at either side, to the left and right, under the arching roof, were open tunnels. From one tunnel opening to the other ran a pair of gleaming rails. We were standing on a subway platform.

Dot walked to the end of the platform and shined the flashlight up the tunnel. The rails gleamed away into the distance.

"This doesn't look like the safe," I said.

"Maybe it's a bomb shelter," Dot said.

Before I could figure out a polite way to laugh at her, I noticed a light growing from the tunnel. A slight breeze kicked up. The light grew like an approaching headlight, and with it a hum in the air. I backed toward the stairs, but Dot just peered down the tunnel. "Dot!" I called. She waved a hand at me, and though she dropped back a step she kept watching. Out of the tunnel glided a car that slid to a stop in front of us. It was no bigger than a pickup. Teardrop shaped, made of gleaming silver metal, its bright single light glared down the track. The car had no windows, but as we stood gaping at it a door slid open in its side. The inside was dimly lit, with plush red seats.

Dot stepped forward and stuck her head inside.

"What are you doing?" I asked.

"It's empty," Dot said. "No driver. Come on."

"Get serious."

Dot crouched and got inside. She turned and ducked her head to look at me out of the low doorway. "Don't be a pussy, Sid."

"Don't be crazy, Dot. We don't even know what this thing is."

"Ain't you ever been out of Mayberry? It's a subway."

"But who built it? Where does it go? And what the hell is it doing in Jackson County?"

"How should I know? Maybe we can find out."

The car just sat there. The air was still. The ruby light from behind her cast Dot's face in shadow. I followed her into the car. "I don't know about this."

"Relax."

There were two bench seats, each wide enough to hold two people, and just enough space on the door side to move from one to the other. Dot sat on one of the seats with her big purse in her lap, calm as a Christian holding four aces. I sat down next to her. As soon as I did, the door slid shut and the car began to move, picking up speed smoothly, pushing us back into the firm upholstery. The only sound was a gradually increasing hum that reached a middle pitch and stayed there. I tried to breathe. There was no clack from the rails, no vibration. In front of us the car narrowed to a bullet-nosed front, and in the heart of that nose was a circular window. Through the window I saw only blackness. After a while I wondered if we were still moving, until a light appeared ahead, first a small speck, then grew brighter and larger until it slipped off past us to the side at a speed that told me the little car was moving faster than I cared to figure.

"These people who own the house," I asked Dot, "where on Mars did you say they came from?"

Dot reached in her purse and took out a pistol, set it down on her lap, and fumbled around in the bag until she pulled out a pack of Juicy Fruit. She pulled out a stick, then held the pack out to me. "Gum?"

"No thanks."

She put the pack back in the purse, and the pistol, too. She slipped the yellow paper sleeve off her gum, unwrapped the foil, and stuck the gum into her mouth. After refolding the foil neatly, she slid it back into the gum sleeve and set the now empty stick on the back of the seat in front of us.

I was about to scream. "Where the fuck are we going, Dot? What's going on here?"

"I don't have any idea where we're going, Sid. If I knew you were going to be such a wuss, I would never of called you."

"Did you know about any of this?"

"Of course not. But we're going to be somewhere soon, I bet."

I got off the seat and moved to the front bench, my back to her. That didn't set my nerves any easier. I could hear her chewing her gum, and felt her eyes on the back of my neck. The car sped into blackness, broken only by the occasional spear of light flashing past. As we did not seem to be getting anywhere real soon, I had some time to contemplate the ways in which I was a fool, number one being the way I let an ex-lap dancer from Mebane lead me around by my imagination for the last ten years.

Just when I thought I couldn't get any more pissed, Dot moved up from the backseat, sat down next to me, and took my hand. "I'm sorry, Sid. Someday I'll make it up to you."

"Yeah?" I said. "So give me some of that gum." She gave me a stick. Her tidy gum wrapper had fallen onto the seat between us; I crumpled the wrapper of my own next to hers.

I had not started in on chewing when the hum of the car lowered and I felt us slowing down. The front window got a little lighter, and the car came to a stop. The door slid open.

The platform it opened onto was better lit than the one under the house in the Blue Ridge. Standing on it waiting were three people, two men and a woman. The two men wore identical dark suits of the kind bankers with too much money wore in downtown Charlotte: the suits hung the way no piece of clothing had ever hung on me—tailored closer than a mother's kiss. The woman, slender, with blond hair done up tight as a librarian's—yet there was no touch of the librarian about her—wore a dark blue dress. They stood there for a moment, then one of the men said, "Excuse me? You're here. Are you getting out?"

Dot got up and nudged me, and I finally got my nerveless legs to work. We stepped out onto the platform, and the three people got into the car, the door slid shut, and it glided off into the darkness.

It was cold on the platform, and a light breeze came from an archway across from us. Instead of rough concrete like the tunnel under the house, here the ceiling and walls were smooth stucco. Carved above the arch was a crouching man wearing some kind of Roman or Greek toga, cradling a book under one arm and holding a torch in the other. He had a wide brow and a long, straight nose and looked like a guard in Central named Pisarkiewicz, only a lot smarter. Golden light filtered down from fixtures like frogs' eggs in the ceiling.

"What now?" I asked.

Dot headed for the archway. "What have we got to lose?"

Past the arch a ramp ran upward, switchbacking every forty feet or so. A couple of women, as well dressed as the one we'd seen on the platform, passed us going the other way. We tried to look like we belonged there, though Dot's hair was a rat's nest, I was dressed in jeans and sneakers, I had not shaved since morning, and my breath smelled of scotch and Juicy Fruit.

At the top of the third switchback, the light brightened. From ahead of us came the sound of voices, echoing as if in a very large room. We reached the final archway, the floor leveled off, and we stepped into the hall.

I did not think there were so many shades of marble. The place was as big as a train station, a great open room with polished stone floors, a domed ceiling a hundred feet above us, a dozen Greek half-columns set into the far wall. Bright sun shining through tall windows between them fell on baskets of flowers and huge potted palms. Around the hall stood a number of booths like information kiosks, and grilled counters like an old-fashioned bank, at which polite staff in pale green shirts dealt with the customers. But it was not all business. Mixed among people carrying briefcases stood others in groups of three or four holding pale drinks in tall glasses or leaning casually on some counter chatting one-on-one with those manning the booths. In one corner a man in a green suit played jazz on a grand piano.

It was a cross between Grand Central Station and the ballroom at the Biltmore House. Dot and I stood out like plow horses at a cotillion. The couple hundred people scattered through the great marble room were big-city dressed. Even the people who dressed down wore hundred-dollar chinos with cashmere sweaters knotted casually around their necks. The place reeked of money.

Dot took my hand and pulled me across the floor. She spotted a table with a fountain and a hundred wine glasses in rows on the starched white tablecloth. A pink marble cherub with pursed lips like a cupid's bow poured pale wine from a pitcher into the basin that surrounded his feet. Dot handed me one of the glasses and took one for herself, held it under the stream falling from the pitcher.

She took a sip. "Tastes good," she said. "Try it."

As we sipped wine and eyed the people, a man in a uniform shirt with a brass name pin that said "Brad" came up to us. "Would you like to wash and brush up? Wash and Brush Up is over there," he said, pointing across the hall to another marble archway. He had a British accent.

"Thanks," said Dot. "We just wanted to wet our whistles first."

The man winked at her. "Now that your whistle is wet, don't be afraid to use it any time I can be of service." He smirked at me. "That goes for you too, sir."

"Fuck you," I said.

"It's been done already," the man said, and walked away.

I put down the wineglass. "Let's get out of here," I said.

"I want to go to see what's over there."

Wash and Brush Up turned out to be a suite of rooms where we were greeted by a young woman named Elizabeth and a young man named Martin. You need to clean up, they said, and separated us. I wasn't going to have any of it, but Dot seemed to have lost her mind—she went off with Martin. After grumbling for a while, I let Elizabeth take me to a small dressing room, where she made me strip and put on a robe. After that came the shower, the haircut, the steambath, the massage. Between the steambath and massage they brought me food, something like a cheese quesadilla only much better than anything like it I had ever tasted. While I ate, Elizabeth left me alone in a room with a curtained window. I pulled the curtain aside and looked out.

The window looked down from a great height on a city unlike any I had ever seen. It was like a picture out of a kid's book, something Persian about it, and something Japanese. Slender green towers, great domed buildings, long, low structures like warehouses made of jade. The sun beat down pitilessly on citizens who went from street to street between the fine buildings with bowed heads and plodding steps. I saw a team of four men in purple shirts pulling a cart; I saw other men with sticks herd children down to a park; I saw vehicles rumble past tired street workers, kicking up clouds of yellow dust so thick that I could taste it.

The door behind me opened, and Elizabeth stuck her head in. I dropped the curtain as if she had caught me whacking off. "Time for your massage," she said.

"Right," I said, and followed.

When I came out, there was Dot, tiny in her big plush robe, her hair clean and combed out and her finger and toenails painted shell pink. She looked about fourteen.

"Nice haircut," she said to me.

"Where are our clothes?" I demanded of Martin.

"We'll get them for you," he said. He gestured to one of the boys. "But for now, come with me."

Then they sat us down in front of a large computer screen and showed us a catalog of clothing you could not find outside of a Neiman Marcus. They had images of us, like 3D paper dolls, that they called up on the screen and that they could dress any way they liked so you could see how you would look. Dot was in hog heaven. "What's this going to cost us?" I said.

Martin laughed as if I had made a good joke. "How about some silk shirts?" he asked me. "You have a good build. I know you're going to like them."

By the time we were dressed, the boy had come back with two big green shopping bags with handles. "What's this?" Dot asked, taking hers.

"Your old clothes," Martin said.

I took mine. I looked at myself in the mirror. I wore a blue shirt, a gray tie with a skinny knot and a long, flowing tail, ebony cuff links, a gunmetal gray silk jacket, and black slacks with a crease that would cut ice. The shoes were of leather as soft as a baby's skin and as comfortable as if I had broken them in for three months. I looked great.

Dot had settled on a champagne-colored dress with a scoop neckline, pale pumps, a simple gold necklace, and earrings that set off her dark hair. She smelled faintly of violets and looked better than lunch break at a chocolate factory.

"We've got to get out of here," I whispered to her.

"Thanks for stopping by!" Elizabeth and Martin said in unison. They escorted us to the door. "Come again soon!"

The hall was only slightly less busy than it had been. "All right, Dot. We head right for the subway. This place gives me the creeps."

"No," said Dot. She grabbed me by the arm that wasn't carrying my old clothes and dragged me across the floor toward one of the grilled windows. No one gave us a second glance. We were dressed the same as everyone else, now, and fit right in.

At the window another young woman in green greeted us. "I am Miss Goode. How may I help you?"

"We came to get our money," said Dot.

"How much?" Miss Goode asked.

Dot turned to me. "What do you say, Sid? Would twenty million be enough?"

"We can do that," said Miss Goode. "Just come around behind the counter to my desk."

Dot started after her. I grabbed Dot's shoulder. "What the fuck are you talking about?" I whispered.

"Just go along and keep quiet."

Miss Goode led us to a large glass-topped desk. "We'll need a photograph, of course. And a number." She spoke into a phone: "Daniel, bring out two cases. . . . That's right." She called up a page on her computer and examined it. "Your bank," she said to me, "is Banque Thaler, Geneva. Your number is PN68578443. You'll have to memorize it eventually. Here, write it on your palm for now." She handed me a very nice ballpoint pen. Then she gave another number to Dot.

While she was doing this, a man came out of a door in the marble wall behind her. He carried two silver metal briefcases and set them on the edge of Miss Goode's desk in front of Dot and me.

"Thank you, Daniel," she said. She turned to us. "Go ahead. Open them!"

I pulled the briefcase toward me and snapped it open. It was filled with tight bundles of crisp new one-hundred-dollar bills. Thirty of them.

"This is wonderful," Dot said. "Thank you so much!"

I closed my case and stood up. "Time to go, Dot."

"Just a minute," said Miss Goode. "I'll need your full name."

"Full name? What for?"

"For the Swiss accounts. All you've got there is three hundred thousand. The rest will be in your account. We'll need your photograph, too."

Dot tugged my elegant sleeve. "Sid forgot about that," she explained to Miss Goode. "Always in such a hurry. His name is Sidney Xavier Dubose. D-U-B-O-S-E. I'm Dorothy Gale."

I had reached my breaking point. "Shut up, Dot."

"Now for the photographs . . ." Miss Goode began.

"You can't have my photograph." I pulled away from Dot. I had the briefcase in my right hand and my bag of clothes under my left.

"That's all right," said Miss Goode. "We'll use your photographs from the tailor program. Just run along. But come again!"

I was already stalking across the floor, my new shoes clipping along like metronomes. People parted to let me by. I went right for the ramp that led to the subway. A thin man smoking a long cigarette watched me curiously as I passed one of the tables; I put my hand against his chest and knocked him down. He sprawled there in astonishment, but did nothing; nor did anyone else.

By the time I hit the ramp I was jogging. At the bottom the platform was deserted; the bubble lights still shone gold, and you could not tell whether it was night or day. Dot came up breathlessly behind me.

"What is wrong with you!" she shouted.

I felt exhausted. I could not tell how long it had been since we broke into the mountain house. "What's wrong with me? What's wrong with this whole setup? This is crazy. What are they going to do to us? This can't be real; it has to be some kind of scam."

"If you think it's a scam, just give me that briefcase. I'll take care of it for you, you stupid redneck bastard."

I stood there sullenly. I didn't know what to say. She turned from me and went to the other end of the platform, as far away as she could get.

After a few minutes the light grew in the tunnel, and the car, or one just like it, slid to a stop before us. The door opened. I got in immediately, and Dot followed. We sat next to each other in silence. The door shut, and the vehicle picked up speed until it was racing along as insanely as it had so many hours ago.

Dot tried to talk to me, but I just looked at the floor. Under the seat I saw the two gum wrappers, one of them crumpled into a knot, the other neatly folded as if it were still full.

That was the last time I ever saw Dot. I live in France now, but I have a house in Mexico and one in Toronto. In Canada I can still go to stock car races. Somehow that doesn't grab me the way it used to.

Instead I drink wine that comes in bottles that have corks. I read books. I listen to music that has no words. All because, as it turned out, I did have a ten-million-dollar Swiss bank account. The money changed everything, more than I ever could have reckoned. It was like a sword hanging over my head, like a wall between me and who I used to be. Within a month I left North Carolina: it made me nervous to stay in the state knowing that the house in the Blue Ridge was still there.

Sometimes I'm tempted to go back and see whether there really is a door in the back of that closet.

When Dot and I climbed the concrete stairs and emerged into the house, it was still night. It might have been only a minute after we went down. I went out to the living room, sat in the rustic leather chair, picked up the glass I had left next to it, and filled it to the brim with scotch. My briefcase full of three hundred thousand dollars stood on the hardwood floor beside the chair. I was dressed in a couple of thousand dollars' worth of casual clothes; my shoes alone probably cost more than a month's rent on any place that I had ever lived.

Dot sat on the sofa and poured herself a drink, too. After a while, she said, "I told you I'd make it up to you someday."

"How did you know about this?" I asked. "What is it?"

"It's a dream come true," Dot said. "You don't look a dream come true in the mouth."

"One person's dream come true is somebody else's nightmare," I said. "Somebody always has to pay." I had never thought that before, but as I spoke it I realized it was true.

Dot finished her scotch, picked up her briefcase and the green bag with her old skirt, sweater, and shoes, and headed for the door. She paused there and turned to me. She looked like twenty million bucks. "Are you coming?"

I followed her out. There was still enough light from the moon that we were able to make our way down the dirt road to my car. The insects chirped in the darkness. Dot opened the passenger door and got in.

"Wait a minute," I said. "Give me your bag."

Dot handed me her green bag. I dumped it out on the ground next to the car, then dumped my own out on top of it. I crumpled the bags and shoved them under the clothes for kindling. On top lay the denim jacket I had been wearing the night I got arrested in the Sears, that the state had kept for me while I served my time, and that I had put back on the day I left stir.

"What are you doing?" Dot asked.

"Bonfire," I said. "Goodbye to the old Dot and Sid."

"But you don't have any matches."

"Reach in the glove compartment. There's a box of Blue Tips."

Every Angel Is Terrifying

Bobby Lee grabbed the grandmother's body under the armpits and dragged her up the other side of the ditch. "Whyn't you help him, Hiram," Railroad said.

Hiram took off his coat, skidded down into the ditch after Bobby Lee, and got hold of the old lady's legs. Together he and Bobby Lee lugged her across the field toward the woods. Her broken blue hat was still pinned to her head, which lolled against Bobby Lee's shoulder. The woman's face watched Railroad all the way into the shadow of the trees.

Railroad carried the cat over to the Studebaker. It occurred to him that he didn't know the cat's name, and now that the whole family was dead he never would. It was a calico, gray striped with a broad white face and an orange nose. "What's your name, puss-puss?" he whispered, scratching it behind the ears. The cat purred. One by one Railroad went round and rolled up the windows of the car. A fracture zigzagged across the windshield, and the front passenger's vent window was shattered. He stuffed Hiram's coat into the hole. Then he put the cat inside the car and shut the door. The cat put its front paws up on the dashboard and, watching him, gave a silent meow.

Railroad pushed up his glasses and stared off toward the tree line. The place was hot and still, silence broken only by birdsong from somewhere up the embankment. He squinted up into the cloudless sky. Only a couple of hours of sun left. He rubbed the spot on his shoulder where the grandmother had touched him. Somehow he had wrenched it when he jerked away from her.

The last thing the grandmother had said picked at him: "You're one of my own children." The old lady looked familiar, but nothing like his mother. But maybe his father had sown some wild oats in the old days— Railroad knew he had—could the old lady have been his mother, for real?

It would explain why the woman who had raised him, the sweetest of women, was saddled with a son as bad as he was.

The idea caught in his head. He wished he'd had the sense to ask the grandmother a few questions. The old woman might have been sent to tell him the truth.

When Hiram and Bobby Lee came back, they found Railroad leaning under the hood of the car.

"What we do now?" Bobby Lee asked.

"Police could be here any minute," Hiram said. Blood was smeared on the leg of his khaki pants. "Somebody might of heard the shots."

Railroad pulled himself out from under the hood. "Onliest thing we got to worry about now, Hiram, is how we get this radiator to stop leaking. You find a tire iron and straighten out this here fan. Bobby Lee, you get the belt off the other car."

It took longer than the half hour Hiram had estimated to get the people's car back on the road. By the time they did it was twilight, and the red-dirt road simmered in the shadows of the pinewoods. They pushed the stolen Hudson they'd been driving off into the trees and got into the Studebaker.

Railroad gripped the wheel of the car and they bounced down the dirt road toward the main highway. Beside him, hat pushed back on his head, Hiram went through the dead man's wallet, while in the back seat Bobby Lee had the cat on his lap and was scratching it under the chin. "Kitty-kitty-kitty-kitty-kitty," he murmured.

"Sixty-eight dollars," Hiram said. "With the twenty-two from the purse, that makes ninety." He turned around and handed a wad of bills to Bobby Lee. "Get rid of that damn cat," he said. "Want me to hold yours for you?" he asked Railroad.

Railroad reached over, took the bills, and stuffed them into the pocket of the yellow shirt with bright blue parrots he wore. It had belonged to the husband who'd been driving the car. Bailey Boy, the grandmother had called him. Railroad's shoulder twinged.

The car shuddered; the wheels had been knocked out of kilter when it rolled. If he tried pushing past fifty, it would shake itself right off the road. Railroad felt the warm weight of his pistol inside his belt, against his belly. Bobby Lee hummed tunelessly in the back seat. Hiram was quiet,

fidgeting, looking out at the dark trees. He tugged his battered coat out
of the vent window, tried to shake some of the wrinkles out of it. "You
oughtn't to use a man's coat without saying to him," he grumbled.

Bobby Lee spoke up. "He didn't want the cat to get away."

Hiram sneezed. "Will you throw that damn animal out the damn
window?"

"She never hurt you none," Bobby Lee said.

Railroad said nothing. He had always imagined that the world was
slightly unreal, that he was meant to be a citizen of some other place. His
mind was a box. Outside the box was a realm of distraction, amusement,
annoyance. Inside the box his real life went on, the struggle between
what he knew and what he didn't know. He had a way of acting—polite,
detached—because that way he wouldn't be bothered. When he was
bothered, he got mad. When he got mad, bad things happened.

He had always been prey to remorse, but now he felt it more fully than
he had since he was a boy. He hadn't paid enough attention. He'd pegged
the old lady as a hypocrite and had gone back into his box, thinking her
just another fool from that puppet world. But the moment of her touching
him—she wanted to comfort him. And he'd shot her.

What was it the woman had said? "You could be honest if you'd
only try. . . . Think how wonderful it would be to settle down and live a
comfortable life and not have to think about somebody chasing you all
the time."

He knew she was only saying that to save her life. But that didn't
mean it couldn't be a message.

Outside the box, Hiram asked, "What was all that yammer yammer
with the grandmother about Jesus? We doing all the killing while you
yammer."

"He did shoot the old lady," Bobby Lee said.

"And made us carry her to the woods, when if he'd of waited she
could of walked there like the others. We're the ones get blood on our
clothes."

Railroad said quietly, "You don't like the way things are going, son?"

Hiram twitched against the seat like he was itchy between the shoulder
blades. "I ain't sayin' that. I just want out of this state."

"We going to Atlanta. In Atlanta we can get lost."

"Gonna get me a girl!" Bobby Lee said.

"They got more cops in Atlanta than the rest of the state put together," Hiram said. "In Florida . . ."

Without taking his eyes off the road, Railroad snapped his right hand across the bridge of Hiram's nose. Hiram jerked, more startled than hurt, and his hat tumbled off into the back seat.

Bobby Lee laughed, and handed Hiram his hat.

It was after 11:00 when they hit the outskirts of Atlanta. Railroad pulled into a diner, the Sweet Spot, red brick and an asbestos-shingled roof, the air smelling of cigarettes and pork barbecue. Hiram rubbed some dirt from the lot into the stain on his pants leg. Railroad unlocked the trunk and found the dead man's suitcase, full of clothes. He carried it in with them.

On the radio that sat on the shelf behind the counter, Kitty Wells sang "It Wasn't God Who Made Honky-Tonk Angels." Railroad studied the menu, front and back, and ordered biscuits and gravy. While they ate Bobby Lee ran on about girls, and Hiram sat smoking. Railroad could tell Hiram was getting ready to do something stupid. Railroad didn't need either of them anymore. So after they finished eating, he left the car keys on the table and took the suitcase into the men's room. He locked the door. He pulled his .38 out of his waistband, put it on the sink, and changed out of the too-tight dungarees into some of the dead husband's baggy trousers. He washed his face and hands. He cleaned his glasses on the tail of the parrot shirt, then tucked in the shirt. He stuck the .38 into the suitcase and came out again. Bobby Lee and Hiram were gone, and the car was no longer in the parking lot. The bill on the table, next to Hiram's still-smoldering cigarette, was for six dollars and eighty cents.

Railroad sat in the booth drinking his coffee. In the window of the diner, near the door, he had noticed a piece of cardboard saying, "WANTED: FRY COOK." When he was done with the coffee, he untaped the sign and headed to the register. After he paid the bill he handed the cashier the sign. "I'm your man," he said.

The cashier called the manager. "Mr. Cauthron, this man says he's a cook."

Mr. Cauthron was maybe thirty-five years old. His carrot red hair stood up in a pompadour like a rooster's comb, and a little belly swelled out over his belt. "What's your name?"

"Lloyd Bailey."

"Lloyd, what experience do you have?"

"I can cook anything on this here menu," Railroad said.

The manager took him back to the kitchen. "Stand aside, Shorty," the manager said to the tall black man at the griddle. "Fix me a Denver omelet," he said to Railroad.

Railroad washed his hands, put on an apron, broke two eggs into a bowl. He threw handfuls of chopped onion, green pepper, and diced ham onto the griddle. When the onions were soft, he poured the beaten eggs over the ham and vegetables, added salt and cayenne pepper.

When he slid the finished omelet onto a plate, the manager bent down over it as if he were inspecting the paint job on a used car. He straightened up. "Pay's thirty dollars a week. Be here at six in the morning."

Out in the lot Railroad set down his bag and looked around. Cicadas buzzed in the hot city night. Around the corner from the diner he'd spotted a big Victorian house with a sign on the porch, "Rooms for Rent." He was about to start walking when, out of the corner of his eye, he caught something move by a trash barrel. He peered into the gloom and saw the cat leap up to the top to get at the garbage. He went over, held out his hand. The cat didn't run; it sniffed him, butted its head against his hand.

He picked it up, cradled it under his arm, and carried it and the bag to the rooming house. Under dense oaks, it was a big tan clapboard mansion with green shutters and hanging baskets of begonias on the porch, and a green porch swing. The thick oval leaded glass of the door was beveled around the edge, the brass of the handle dark with age.

The door was unlocked. His heart jumped a bit at the opportunity, but at the same time he wanted to warn the proprietor against such foolishness. Off to one side of the entrance was a little table with a doily, vase, and dried flowers; across from it a brass plate on a door said, "Manager."

Railroad knocked. After a moment the door opened and a woman with the face of an angel appeared. She was not young, perhaps forty, with very white skin and blond hair. She looked at him, smiled, saw the cat under his arm. "What a sweet animal," she said.

"I'd like a room," he said.

"I'm sorry. We don't cater to pets," the woman said, not unkindly.

"This here's no pet, ma'am," Railroad said. "This here's my only friend in the world."

The landlady's name was Mrs. Graves. The room she rented him was twelve feet by twelve feet, with a single bed, a cherry veneer dresser, a wooden table and chair, a narrow closet, lace curtains on the window, and an old pineapple quilt on the bed. The air smelled sweet. On the wall opposite the bed was a picture in a dime-store frame, of an empty rowboat floating in an angry gray ocean, the sky overcast, only a single shaft of sunlight in the distance from a sunset that was not in the picture.

The room cost ten dollars a week. Despite Mrs. Graves's rule against pets, like magic she took a shine to Railroad's cat. It was almost as if she'd rented the room to the cat, with Railroad along for the ride. After some consideration, he named the cat Pleasure. It was the most affectionate animal Railroad had ever seen. It wanted to be with him, even when Railroad ignored it. The cat made him feel wanted; it made him nervous. Railroad fashioned a cat door in the window of his room so that Pleasure could go out and in whenever it wanted, and not be confined to the room when Railroad was at work.

The only other residents of the boarding house were Louise Parker, a schoolteacher, and Claude Foster, a lingerie salesman. Mrs. Graves cleaned Railroad's room once a week, swept the floors, alternated the quilt every other week with a second one done in a rose pattern that he remembered from his childhood. He worked at the diner from six in the morning, when Maisie, the cashier, unlocked, until Shorty took over at three in the afternoon. The counter girl was Betsy, and Service, a Negro boy, bussed tables and washed dishes. Railroad told them to call him Bailey, and didn't talk much.

When he wasn't working, Railroad spent most of his time at the boardinghouse, or evenings in a small nearby park. Railroad would take the Bible from the drawer in the boarding-house table, buy an afternoon newspaper, and carry them with him. Pleasure often followed him to the park. The cat would lunge after squirrels and shy away from dogs, hissing sideways. Cats liked to kill squirrels, dogs liked to kill cats, but there was no sin in it. Pleasure would not go to hell, or heaven. Cats had no souls.

The world was full of stupid people like Bobby Lee and Hiram, who killed without knowing why. Life was a prison. Turn to the right, it was a wall. Turn to the left, it was a wall. Look up it was a ceiling, look down it was a floor. Railroad had taken out his imprisonment on others, but he was not deceived in his own behavior.

He did not believe in sin, but somehow he felt it. Still, he was not a dog or a cat, he was a man. *You're one of my own children.* There was no reason why he had to kill people. He only wished he'd never have to deal with any Hirams or Bobby Lees anymore. He gazed across the park at the Ipana toothpaste sign painted on the wall of the Piggly Wiggly. *Whiter than white.* Pleasure crouched at the end of the bench, haunches twitching as it watched a finch hop across the sidewalk.

Railroad picked it up, rubbed his cheek against its whiskers. "Pleasure, I'll tell you what," he whispered. "Let's make us a deal. You save me from Bobby Lee and Hiram, and I'll never kill anybody again."

The cat looked at him with its clear yellow eyes.

Railroad sighed. He put the cat down. He leaned back on the bench and opened the newspaper. Beneath the fold on the front page he read:

Escaped Convicts Killed in Wreck

Valdosta—Two escaped convicts and an unidentified female passenger were killed Tuesday when the late model stolen automobile they were driving struck a bridge abutment while being pursued by State Police.

The deceased convicts, Hiram Leroy Burgett, 31, and Bobby Lee Ross, 21, escaped June 23 while being transported to the State Hospital for the Criminally

Insane for psychological evaluation. A third
escapee, Ronald Reuel Pickens, 47, is still
at large.

The lunch rush was petering out. There were two people at the counter and four booths were occupied, and Railroad had set a BLT and an order of fried chicken with collards up on the shelf when Maisie came back into the kitchen and called the manager. "Police wants to talk to you, Mr. C."

Railroad peeked out from behind the row of hanging order slips. A man in a suit sat at the counter, sipping sweet tea. Cauthron went out to talk to him.

"Two castaways on a raft," Betsy called to Railroad.

The man spoke with Cauthron for a few minutes, showed him a photograph. Cauthron shook his head, nodded, shook his head again. They laughed. Railroad eyed the back door of the diner, but turned back to the grill. By the time he had the toast up and the eggs fried, the man was gone. Cauthron stepped back to his office without saying anything.

At the end of the shift he pulled Railroad aside. "Lloyd," he said. "I need to speak with you."

Railroad followed him into the cubbyhole he called his office. Cauthron sat behind the cluttered desk and picked up a letter from the top layer of trash. "I just got this here note from Social Security saying that number you gave is not valid." He looked up at Railroad, his china-blue eyes unreadable.

Railroad took off his glasses and rubbed the bridge of his nose with his thumb and forefinger. He didn't say anything.

"I suppose it's just some mixup," Cauthron said. "Same as that business with the detective this afternoon. Don't you worry about it."

"Thank you, Mr. Cauthron."

"One other thing, before you go, Lloyd. Did I say your salary was thirty a week? I meant twenty-five. That okay with you?"

"Whatever you say, Mr. Cauthron."

"And I think, in order to encourage trade, we'll start opening at five. I'd like you to pick up the extra hour. Starting Monday."

Railroad nodded. "Is that all?"

"That's it, Lloyd." Cauthron seemed suddenly to enjoy calling Railroad

"Lloyd," rolling the name over his tongue and watching for his reaction. "Thanks for being such a Christian about it."

Railroad went back to his room in the rooming house. Pleasure mewed for him, and when he sat on the bed, hopped into his lap. But Railroad just stared at the picture of the rowboat on the opposite wall. After a while the cat hopped onto the window sill and out through her door onto the roof.

Only a crazy person would use the knowledge that a man was a murderer in order to cheat that man out of his pay. How could he know that Railroad wouldn't kill him, or run away, or do both?

Lucky for Cauthron that Railroad had made his deal with Pleasure. But now he didn't know what to do. If the old lady's message was indeed from God, then maybe this was his first test. Nobody said being good was supposed to be easy. Nobody said, just because Railroad was turning to good, everybody he met forever after would be good. Railroad had asked Pleasure to save him from Bobby Lee and Hiram, not Mr. Cauthron.

He needed guidance. He slid open the drawer of the table. Beside the Bible was his .38. He flipped open the cylinder, checked to see that all the chambers were loaded, then put it back into the drawer. He took out the Bible, flipped through its pages with his eyes closed, and stabbed his index finger down on a verse.

He opened his eyes. The verse he'd been directed to was from Deuteronomy: "These you may eat of all that are in the waters: you may eat all that have fins and scales. And whatever does not have fins and scales you shall not eat."

There was a knock at the door. Railroad looked up. "Yes?"

"Mr. Bailey?" It was Mrs. Graves. "I thought you might like some tea."

Keeping his finger in the Bible to mark his page, Railroad got up and opened the door. Mrs. Graves stood there with a couple of tall glasses, beaded with sweat, on a tray.

"That's mighty kind of you, Miz Graves. Would you like to come in?"

"Thank you, Mr. Bailey." She set the tray down on the table, gave him a glass. It was like nectar. "Is it sweet enough?"

"It's perfect, ma'm."

She wore a yellow print dress with little flowers on it. Her every movement showed a calm he had not seen in a woman before, and her gray eyes exuded compassion, as if to say, I know who you are but that doesn't matter.

They sat down, he on the bed, she on the chair, the door to the room carefully open. She saw the Bible in his hand. "I find much comfort in the Bible."

"I can't say as I find much comfort in it, ma'm. Too many bloody deeds."

"But many acts of goodness."

"You said a true word."

"Sometimes I wish I could live in the world of goodness." She smiled. "But this world is good enough."

Did she really think that? "Since Eve ate the apple, ma'm, it's a world of good and evil. How can the good make up for the bad? That's a mystery to me."

She sipped her tea. "Of course it's a mystery. That's the point."

"The point is, something's always after you, deserve it or not."

"What a sad thought, Mr. Bailey."

"Yes'm. From minute to minute, we fade away. Only way to get to heaven is to die."

After Mrs. Graves left he sat thinking about her beautiful face. Like an angel. Nice titties, too. And yet he didn't want to hurt her.

He would marry her. He would settle down, like the grandmother said. But he would have to get an engagement ring. If he'd been thinking, he could have taken the grandmother's ring—but how was he supposed to know when he'd killed her that he was going to fall in love so soon?

He opened the dresser, felt among the dead man's clothes until he found the sock, pulled out his savings. It was only forty-three dollars.

The only help for it was to ask Pleasure. Railroad paced the room. It was a long time, and Railroad began to worry, before the cat came back. The cat slipped silently through her door, lay down on the table, simple as you please, in the wedge of sunlight coming in the window. Railroad got down on his knees, his face level with the tabletop. The cat went "Mrrph?" and raised its head. Railroad gazed into its steady eyes.

"Pleasure," he said. "I need an engagement ring, and I don't have enough money. Get one for me."

The cat watched him.

He waited for some sign. Nothing happened.

Then, like a dam bursting, a flood of confidence flowed into him. He knew what he would do.

The next morning he whistled as he walked down to the Sweet Spot. He spent much of his shift imagining when and how he would ask Mrs. Graves for her hand. Maybe on the porch swing, on Saturday night? Or at breakfast some morning? He could leave the ring next to his plate and she would find it, with his note, when clearing the table. Or he could come down to her room in the middle of the night, and he'd ram himself into her in the darkness, make her whimper, then lay the perfect diamond on her breast.

At the end of the shift he took a beefsteak from the diner's refrigerator as an offering to Pleasure. But when he entered his room the cat was not there. He left the meat wrapped in butcher paper in the kitchen downstairs, then went back up and changed into Bailey Boy's baggy suit. At the corner he took the bus downtown and walked into the first jewelry store he saw. He made the woman show him several diamond engagement rings. Then the phone rang, and when the woman went to answer it he pocketed a ring and walked out. No clerk in her right mind should be so careless, but it went exactly as he had imagined it. As easy as breathing.

That night he had a dream. He was alone with Mrs. Graves, and she was making love to him. But as he moved against her, he felt the skin of her full breast deflate and wrinkle beneath his hand, and he found he was making love to the dead grandmother, her face grinning the same vacant grin it had when Hiram and Bobby Lee hauled her into the woods.

Railroad woke in terror. Pleasure was sitting on his chest, face an inch from his, purring loud as a diesel. He snatched the cat up in both hands and hurled it across the room. It hit the wall with a thump, then fell to the floor, claws skittering on the hardwood. It scuttled for the window, through the door onto the porch roof.

It took him ten minutes for his heart to slow down, and then he could not sleep.

Someone is always after you. That day in the diner, when Railroad was taking a break, sitting on a stool in front of the window fan sipping ice water, Cauthron came out of the office and put his hand on his shoulder, the one that still hurt occasionally. "Hot work, ain't it boy?"

"Yessir." Railroad was ten or twelve years older than Cauthron.

"What is this world coming to?" Maisie said to nobody in particular. She had the newspaper open on the counter and was scanning the headlines. "You read what it says here about some man robbing a diamond ring right out from under the nose of the clerk at Merriam's Jewelry."

"I saw that already," Mr. Cauthron said. And after a moment, "White fellow, wasn't it?"

"It was," sighed Maisie. "Must be some trash from the backwoods. Some of those poor people have not had the benefit of a Christian upbringing."

"They'll catch him. Men like that always get caught." Cauthron leaned in the doorway of his office, arms crossed above his belly. "Maisie," Cauthron said. "Did I tell you Lloyd here is the best short-order cook we've had in here since 1947? The best *white* short-order cook."

"I did hear you say that."

"I mean, makes you wonder where he was before he came here. Was he short-order cooking all round Atlanta? Seems like we would of heard, don't it? Come to think, Lloyd never told me much about where he was before he showed up that day. He ever say much to you, Maisie?"

"Can't say as I recall."

"You can't recall because he hasn't. What you say, Lloyd? Why is that?"

"No time for conversation, Mr. Cauthron."

"No time for conversation? You carrying some resentment, Lloyd? We ain't paying you enough?"

"I didn't say that."

"Because, if you don't like it here, I'd be unhappy to lose the best white short-order cook I had since 1947."

Railroad put down his empty glass and slipped on his paper hat. "I can't afford to lose this job. And, you don't mind my saying, Mr. Cauthron, you'd come to regret it if I was forced to leave."

"Weren't you listening, Lloyd? Isn't that what I just said?"

"Yes, you did. Now maybe we ought to quit bothering Maisie with our talk and get back to work."

"I like a man that enjoys his job," Cauthron said, slapping Railroad on the shoulder again. "I'd have to be suicidal to make a good worker like you leave. Do I look suicidal, Lloyd?"

"No, you don't look suicidal, Mr. Cauthron."

"I see Pleasure all the time going down the block to pick at the trash by the Sweet Spot," Mrs. Graves told him as they sat on the front porch swing that evening. "That cat could get hurt if you let it out so much. That is a busy street."

Foster had gone to a ball game, and Louise Parker was visiting her sister in Chattanooga, so they were alone. It was the opportunity Railroad had been waiting for.

"I don't want to keep her a prisoner," he said. The chain of the swing creaked as they rocked slowly back and forth. He could smell her lilac perfume. The curve of her thigh beneath her print dress caught the light from the front room coming through the window.

"You're a man who has spent much time alone, aren't you," she said. "So mysterious."

He had his hand in his pocket, the ring in his fingers. He hesitated. A couple walking down the sidewalk nodded at them. He couldn't do it out here, where the world might see. "Mrs. Graves, would you come up to my room? I have something I need to show you."

She did not hesitate. "I hope there's nothing wrong."

"No, ma'm. Just something I'd like to rearrange."

He opened the door for her and followed her up the stairs. The clock in the hall ticked loudly. He opened the door to his room and ushered her in, closed the door behind them. When she turned to face him he fell to his knees.

He held up the ring in both hands, his offering. "Miz Graves, I want you to marry me."

She looked at him kindly, her expression calm. The silence stretched. She reached out; he thought she was going to take the ring, but instead she touched his wrist. "I can't marry you, Mr. Bailey."

"Why not?"

"Why, I hardly know you."

Railroad felt dizzy. "You could some time."

"Oh, Mr. Bailey. Lloyd. You don't understand—I'll never marry again. It's not you."

Not him. It was never him, had never *been* him. His knees hurt from the hardwood floor. He looked at the ring, lowered his hands, clasped it in his fist. Mrs. Graves moved her hand from his wrist to his shoulder, squeezed it. A knife of pain ran down his arm. Without standing, he punched her in the stomach.

She gasped and fell back onto the bed. He was on her in a second, one hand over her mouth while he ripped her dress open from the neck. She struggled, and he pulled the pistol out from behind his back and held it to her head. She lay still.

"Don't you stop me, now," he muttered. He tugged his pants down and did what he wanted.

She hardly made a sound. How ladylike of her to keep so silent.

Much later, lying on the bed, eyes dreamily focused on the light fixture in the center of the ceiling, it came to him what had bothered him about the grandmother. She had ignored the fact that she was going to die. "She would of been a good woman, if it had been somebody there to shoot her every minute of her life," he'd told Bobby Lee. And that was true. But then, for that last moment, she *became* a good woman. The reason was that, once Railroad convinced her she was going to die, she could forget about it. In the end, when she reached out to him, there was no thought in her mind about death, about the fact that he had killed her son and daughter-in-law and grandchildren and was soon going to kill her. All she wanted was to comfort him. She didn't even care if he couldn't be comforted. She was living in that exact instant, with no memory of the past or regard for the future, out of the instinct of her soul and nothing else.

Like the cat. Pleasure lived that way all the time. The cat didn't know about Jesus' sacrifice, about angels and devils. That cat looked at him and saw what was there.

He raised himself on his elbows. Mrs. Graves lay very still beside him, her blond hair spread across the pineapple quilt. He felt her neck for a pulse.

It was dark night now: the whine of insects in the oaks outside the window, the rush of traffic on the cross street, drifted in on the hot air.

Quietly, Railroad slipped out into the hall and down to Foster's room. He put his ear to the door and heard no sound. He came back to his own room, wrapped Mrs. Graves in the quilt and, as silently as he could, dragged her into his closet. He closed the door.

Railroad heard purring, and saw Pleasure sitting on the table, watching. "God damn you. God damn you to hell," he said to the cat, but before he could grab it the calico had darted out the window.

He figured it out. The idea of marrying Mrs. Graves had been only a stage in the subtle revenge being taken on him by the dead grandmother, through the cat. The wishes Pleasure had granted were the bait, the nightmare had been a warning. But he hadn't listened.

He rubbed his sore shoulder. The old lady's gesture, like a mustard-seed, had grown to be a great crow-filled tree in Railroad's heart.

A good trick the devil had played on him. Now, no matter how he reformed himself, he could not get rid of what he had done.

It was hot and still, not a breath of air, as if the world were being smothered in a fever blanket. A milk-white sky. The kitchen of the Sweet Spot was hot as the furnace of Hell; beneath his shirt Railroad's sweat ran down to slick the warm pistol slid into his belt. Railroad was fixing a stack of buttermilk pancakes when the detective walked in.

The detective sauntered over to the counter and sat down on one of the stools. Maisie was not there; she was probably in the ladies' room. The detective took a look around, then plucked a menu from behind the napkin holder in front of him and started reading. On the radio Hank Williams was singing "I'm So Lonesome I Could Cry."

Quietly, Railroad untied his apron and slipped out of the back door. In the alley near the trash barrels he looked out over the lot. He was about to hop the chain-link fence when he saw Cauthron's car stopped at the light on the corner.

Railroad pulled out his pistol, crouched behind a barrel, and aimed at the space in the lot where Cauthron usually parked. He felt something bump against his leg.

It was Pleasure. "Don't you cross me now," Railroad whispered, pushing the animal away.

The cat came back, put its front paws up on his thigh, purring.

"Damn you! You owe me, you little demon!" he hissed. He let the gun drop, looked down at the cat.

Pleasure looked up at him. "Miaow?"

"What do you want! You want me to stop, do you? Then make it go away. Make it so I never killed nobody."

Nothing happened. It was just an animal. In a rage, he dropped the gun and seized the cat in both hands. It twisted in his grasp, hissing.

"You know what it's like to hurt in your heart?" Railroad tore open his shirt and pressed Pleasure against his chest. "Feel it! Feel it beating there!" Pleasure squirmed and clawed, hatching his chest with a web of scratches. "You owe me! You owe me!" Railroad was shouting now. "Make it go away!"

Pleasure finally twisted out of his grasp. The cat fell, rolled, and scurried away, running right under Cauthron's car as it pulled into the lot. With a little bump, the car's left front tire ran over it.

Cauthron jerked the car to a halt. Pleasure howled, still alive, writhing, trying to drag itself away on its front paws. The cat's back was broken. Railroad looked at the fence, looked back.

He ran over to Pleasure and knelt down. Cauthron got out of the car. Railroad tried to pick up the cat, but it hissed and bit him. Its sides fluttered with rapid breathing. Its eyes clouded. It rested its head on the gravel.

Railroad had trouble breathing. He looked up from his crouch to see that Maisie and some customers had come out of the diner. Among them was the detective.

"I didn't mean to do that, Lloyd," Cauthron said. "It just ran out in front of me." He paused a moment. "Jesus Christ, Lloyd, what happened to your chest?"

Railroad picked up the cat in his bloody hands. "Nobody ever gets away with nothing," he said. "I'm ready to go now."

"Go where?"

"Back to prison."

"What are you talking about?"

"Me and Hiram and Bobby Lee killed all those folks in the woods and took their car. This was their cat."

"What people?"

"Bailey Boy and his mother and his wife and his kids and his baby."

The detective pushed back his hat and scratched his head. "You all best come in here and we'll talk this thing over."

They went into the diner. Railroad would not let them take Pleasure from him until they gave him a cardboard box to put the body in. Maisie brought him a towel to wipe his hands, and Railroad told the detective, whose name was Vernon Shaw, all about the State Hospital for the Criminally Insane, and the hearselike Hudson, and the family they'd murdered in the backwoods. Mostly he talked about the grandmother and the cat. Shaw sat there and listened soberly. At the end he folded up his notebook and said, "That's quite a story, Mr. Bailey. But we caught the people who did that killing, and it ain't you."

"What do you mean? I know what I done."

"Another thing, you don't think I'd know if there was some murderer loose from the penitentiary? There isn't anyone escaped."

"What were you doing in here last week, asking questions?"

"I was having myself some pancakes and coffee."

"I didn't make this up."

"So you say. But seems to me, Mr. Bailey, you been standing over a hot stove too long."

Railroad didn't say anything. He felt as if his heart were about to break.

Mr. Cauthron told him he might just as well take the morning off and get some rest. He would man the griddle himself. Railroad got unsteadily to his feet, took the box containing Pleasure's body, and tucked it under his arm. He walked out of the diner.

He went back to the boarding house. He climbed the steps. Mr. Foster was in the front room reading the newspaper. "Morning, Bailey," he said. "What you got there?"

"My cat got killed."

"No! Sorry to hear that."

"You seen Miz Graves this morning?" he asked.

"Not yet."

Railroad climbed the stairs, walked slowly down the hall to his room. He entered. Dust motes danced in the sunlight coming through the window. The ocean rowboat was no darker than it had been the day before. He set the dead cat down next to the Bible on the table. The pineapple quilt was no longer on the bed; now it was the rose. He reached into his pocket and felt the engagement ring.

The closet door was closed. He went to it, put his hand on the doorknob. He turned it and opened the door.

The Red Phone

The red phone rings. You pick up the receiver. "Hello?"

A woman's voice. "I want to speak with Edwin Persky."

"Just a minute." You put her on hold, then punch in the letters: P-E-R-S-K-Y. The sound of a phone ringing. A woman answers. "Hello?"

"Edwin Persky, please."

"Hold on."

She puts you on hold and you listen to a pop orchestral recording of "Try to Remember" while she connects with Persky. Pretty soon she's back. "This is Edwin Persky," she says. "What can I do for you?"

You go back to the woman on hold, and say to her, "This is Edwin Persky. What can I do for you?"

The woman's voice becomes seductive. "I want to have sex with you."

You switch back to Persky's interlocutor. "I want to have sex with you."

She speaks with Persky, then relays his response. "What are you wearing right now?"

Back to woman one. "What are you wearing right now?"

"I'm wearing black lace panties and a garter belt. And nothing else."

You wish these people would show a little more imagination. And why the garter belt if she's not wearing hose? You can see her as she really is, sitting in her kitchen wearing a ragged sweatsuit, eating cookie dough out of a plastic container.

You tell Persky's rep: "I'm wearing black lace panties and a garter belt. And nothing else."

"Jesus," she sighs. Something about the way she sighs conveys more intimacy than you've felt from anyone in six months. A shiver runs down your spine.

She relays the come-on, then replies. "I'm taking off my pants. My mammoth erection thrusts out of my tight boxers. I fall to my knees and rub my three-day growth of beard against your belly."

You pass along the message. Cookie-dough woman says, "I come down on top of you and take your organ into my mouth. My tongue runs over the throbbing veins." It's too much. "Don't say that," you tell her. Say, "I grab the term insurance policy from off your cluttered desk and roll it into a tube. I place the tube over your dick, put one end into my mouth, and begin humming 'The Girl from Ipanema.'"

"'The Girl from Ipanema?' What's that?"

"Don't worry. Just say it."

The woman hesitates, then says, "I grab the insurance policy—"

"—term insurance."

It takes her three tries to get it right. You pass it along to Persky's rep.

"That took a while," she says, after she passes it on. "At least it's original."

You snicker. "I had to help her. What's Persky doing?"

"I expect he's whacking off. Shall we speculate?"

"So does he have a reply?"

"Let's see—'I'm thrusting, thrusting, into your red mouth. I pinch your nipples and'—Jesus, I can't say this. Tell her he says, 'I smear warm guava jelly over your perky earlobes while transferring three hundred thousand in post-coital debentures to your trust fund.'"

"Debentures—I like that."

"Thanks," she says.

You relay the message to cookie-dough woman. She replies with something about waves of pink pleasure. You don't bother to get her on board this time, as you tell Persky's interlocutor, "I double your investment, going short Euros in the international currency markets while shaving your balls with a priceless ancient bronze Phonecian razor of cunning design."

She comes back: "My amygdala vibrates with primal impulse as the sensory overload threatens to reduce my IQ by forty points."

Now this is what you call action. And a challenge. You are inspired, and come back with a fantasy about Peruvian nights and the downy fur of the newborn alpaca. It goes on like this for a while. Cookie-dough starts gasping, and the pauses between Persky's replies stretch. Soon his interlocutor and I have time on our hands.

"Are you working this Tuesday?" you ask her.

"No. You?"

"*Nihil obstat.* Take in a movie?"

"Sounds good. I'm Janice."

"Sid. Meet me at the Visual Diner on McMartin. Seven-thirty?"

"How will I know you?"

"I'll be wearing lace panties and a garter belt," you tell her.

"Okay," Janice says. "Look for my throbbing organ."

The Invisible Empire

Inspired by Karen Joy Fowler's story
"Game Night at the Fox and Goose"

When Henrietta and Hiram Patterson arrived at church that Sunday, Henrietta's arm was bound to a splint, tied up in a sling made from a blue kerchief. In the quiet chat of the congregation before we entered, Henrietta allowed as how she had been kicked by the mule, but I was not the only observer to notice Hiram's sidelong watchfulness, and the fact that their two boys kept their mother between themselves and their father at all times.

The congregation was subdued in the wake of the news of that week. Robert and I sat in the third pew; Sarah sat with her husband and three children a row ahead of us. Lydia Field, her black hair piled high beneath a modest straw hat, kept watch from the choir loft. Beautiful Iris sat in front with her beau Henry Fletcher. Louellen was not a churchgoer, and Sophonsiba attended the colored church.

As the Pattersons took seats in our pew, I nodded toward them. Hiram, shaved clean and his hair parted neatly in the middle, nodded gravely back. Henrietta avoided my gaze. Their older boy took up a hymnal and paged through it.

The service began with the singing of "When Adam Was Created."

> When Adam was created,
> He dwelt in Eden's shade;
> As Moses has related,
> Before a bride was made.

I looked up at Lydia in the choir. Eyes closed, she sang as sweetly

36

as an angel; one would think her the picture of feminine submission. Another angel was Sarah, mother and homemaker. Certainly Henry Fletcher considered Iris an angel, sent from heaven to entice him.

I felt for Robert's hand, and held it as I sang.

> This woman was not taken
> From Adam's head, we know;
> And she must not rule o'er him,
> It's evidently so.
>
> The husband is commanded
> To love his loving bride;
> And live as does a Christian,
> And for his house provide.
> The woman is commanded
> Her husband to obey,
> In every thing that's lawful,
> Until her dying day.

As the song ended the Reverend Hines climbed to the pulpit. He stared down for some time without speaking, the light from the clerestory gleaming off his bald pate. Finally he began.

"I take my text, on this day of retribution, from the letter of St. Paul to the Ephesians, Chapter 5. 'Wives, submit yourselves unto your own husbands, as unto the Lord. For the husband is the head of the wife, even as Christ is the head of the church: and he is the saviour of the body. Therefore as the church is subject unto Christ, so let the wives be to their own husbands in every thing.'"

The minister rested his hand on the Bible. "My brothers and sisters, the sword of a righteous God is raised over the heads of those rebellious women who walk among us today. They think that by hiding in the dark, we will not see them. But to the Lord God Almighty, there is no darkness but the darkness of eternal perdition to which those women condemn themselves. God saw Eve when she ate of the forbidden fruit; He sees you now."

Did God see when a father in Bristol, Connecticut knocked the teeth of his eighteen-year-old daughter down her throat because she entertained the attentions of a boy he did not approve? Did He see when Charles S. Smith, a married man, got with child the simple-minded eleven-year-old Edith Wilson in Otsego County, New York?

"But my message today is not only to the wives," Hines went on. "Brothers, I ask you: Why was Adam cast from the garden? It was not because he ate of the apple! I put it to you that he was cast out because he sacrificed his judgment to that of his wife. The minute Adam saw Eve with the apple of which she had eaten, he knew she was damned. Adam's sin was that he loved Eve too much. He loved her so much that, despite his knowledge that in violating the injunction of the Lord God she had committed the gravest crime, he could not bear to lose her. So he ate of the apple, too, and damned himself, and all of his posterity, with her.

"From that one act of submission to a wrongheaded woman have come five thousand years of suffering.

"My word today to you wives is obvious: obey your husband. His hand is the hand of the Lord. When you turn against a man, you turn against the utmost power of the universe. If you have sinned, the Lord demands that you confess. Remember, Jesus forgave even the woman taken in adultery; he awaits your repentance with arms open in sweet forgiveness. For those whose hearts are hardened, only death awaits. Speak now, and be saved, or hold your tongues and be damned for all eternity.

"My word today to you husbands, in particular and most direly to those who know of the sins of your wives yet keep silent out of love, is simply this: you must act! You bear the burden of the Lord's command, to be the head of your wife. Your own salvation, her salvation, and the salvation of the community depend on it. Do not think that, by protecting her, you show mercy, any more than by joining Eve, Adam did. By protecting evil, you condemn yourself, and your children, and the children of every other man, to evil.

"Across our land, in these days of rebellion, this challenge is put to all, male and female. 'Be not deceived; God is not mocked: for whatsoever a man soweth, that shall he also reap.'

"Let us pray."

As Reverend Hines led the Lord's Prayer, I bowed my head and recited the words with the others, but my ears burned. Beside me, Robert's eyes were closed. I glanced up and saw Lydia held her head rigidly.

After the prayer, the reverend called on the congregation to testify. "Now is the time! Do not be afraid of your neighbors' reaction. Do not wait, thinking perhaps that tomorrow, or next week, will be soon enough. Tomorrow you may be dead and burning in hell; no man knows the hour of his judgment!"

He waited. The church lay silent. I saw Iris's golden head tremble; Iris is a foolish girl. I remembered how she had fretted at the talk she had aroused when she'd worn red bloomers to the cotillion. Her commitment went little farther than reading smuggled copies of *Woodhull and Claflin's Weekly*. But she did not rise.

In the end, no one did. Reverend Hines's scowl told all that was needed of his displeasure.

After the service, as we stood beneath the big oak outside, I made a special point to take the reverend's hand. I thanked him for calling us to our consciences and deplored the lack of a response from the congregation.

"God have mercy on their souls," he said. "For I will have none."

"I hope their silence only signifies the personal repentance that must precede the public one," I said, and stepped aside.

As Robert shook hands with Hines, Lydia touched my arm, and mentioned to me that the quilting circle needed to get together soon.

Robert is a carpenter: he built our house with his own hands, on an acre of ground a mile outside of town. It is a finer house than our income warrants, with extra bedrooms that we have not had cause to use. In truth, the house, like our lives, is a work in progress, perhaps never to be finished. In the evenings, after quitting his shop, Robert works laying oak flooring, mounting crown molding, trimming windows.

I fell in love with Robert when I saw him work. He is never a talkative man, but in his workshop he becomes a silent one, except for the aimless and off-key tunes that he hums, unaware.

He leans over the bench, feeds a long strip of maple through the saw, pumping the treadle steadily with his foot. He inspects the result, measures it, marks it, and slides it into the miter box. His eyes are quiet. His lips close in an expression that is the faintest prelude to a smile, but not a smile itself. His hands are precise. He takes up a box saw. He does not hurry, he does not dawdle. A shock of hair falls into his eyes, he brushes it away, and it falls back. In the mornings I shake sawdust from his pillow.

After we had returned from the church and had eaten our dinner, Robert changed out of his Sunday suit and went to work on the stair rail in the front hall.

"It's Sunday," I said, wiping my hands. "The day of rest."

"But we aren't the sort who regulate our lives by the Bible, are we."

He did not return my stare. "Would you have me be the kind of woman Jordan Hines prefers?"

He shrugged the canvas strap from his shoulder and set down his long toolbox. "I don't look to Jordan Hines for guidance. But some things are wrong. Killing a man in cold blood is wrong."

"But killing a woman in hot passion is all right. And breaking her arm is not worth notice."

"Don't put words in my mouth."

"Henrietta Patterson is a mouse; she wouldn't take a step outside her kitchen without her husband's leave—more's the pity. Name a man in this town who has been killed."

"Susannah, can you blame me if I'm troubled? This cannot go on much longer before you are found out."

"For every woman found out a hundred more will rise. Laura D. Fair was murdered by a mob in Seneca Falls ten years ago. Did that stop anything?"

He knelt beside the box and took up one of the balusters he had turned on the lathe that week. "I did not marry Laura D. Fair. At least, I didn't think I was marrying her. I married for love and a family, not revenge and violence."

I turned from him and went to the kitchen. He laid down the baluster and followed me. As I stood with my back to him, he touched my shoulder.

"I didn't mean it that way," he said. "If we never have a child, I'll still have you. That's why I'm worried. I could not bear to lose you."

I had not seen my woman's bleeding in more than a month, but I wouldn't get our hopes up only to suffer another loss. "I won't sit by and watch a woman like Henrietta Patterson pretend to be kicked by a mule when everyone in town knows it was her drunken husband." I turned from him and went to our room.

"Susannah!"

I closed the door and lay on the bed, dry eyed, heavy with fatigue. He did not follow. After a while I heard the sound of his boots in the hall, and the snick of his folding rule. Our cat Dinah jumped onto the bed and curled up beside me. As the afternoon declined I fell asleep.

When I woke it was evening. I took off my dress and donned a pair of men's trousers and a man's shirt. Worn, sturdy shoes, leather work gloves. I found Robert in the kitchen, the sleeves of his work shirt rolled to his elbows, eating bread and cheese. On the table lay the newspaper from the day before.

'SISTERS OF FURY' EXECUTED

◆

Presidential Assassins Hanged in Philadelphia

◆

The 'Drop' Falls at Three Minutes Past Six O'Clock

◆

President Hendricks Declares 'Justice Done'

◆

Female Protests Quelled

Philadelphia, July 22

The last chapter of the conspiracy to assassinate the President is finished.

Saturday, at six in the morning, the

twelve women convicted of treason and murder in the assassination of President Cleveland were put to death. In execution of the sentence of the Military Commission, duly approved by the President, the prisoners were hanged by the neck until dead in the courtyard of the federal penitentiary in Philadelphia, Pennsylvania. The painful scene was unattended by either extraordinary accident or incident, and was conducted in the most solemn and quiet manner.

Witnesses report that the last words of Helen Araminta Macready, leader of the hooded women who assaulted the President last May during the monthly tea held on the White House lawn, were "Death to all seducers."

Robert looked up at me. His eyes slowly took in my clothing. "I am going out tonight," I told him. "Don't wait up for me."

The six of us gathered at the barn at the Compton place at midnight. In the fields remained only twisted, dry stalks of last year's corn; the burnt shell of the house stood stark in the moonlight, the chimney rising like a sentinel over the ruin.

Sophonsiba crawled into the hearth and pulled our robes out of the chimney. She hurried back to the barn, her dark face gleaming, and handed around the robes and hoods.

Lydia and Iris had brought the horses, and we mounted and rode east along the Maryville Road. I am not the best rider—Lydia has been a horsewoman since her youth—but my skill exceeded that of the awkward Sarah and Louellen. Still, we had all made progress in the last year. The night air hung heavy with not a breath of breeze. I felt the sweat gather at the back of my neck. Cicadas buzzed in the oaks along the road.

The Patterson farm stood near the junction of Smokes Creek and the

Manahoc, forty poorly tended acres of cleared forest planted to corn and beans. We tied the horses in the woods near the road and moved silently up to the ramshackle house.

The back door was open. We crept through the kitchen, past the room where the boys slept, to their parents' room. Henrietta lay on her back cradling the broken forearm against her breast, waiting for us, her eyes glinting in the dark.

Sophonsiba motioned her to be quiet. Patterson stank of whiskey, and snored loudly, lost to the world. We fell upon him: One woman to each arm, and a pillow over his face.

"No!" Henrietta cried, "don't hurt him!" But it was mostly show.

"Megaera!" Lydia told Louellen. "Hold her back." Louellen pulled Henrietta away from the bed. Patterson struggled, but in a moment we had him bound and gagged. Lydia lit a lamp; when he saw the hooded figures standing around the bed, his eyes went wide.

We dragged him to his feet and pushed him out into the yard. "No, please," Henrietta whimpered.

The oldest boy, no more than eight or nine, woke and ran after us. His mother had to hold him back, wrapping her good arm about him. He stood barefoot in the dirt watching us with big eyes. His little brother came out and clutched his mother's nightgown. "Mama?" he asked.

"Hush," his mother said, weeping.

Sarah and Iris fetched the horses. Sophonsiba knocked Patterson's feet out from under him and the drunken man fell hard. He cursed through the gag, rolling in the dust as Lydia tied him by a long rope to the pommel of her saddle.

We dragged him out to the bridge over the creek. There we stripped him naked and tied him to a bridge post.

"His figure falls far short of the Greek ideal," Iris said slyly.

"Be quiet, Tisiphone," Lydia commanded in a guttural voice. I do think that Lydia could find work as a medium, and it would not be a show—for I had seen enough of her to know that, when she spoke like this, she was indeed being moved by some spirit that was not quite herself.

"Hiram Patterson," Lydia growled, "we are the ghosts of women dead at the hands of men. We are told you come of a good family. If that is so, it is time for you to get down on your knees in church next

Sunday, confess your sins, and beg the forgiveness of your dear wife. You are marked. We will be watching. If you fail, rest assured that there is no place in Greene County that is beyond our reach."

Lydia extended her arm, pointing a black-gloved finger at him. "You will not receive another warning. We *will* have good husbands, or we will have none."

Then she turned to me. "Alecto," she said. "Do your work."

Sophonsiba advanced with the torch. I took out the straight razor and unfolded the blade. When Patterson saw the torchlight gleam along it, he let out a muffled howl and lost control of his bladder. The urine splashed down the front of my robe. I slapped his face.

Disgusted, I crouched before him. He writhed. "Keep still, or this will not go well for you!" I said. His legs trembled like those of a man palsied. When I touched the razor to his groin, he fainted. His body slumped, and he fell against the blade. Blood welled and ran down his leg.

"I'm afraid I have nicked him," I said.

"Finish quickly."

He bled a deal, but the wound was far from mortal. I shaved his pubic hair, and delicately cut a circle and dependent cross on his chest.

I was withdrawing the bloody razor from my work when Louellen hissed, "Someone's coming!"

A half dozen horses came galloping down the road.

Sophonsiba hurled the torch into the creek while the rest of us ran to our mounts. My horse shied from the flash of our robes, tossing his head and flipping the reins from my fingers. I stumbled forward and grasped them, then awkwardly pulled myself into the saddle.

"Halt!" one of the men shouted. A gunshot cracked; Sarah's head snapped back and she dropped like a stone from her horse, her foot caught in her stirrup. The horse began to run, dragging her.

Sophonsiba pulled a pistol from beneath her robe and fired at the men; at the sound of the shot her horse reared, almost throwing her. The men drew up and fired back. Louellen and Iris were already gone, and Sophonsiba kicked her horse's flanks and surged away. I hesitated, thinking of Sarah, but Lydia grabbed my robe and tugged. "Ride!" she shouted, and we were off.

We galloped down the road toward Parson's Knob, away from the creek. A couple more shots whizzed past us. When we crested the ridge, I spied Sophonsiba, Louellen, and Iris ahead of us. Instead of following, Lydia veered right, into the trees.

"This way," she called. I jerked the reins, almost losing my saddle, and swerved with her between the trees.

Clouds had blown in, and a wind had picked up. In the dark it was hard to see the branches that whipped across us; I ducked and dodged trying to keep up. We descended through a series of gullies toward the river. After ten frantic minutes Lydia halted, and held up a hand for me to be quiet. We heard further shots in the distance.

"The men must have been covering the road," Lydia said. "They wanted us to flee that way. Louellen rode them right into an ambush."

"Will they tell?" We had all vowed death before betrayal.

Lydia's masked face turned toward me. "Louellen will not. Sophonsiba most definitely will not. Iris would—if she hasn't already."

"What?"

"Do you think they came upon us by accident? They were forewarned. We have a traitor among us."

"It can't be. If they knew, why weren't they waiting when we came for Patterson?"

"I don't know."

We rode north along the river, picking our way quietly through the trees. The foliage was so thick here we had to dismount and lead the horses, and eventually we moved away from the river so as not to come out onto the road near the ferry landing.

Leaves rustled in the stiffening breeze, broken by the occasional hoot of an owl. The temperature was falling and it felt like rain.

I pondered what had happened to the others. Sarah was surely dead. If caught, Sophonsiba would be summarily shot—and the others? Last winter the Martyred Marys had been hanged in Trenton. The governor had vowed "to expunge the viper of female vigilance organizations" from the state. Victoria Woodhull's press had been destroyed; even Bloomer's timid *The Lily* was forced to print in secret. In the aftermath of the president's assassination, every man in the country would be on the alert.

My horse nickered nervously, tossed his head, and I shortened my grip on the reins. Lydia held up a hand. "Willets Road," she whispered and, handing me her horse's reins, crept forward to peer into the clearing in the trees, looking, in her black robe, for all the world like some monstrous crow.

She came back. "It's clear. Let's try to make it to the barn. I'll take the horses from there and we can creep back into town before first light."

We remounted and rode west, away from the river. The road was deserted, and the sinking moon, dipping beneath the gathering clouds, shone eerily, the oak trees with their sprays of leaves black against the sky. Twenty minutes later, as the Compton place arose out of the darkness, we heard the sound of horses.

"Quickly!" Lydia hissed, and kicked her horse into a canter, heading for the barn just as the clouds opened and the rain began. I raced after her, and we jumped off the horses, pulling them inside. We peered out toward the road a hundred yards away through the increasing downpour as lightning revealed three horsemen trotting by from the direction we had come. One of them towed a horse that looked like it might have a body thrown over the saddle.

The rain drummed on the roof, drizzling through gaps in the boards. Neither of us spoke for some time. Lydia took off her robe and tucked it under her saddle pad. Mine reeked of Patterson's urine. I buried it in some rotting straw in the corner of a stall and tucked the hood into the waistband of my trousers. "I'll take the horses back to Martha's stable," Lydia said. "You can get back to town on foot."

"Who do you think those men were?" I asked. "I don't think they are from our town."

"I expect they are from Maryville. Maybe joined by a few from town, but not many. We'll find out tomorrow."

"I don't believe Iris betrayed us. The men fired as soon as they saw us. Would they shoot at their own informer?"

"I would not hazard to guess what a man might do," Lydia said.

I sat back in the straw of the barn's floor. The darkness was profound. I felt a spider's web against my cheek as I leaned against a stall. "I begin to wonder if we can ever change them."

Lydia turned to me; her voice was fierce. "If men were capable of change, then reason would have done it years ago. For most, the only answer is death."

"How can you say that?"

"You and your precious Robert! What do you think we have been doing? We aren't changing their minds—we're forcing them to stop abusing us because they know if they don't stop they will be punished."

"No. I don't believe that."

"Do you think Patterson is capable of having his mind changed?"

"Maybe not Patterson—but other men."

"Any men persuaded are regarded by others with contempt. Men like Patterson run the world."

I wanted to protest, to point out that no one had come forward in answer to Hines's call at church. Instead I brooded. "If it comes to war between men and women, women will lose."

She tugged at the hood at my waist. "Why do you think you wear this?"

Just then my horse neighed and backed up into the darkness. Through the sound of the rain came voices from the road. We peered through the barn door, and were just able to make out three figures pulled up, sitting motionless in their saddles. I prayed they would pass. Instead they moved off the road toward us.

Lydia found her horse's reins, fitted her boot into the stirrup, and pulled herself astride. "Sneak out the back. Stick to the woods. I'll ride out front and outrun them."

Without waiting for my protest she kicked her horse's flanks, crouched behind his head, and raced out of the barn. The men were startled; Lydia veered past them and out to the road. One drew a pistol and fired; I saw the muzzle flash in the dark.

I did not wait to see what happened next. I crawled out the back of the barn and ran slipping through the mud for the tree line fifty yards away through Compton's abandoned cornfield. I did not look back until I was under the trees; the men were gone, chasing after Lydia down the Maryville Road.

I ran for a long time. I had played in these woods as a girl, running with the boys, climbing trees, building forts, fighting General Lee and Napoleon and wicked King John in a thousand childish games. But though I knew the woods well, in the darkness and rain it was hard for me to keep my direction, and I got lost. Perhaps it was a delayed reaction, or fear, or some late understanding of how mad our project had been, but I found myself sitting beneath the trees, soaked to the skin, sobbing. When I closed my eyes, I again saw Sarah's head snap back from the force of the shot. I prayed that Lydia was wrong about Iris. I wondered if the others had escaped, and realized that, if they had not, it would be better for me if they had been killed. Yet how could I face the day hoping for such a disaster?

As dawn approached the rain stopped and the clouds blew away. I could make out my surroundings and realized I was not far from home. I tried to stand, but a wave of nausea swept over me and I leaned one hand against the bole of a tree, bent over, vomiting.

I stuffed my hood into a hollow log and made my way in the lessening darkness back home. My legs felt as heavy as iron.

When I reached the house, I crept quietly into the kitchen, undressed, and washed my face and hands with water from the kitchen pump. Dinah came in and sat on her haunches, watching me with feline imperturbability. I crammed my shirt and trousers into the bottom of the laundry basket.

As I climbed back into bed, Robert lifted his head. "I've been lying awake all night. Will this ever stop, Susannah?"

"It's stopped," I said, resting my head against his arm.

"Thank God," he said. "Are you all right?"

"I'm fine."

He kissed me on the cheek, and fell asleep. I lay there waiting for the dawn, my hand resting on my belly, thinking about whether I wanted it to be a boy, or a girl, or nothing at all.

The Juniper Tree

The Juniper Tree

One of the most successful transplants to the colony established by the Society of Cousins on the far side of the moon was the juniper tree. Soon after Jack Baldwin and his daughter Rosalind emigrated in 2085, a project under Baldwin's direction planted junipers on the inside slopes of the domed crater, where they prospered in the low-moisture environment. Visitors to the Society today may be excused if, strolling the woods above the agricultural lands of the crater floor, the fragrance of the foliage, beneath the projected blue sky of the dome, makes them think for a moment that they are in some low-gravity dream of New Mexico.

It was under a juniper tree that Jack disposed of the remains of Carey Evasson, the fourteen-year-old boy he killed.

Ice

The blue squad's centering pass slid through the crease, where Maryjane fanned on the shot. The puck skidded to the boards, bounced into the neutral zone, and Roz, who had been promoted to the red team for today's practice, picked it up to start a rush the other way. Carey spotted her from across the rink and set off parallel to her. They'd caught the blues off guard, with only Thabo between them and the goalie. Thabo came up to check her. Roz swerved right, then left a drop pass for Carey.

But Thabo poked his stick between Roz's legs and deflected the pass. While Roz and Carey overran the play, Thabo passed the puck back the other way to Maryjane.

Their breakaway was interrupted by the shriek of Coach Ingasdaughter's whistle. The coach skated onto the ice, yelling at Roz. "What kind of a play was that? You've got a two-on-one and you go for the drop pass? SHOOT THE PUCK!"

"But if Thabo had followed me Carey would have had an open net."

"If if if!" She raised her eyes to the roof of the cavern far overhead. "Why do you think Thabo didn't follow you? He knew you would pass, because you NEVER shoot! If you don't establish that you're a threat, they're always going to ignore you. For once, let the BOY get the rebound!"

Roz's face burned. The blue and red squads stood around watching her take the heat. Carey was looking down, brushing the blade of his stick across the ice.

Coach Ingasdaughter suddenly grabbed Roz by the shoulders, pulled her forward, and planted a kiss on her lips. "But what can I expect from a girl whose parents were married?" she said, letting Roz go. Someone snickered. "Ten-minute break," Ingasdaughter said, and turned away.

Roz almost took a slash at her retreating back. Instead she looked past the coach to the bleachers where a few off-shift pressure workers sat, helmets thrown back over their shoulders, watching the practice. Beyond the rink, the floor of the cave was one huge mass of blue ice, humped and creased, refracting the lights and fading into the distance. The coach skated over to talk with her assistant. Most of the team went over to the cooler by the home bench. Roz skated to the penalty box, flipped the door open, and sat down.

It was hard being the only immigrant on the hockey team. The cousins teased her, called her "High-G." Roz had thought that going out for hockey would be a way for her to make some girlfriends who could break her into one of the cliques. You needed a family to get anywhere among the cousins. You needed a mother. A father was of no consequence— everybody had a dozen fathers, or none at all.

Instead she met Carey. And, through dumb luck, it had seemed to work. Carey's grandmother, Margaret Emmasdaughter, had known Nora Sobieski personally. His mother was Eva Maggiesdaughter, chair of the Board of Matrons, by some measures the most powerful woman in the colony.

Some of the players started skating big circles on the oversized rink. She watched Carey build up a head of steam, grinning, his blond hair flying behind him. On the next time round he pulled off his glove, skated past the penalty box, winked, and gave her five as he flew by. The heavy gold ring he wore left a welt on her palm; just like Carey to hurt her without meaning to, but she could not help but smile.

The first time she had met Cary she nearly killed him. Roz had not gotten completely adjusted to skating in one-sixth G, how it was harder to start and stop, but also how much faster you got going than on Earth. Carey had taken the full brunt of her check and slammed headfirst into the boards. Play stopped. Everyone gathered around while he lay motionless on the ice.

Carey turned over and staggered to his feet, only his forehead showing above his shoulder pads. His voice came from somewhere within his jersey. "Watch out for those Earth women, guys."

Everyone laughed, and Carey poked his head out from below his pads. His bright green eyes had been focused on Roz's, and she burst out laughing, too.

When her father moved in with Eva, Carey became the brother she had never had, bold where she was shy, funny where she was sober.

Coach blew her whistle and they did two-on-one drills for the rest of the practice. Afterward Roz sat on a bench in the locker room taping the blade of her stick. At the end of the bench Maryjane flirted with Stella in stage whispers. Roz tried to ignore them.

Carey, wrapped only in a towel, sat down next to Roz and checked to see whether the coaches were in earshot. She liked watching the way the muscles of his chest and arms slid beneath his skin, so much that she tried hard not to look at him. He leaned toward her. "Hey, High-G—you interested in joining the First Imprints club?"

"What's that?"

He touched her on the leg. He always touched her, seemingly chance encounters, elbow to shoulder, knee to calf, his forehead brushing her hair. "A bunch of us are going to meet at the fountains in the dome," Carey said. "When the carnival is real crazy we're going to sneak out onto the surface. You'll need your pressure suit—and make sure its waste reservoir vent is working."

"Waste reservoir? What for?"

"Keep your voice down!"

"Why?"

"We're going to climb Shiva Ridge and pee on the mountaintop." He tapped the finger on her leg. His touch was warm.

"If your mother finds out, you'll be in deep trouble."

He smiled. "You'll never get to be an alpha female with that attitude, High-G. Mother would have invented this club, if she'd thought of it." He got up and went over to talk to Thabo.

God, she was so stupid! It was the beginning of Founders' Week, and she had hoped Carey would be her guide and companion through the carnival. She had worried all week what to wear. Now she'd blown it. She tugged on the green asymmetrically sleeved shirt she had chosen so carefully to set off her red hair.

Roz hung around the edges as Carey joked with the others, trying to laugh in the right places, feeling miserably out of place. After they dressed, she left with Carey, Thabo, and Raisa for the festival. Yellow triangular signs surrounded the pressure lock in the hallway linking the ice cavern to the lava tube. Roz struggled to keep up with Carey who, like all of the kids born on the moon, was taller than Roz. Raisa leaned on Thabo. Raisa had told Roz the day before that she was thinking about moving out and getting her own apartment. Raisa was thirteen, six months younger than Roz.

The lava tube was as much as forty meters wide, thirty tall, and it twisted and turned, rose and fell, revealing different vistas as they went along. Shops and apartments clung to the walls. Gardens grew along the nave beneath heliostats that transformed light transmitted from the surface during the lunar day into a twenty-four-hour cycle. Unless you went outside you could forget whether it was day or night out on the surface.

Now it was "night." As they entered the crater from the lava tube, the full extent of the colony was spread out before them. The crater was nearly two kilometers in diameter. Even in one-sixth G, the dome was a triumph of engineering, supported by a 500-meter-tall central steel and glass spire. Roz could hardly believe it, but the school legend was that Carey had once climbed the spire in order to spray paint the name of a girl he liked on the inside of the dome.

Outside, the dome was covered with five meters of regolith to protect the inside from radiation, and beneath the ribbed struts that spread out from the spire like an umbrella's, the interior surface was a screen on which could be projected a daytime sky or a nighttime starfield. Just now thousands of bright stars shone down. Mars and Jupiter hung in bright conjunction high overhead.

From the west and south sides of the crater many levels of balconied apartments overlooked the interior. Most of the crater floor was given over to agriculture, but at the base of the spire was Sobieski Park, the main meeting ground for the colony's 2,500 inhabitants. An elaborate fountain surrounded the tower. There was an open-air theater. Trees and grass, luxuriantly irrigated in a display of conspicuous water consumption, spread out from the center.

Roz and the others climbed down the zigzag path from the lava tube and through the farmlands to the park. Beneath strings of colored lights hung in the trees, men and women danced to the music of a drum band. Naked revelers wove their way through the crowd. Both sexes wore bright, fragrant ribbons in their hair. The *Cirque Jacinthe* performed low-gravity acrobatics on the amphitheater stage. Little children ran in and out of the fountains, while men and women in twos and threes and every combination of sexes leaned in each other's arms.

On the shadowed grass, Roz watched an old man and a young girl lying together, not touching, leaning heads on elbows, speaking in low voices with their faces inches apart. What could they possibly have to say to each other? Thabo and Raisa faded off into the dancers around the band, and Roz was alone with Carey. Carey brought her a flavored ice and sat down on the grass beside her. The drum band was making a racket, and the people were dancing faster now.

"Sorry the coach is on your case so much," Carey said. He touched her shoulder gently. The Cousins were always touching each other. With them, the dividing line between touching for sex and touching just to touch was erased.

God, she wished she could figure out what she wanted. Was he her brother or her boyfriend? It was hard enough back on Earth; among the cousins it was impossible.

When she didn't answer right away, Carey said, "The invisible girl returns."

"What?"

"You're disappearing again."

Roz watched the girl with the man on the grass. The girl was no older than Roz. The distance between the two had disappeared; now the girl was climbing onto the man.

Carey ran his finger down Roz's arm, then gently nudged her over. Roz pushed him away. "No thanks."

Carey tried to kiss her cheek, and she turned away. "Not now, okay?"

"What's the matter?"

"Does something have to be the matter? Any Cousins girl might tell you no, too. Don't act like it's just because I'm from Earth."

"It is."

"Is not."

"I'm not going to rape you, High-G. Cousins don't rape."

"What's that supposed to mean?"

"Absolutely nothing. But you know how screwed up it is down on Earth."

"Lots of stuff people do here would be wrong on Earth."

"Right. And people there shoot each other if anyone touches them."

Cousins could be so arrogant it made her want to spit. "You've never even seen the Earth—let alone been there."

"I've seen you, Roz."

"You don't own me."

He smiled. "No. Your father does." He nuzzled her neck.

Roz hit him. "Get off me, you pig!" She got up and ran away.

Festival

Forty milligrams of serentol, a whiff or two of THC, and an ounce of grain alcohol: Jack Baldwin wobbled through the crowd of revelers in Sobieski Park. Beneath the somatic night, feeling just an edge of anxiety, he looked for Eva among the faces.

The park was full of young men and women, their perfect bodies in one another's arms. Sex was their favorite pastime, and who could blame them? They went about it as if their lives depended on the next coupling. That was biology at work, he supposed—but if it was just genes having their way with the human body, then why all the emotional turmoil—does she love me who's he sleeping with I can't stand it when she looks at him like that how unfair to treat me like a toy who does he think he is I can't stand it I'll die if I can't have her tonight . . .

Where was Eva? He smiled. Apparently genes did not let go of your mind just because you were pushing forty. Sex had been a problem back on Earth—always some screwup with women coworkers, hassles with his live-ins, distractions. Here, sex was the common coin of interpersonal contact, unjudged as taste in ice cream (but some people made a religion of taste), easy as speech (but speech was not always easy), frequent as eating (but some people starved themselves in the midst of plenty). Where did that leave him? Was he simply a victim of the culture that had raised him? Or was his frustration purely personal?

Where was Eva?

Men and women, naked, oiled, and smiling, wove their way through the celebrants, offering themselves to whoever might wish to take them. It was the one day of the year that the Society of Cousins fit the cliched image of polymorphous orgy that outsiders had of it. One of them, a dark young woman—dark as Eva—brushed her fingers across Jack's cheek, then swirled away on one luscious hip.

But Eva was taller, more slender. Eva's breasts were small, her waist narrow despite the softness of the belly that had borne Carey, and when they made love her hipbones pressed against him. She was forty, and there was gray in her black hair. This girl dancing by could satisfy his lust, and perhaps if he came to know her would become a person as complex as Eva. But she would not be Eva: the combination of idealism and practicality, the temper that got her into trouble because she could not keep her mouth shut. Fierce when she fought for what mattered to her, but open-hearted to those who opposed her, with an inability to be successfully machiavellian that was her saving grace.

He had met Eva a month after he and Roz had arrived at the colony. Jack was working on a new nematode that, combined with a gene-engineered composting process, would produce living soil from regolith more efficiently than the tedious chemical methods that had been used to create Fowler's initial environment. His specialty in nematodes had been the passport for him and Roz into the guarded Cousins society, the last available bridge after a succession of bridges he had burned behind them. He certainly had not planned to end up on the moon. The breakup with Helen. The fight over Roz, ending with him taking her against the court order. The succession of jobs. The forged vita.

Eva, newly elected head of the board, was also head of the environmental subcommittee. She had come by the biotech lab in the outlying bunker. Jack did not know who the tall, striking woman in the web-patterned pressure suit was. She asked questions of Amravati, the head of the project, then came over to observe Jack, up to his ankles in muck, examining bacteria through an electron microscope visor.

Flirting led to a social meeting, more flirting led to sex. Sex—that vortex women hid behind their navels, that place he sometimes had to be so badly that every other thought fell away and he lost himself again. Or was it finding himself? Eva's specialty was physics, some type of quantum imaging that he did not understand and whose practical benefits he could not picture. But a relationship that had started as a mercenary opportunity had, to Jack's surprise, turned to something like love.

As Jack sat on the edge of the fountain, hoping he might find Eva in the crowd, instead he spotted Roz. Her face was clouded; her dark brown eyes large with some trouble. "Roz!" he called.

She heard his voice, looked up, saw him. She hesitated a moment, then walked over.

"What's the matter?" he asked.

"Nothing." She sat down next to him. She was bothered by something.

Across the plaza, two of the acrobats juggled three children in the low gravity the way someone on Earth might juggle beanbags. The kids, tucked into balls, squealed in delight as they rose and fell like the waters of the fountain.

"Isn't this amazing?" Jack asked.

"'Amazing,' Dad—that's very perceptive."

"What?"

"This place is disgusting. Look at that old creep there feeling up that girl."

"The Cousins do things differently. But they don't do anything against anyone's will."

"It's all okay with you, just as long as you're getting laid every night."
He put his hand on her leg. "What's going on?"

She pulled away. "Nothing's going on! I'm just tired of watching you take advantage of people. Mom would never have brought me here."

Roz never mentioned her mother. Jack tried to focus. "I don't know, girl. Your mom had her own problems fitting in."

"The only reason we came here is that you couldn't get a job back on Earth."

He tried to get Roz to look at him, but she was fixed on her outsized plastic shoes. "Aren't we hostile tonight?" he said. She didn't answer. He saw for the first time how much her profile had become that of a grown woman. "I'll admit it. The job had something to do with it. But Roz, you've got a chance to become someone here you could never be on Earth—if you'll make an effort. Women are important here. Hell, women run the place! Do you think I like the idea of being a second-class citizen? I gave up a lot to bring you here."

"All you care about is getting into Eva's bed," Roz told the shoes. "She's using you, and she'll just dump you after she's had enough, like all these other cousins."

"You think that little of my choices?"

That made her look at him. Her face was screwed into a scowl. The music of the drum band stopped suddenly, and the people applauded. "How do you know Eva's not going to try to get me into bed with her, too?"

Jack laughed. "I don't think so."

She stood up. "God, you are so smug! I can't tell you anything!"

"Roz, what is this—"

She turned and stalked off.

"Roz!" he called after her. She did not turn back.

Next to him, a thin black woman holding a toddler had been eavesdropping. Jack walked away to escape her gaze. The band started another song. Inwardly churning, he listened to the music for a few minutes, watching the people dance. Whatever his failings, hadn't he always done his best for Roz? He didn't expect her to agree with him all the time, but she had to know how much he loved her.

The amused detachment with which he'd entered the festival was gone. The steel drums gave him a headache. He crossed the plaza. Before he had gone ten paces he saw Eva. She was in the crowd of dancers, paired with a round-faced woman. The woman was grinning fiercely; she bumped against Eva, slid her belly up against Eva's. Eva had her arms raised into the air and was smiling, too, grinding her hips.

As Jack stood watching, someone sidled up to him. It was Hal Keikosson, who worked in Agriculture. Hal was in his forties and still living with his mother—a common situation among the Cousins.

"Hey, Jack. Who was that girl I saw you talking to? That red hair? Cute."

Jack kept watching Eva and the woman. Eva had not noticed him yet. "That was my daughter," he told Hal.

"Interesting." Hal swayed a bit, clutching a squeeze cup in his sweaty hand.

Jack ought to let it go, but he couldn't. "What does that mean?"

"Nothing. She must be fourteen or fifteen already, right?"

"She's fourteen."

"And maybe she isn't your daughter." Hal giggled.

Jack stared at him. "What?"

"I mean, how could her mother be sure—or maybe she lied to you."

"Shut the fuck up."

"Hey, it's none of my business who you sleep with."

"I'm not sleeping with her."

"Calm down, calm down, cousin." Hal took a sip from his cup. He looked benignly at the figures writhing in the shadows beneath the trees. "That's too bad," he said quietly, and chuckled.

Jack stalked away to keep from taking a swing at him.

The drum band was louder now, and so was the babble of the increasing crowd. He passed a group of drunken singers. Near the amphitheater he saw one of the acrobat children staggering around in circles, giggling. Jamira Tamlasdaughter, a friend of Eva's, tried to say hello, but he passed her by with a wave. Jack's head throbbed. Beyond the trees that marked the border of Sobieski Park he followed a path through fields of dry-lands soybeans, corn, potatoes. There was no one out here—most of the cousins were at the festival now.

A kilometer later the path turned upward into the open lands of the crater slopes. Low, hardy blue-white grass covered the ground. But the sound of the band still floated over the fields, and turning, Jack could see the central tower lit by the colored lights. The slope was side lit only by that distant light and the projected starlight from the dome. Somewhere off to his left a night bird sang in a scraggly pine. He turned his back to the festival.

It was an easy climb in one-sixth G, and when he hit the concrete rim of the crater that supported the dome, he followed the perimeter road around toward the north airlock. He wanted out. The best refuge he could think of was the biotech lab.

Because of the festival, the airlock was deserted. Jack took his pressure suit from his locker, suited up, and cycled through the personnel lock. He passed through the radiation baffles to the surface.

Though it was night inside the dome, out here it was lunar afternoon. Harsh shadows lay beneath the fields of solar collectors lining the road to the labs. Jack skipped along the tracked-up roadway, kicking up a powder of fines. Over the throb of his headache he listened to the sound of his own breathing in his earphones.

The fight he'd had with Roz was just like one of his final spats with Helen, full of buried resentments and false assumptions. Roz's accusations stung because there was an element of truth in them. But Roz was wrong to say Jack didn't care about her. From the moment of her birth Jack had committed himself to Roz without reservation. Clearly he hadn't paid enough attention to her troubles, but he would do anything to protect her.

Roz didn't understand that things were hard for Jack. "All men are boys," the cousins said. In the case of a jerk like Keikosson, he could admit the saying's truth. But it was as much a product of the way they lived as of the men themselves. The women of the Cousins indulged their boys their pleasures, kept them adolescents far into their adulthood. It was a form of control-by-privilege.

Jack chafed at the way a male in the colony was seldom respected for his achievements, but rather for who his mother and grandmother were. He hated the way women deferred to him once it got around that he was Eva Maggiesdaughter's latest partner. He hated the sidelong glances he got about his relationship to Roz. He was Roz's father. He was not anyone's boy.

The biotech labs were located in a bunker a kilometer north of Fowler. He entered the personnel lock, air-blasted the fines from his suit and removed it. Like the airlock, the lab was deserted. He passed through the greenhouse's rows of juniper and piñon seedlings to the soils lab. The temperature on his latest batch of nematode soil was 30 centigrade. He drew on some boots, rolled back the cover on the reservoir, and waded into the loamy earth. The rich smell of nitrogen compounds filled his lungs, and he felt momentarily dizzy with relaxation.

Taking a rake from the tool cabinet, he worked over the surface of the soil. His nematodes were doing their jobs nicely, increasing the water content, breaking down organics and hosting the nitrogen-fixing bacteria. Once his team got the okay from the colony's environmental committee, they would start a trial planting using the soil and the greenhouse seedlings on Fowler's east slope.

He had not been working long when he heard the airlock alert. Startled, he dropped the rake and stood up. Some minutes later a figure emerged from the greenhouse and peered from around the rock crusher. "Jack?"

"Over here, Carey," Jack said.

The boy came over. He was taller than his mother, and blond instead of dark. Jack wondered once again who his father was. Carey was still wearing his pressure suit, helmet off.

"What are you doing here?" Jack asked. "How did you know I was here?"

"I was coming into the north airlock when I saw you cycling out," Carey said. "By the time I got my suit on you were gone, but I figured you might be here. I wanted to speak with you about Roz, Jack."

"What about her?"

"I think she's having a hard time," Carey said. "I think you might want to pay more attention to what's going on with her. Fathers like you do that, right?"

"Fathers like what?"

"Come on, Jack, you know—Earth fathers."

"What's wrong with Roz?" Jack asked.

"She seems to have some sexual hang-ups. She hasn't talked with you about it? She talks about you all the time."

"I don't think there's anything wrong with Roz. Besides, it's none of your business, Carey."

"Well, it sort of is. At least if she's not telling you these things, and you care about her, then I guess I need to tell you. Like after we slept together the first time, she cried."

"You slept with her." Jack's own voice sounded leaden in his ears.

"Sure. I thought you knew." Carey was completely unselfconscious. "I mean, we're all in the same apartment. She didn't tell you that, either?"

"No."

"She needs help. She's making some progress with the kids on the hockey team, but for every step forward she takes one back. I think she's too hung up on you, Jack."

"Don't call me Jack."

Carey looked confused. "Excuse me?"

"Don't call me Jack, you little pissant. You don't know a thing about me and Roz."

"I know you're immigrants and don't understand everything. But a lot of people are starting to think you need to live separately. You don't own Roz."

"What the hell are you talking about?"

"She's a woman. She can make up her own mind."

The boy's face was an open map of earnest, smug innocence. Jack couldn't stand it. "Damn you, she's not your whore!"

Carey laughed. "A whore? That's an·Earth thing, right? One of those sexual ownership practices?"

Jack took one step, grabbed the collar of the boy's pressure suit and yanked him forward. Carey's feet caught on the edge of the reservoir. As he fell, he twisted around; Jack lost his own balance and shoved Carey downward to keep from falling himself. Much faster than normal in lunar-G, Carey hit the ground. His head snapped sideways against the rake.

Catching his balance, Jack waited for Carey to get up. But he didn't get up. Jack crouched over the boy. Carey had fallen onto the head of the rake; one of the six-centimeter ceramic tines had penetrated his temple. Blood seeped into the soil.

Carefully, Jack drew out the tine, rolled him over. Carey shuddered and the blood flowed more freely. The boy's breathing was shallow, his eyes unfocused. As Jack watched, Carey's breathing stopped.

After ten minutes of futile CPR, Jack fell back from Carey's limp body and sat down heavily on the edge of the reservoir.

Jesus Christ. What had he done? What was he going to do now? Eva!—what would she think?

It was an accident. But that didn't matter. He was an immigrant, an outsider, a man. Someone would surely accuse him of murder. They would drug him into insensibility, cut up his brain. At best they would expel him from the colony, and Roz with him—or worse still, they might not expel Roz. He sat there facing the cold reality of his thirty-eight years of screwed-up life.

Carey's head lolled back into the muck, his mouth open. "You arrogant prick," Jack whispered to the dead boy. "You fucked it all up."

He looked around the room. In front of him was the reduction chamber, the crusher, the soil reservoir. Shuddering, he went back to the tool chest and found a machete. He dragged Carey's body over the edge of the reservoir, getting dirt up to his own elbows. The soil was rich with the heat of decomposition.

Jack stripped off Carey's suit. He was about to begin cutting off the boy's arms when the airlock alert sounded again. He panicked. He stumbled out of the reservoir, trying to heft Carey's body into the hopper of the crusher. Before he could conceal the body he heard steps behind him.

It was Roz. She stood for a moment staring at him as he held Carey's bare ankle in his hand. "Dad?"

"Go away, Roz."

She came over to him. "Dad, what's going on?" She saw the body. "Jesus, Dad, what happened?"

"An accident. The less you know about it the better."

She took a couple of steps closer. "Carey? Is he all right?"

"Go *away*, Roz."

Roz put her hand to her mouth. "Is he dead?"

Jack let go of Carey and came over to her. "It was an accident, Roz. I didn't mean to hurt him. He fell down."

"Carey!" She rushed over, then backed away until she bumped into the rock crusher. "He's dead! What happened? Dad! Why did you do this?"

Jack didn't know what to do. He looked back at Carey, lying awkwardly on the concrete floor, the machete beside his leg. "It was an accident, Roz. I grabbed him, he fell. I didn't mean to—"

"Carey," she said. "Carey." She would not look at Jack.

"Roz, I would never have hurt him on purpose. I—"

"What were you fighting about?"

"It wasn't a fight. He told me you had slept together. I was shocked, I guess. I—"

Roz slumped to the floor. "It was my fault?"

"No. It was an accident."

"I don't believe this," she said. She looked at Carey's body. Jack thought about the last time she must have seen him naked. "You're going to go to jail!" Roz said. "They might even kill you. Who's going to take care of me?"

"*I'm* going to take care of you. Please, Roz, don't think about this. You need to get out of here."

"What are we going to do?"

"You're not going to do anything except get out! Don't you understand?"

Roz stared at him a long moment. "I can help."

Jack felt chilled. "I don't want your help! I'm your father, damn it!"

She sat there, her eyes welling with tears. He sat down next to her and put his arm around her. She cried against his shoulder. A long time passed, and neither of them spoke.

Finally she pulled away from him. "It's my fault," she said. "I should have told you I loved him."

Jack closed his eyes. He could hear his own pulse in his ears. The earth of the reservoir smelled rich and fertile. "Please, don't say any more."

"Oh, God, how could you do this?" he heard her whisper. "Carey . . ." She cried against Jack's shoulder some more.

Then, after a while, swallowing her tears, Roz said, "If we get rid of his suit . . . if we get rid of his suit, they'll think he got lost on the surface."

He opened his eyes and looked at her. Now he was scared. Who was this girl?

"What do you mean?" he asked.

Eating

Eva expected Jack would turn up at the festival eventually, and she didn't want to miss the partying. Her mother came by with some of her cronies, and then Eva found herself dancing with Angela Angelasdaughter, the colony's most notorious artist. Ten years ago, any gossip session in the sauna would devote ten minutes to the sexy sculptress and her physicist lover. Since then Angela had gained a potbelly, but her smile was as wicked as ever.

During a break in the music, Eva shared a drink with Jamira Tamlasdaughter. Jamira told Eva she had seen Jack earlier. "He's so handsome, Eva," Jamira said. "You're so lucky. He's like a god."

Eva smiled, thinking of Jack's taut body stretched across her bed. "Where did he go?"

"I don't know. I expect he's here somewhere."

But Jack did not show up. What with one thing and another it was well after midnight when Eva returned to her apartment. Jack was sitting on the floor with a glass in front of him.

"So here you are," Eva said. "I thought we would meet at the festival."

He looked up at her, and his blue eyes were so soulfully sad that she melted. "I couldn't find you," he said quietly.

She sat down next to him. "I got caught up at the lab." She and Victor had been working overtime on assembler programming. "Are Carey and Roz here?"

"No."

"Good. Then we can entertain ourselves—unless this stuff you pour into yourself makes that unnecessary."

Jack put his arms around her, pulled her to him, and rested his forehead against hers. "You know I always need you," he whispered. Eva could smell spiced alcohol on his breath. She pulled him back onto the floor, and they kissed.

They eventually found their way to the bedroom. Afterward, she was ravenously hungry. As a member of the Board, she had earned the privilege of a small kitchen: she padded in, naked, and returned to the room with a plate, a knife, an apple, and a hunk of cheese.

Jack was stretched across the bed just as she had imagined him, the muscles of his belly thrown into relief by the low light. She sat cross-legged beside him, cut a slice from the apple, and offered it to him. "Here we are, in the Garden. Eve offers you an apple."

"No, thanks."

"Come on, Adam. Have some fun."

His eyes flicked away from her, the corner of his mouth twitched. "I've had too much fun already," he said to the ceiling.

She drew the apple slice across his chest, down to his navel. "There's always more where that came from."

"I'm worried about Roz. She shouldn't be out this late."

"Your daughter's too sensible to do anything risky." Eva heard the door to the apartment open, the sound of someone coming down the hall and entering Rosalind's room. "See?" Eva said. "There she is."

"What about Carey?"

"Carey, on the other hand, is no doubt is busy getting into some sort of trouble. We'll deal with him in the morning."

She brushed her hand over his penis, and it stiffened. He said nothing, but eventually his hand came up to touch her hair, and then he pulled close and made love to her with an intensity that left her breathless and relaxed. He fell asleep beside her, and she lay watching the plate and the apple slices in the faint light. Soon, she thought, soon, they would be able to reproduce anything. She would prove that the Cousins were not some backward-looking female-dominated hive. They would stun the world. Dreaming of this, Jack's arm around her, she fell asleep.

In the morning Carey had not returned.

Over breakfast—Eva finished the apple, now turned brown—she asked Roz what had happened after hockey practice. After denying anything, Roz finally admitted that Carey and some others had used the cover of the festival to sneak out of the colony onto the surface. The "First Imprints Club." In the dead lunar surface the marks of their urine in the dust would last as long as if etched in stone.

That sounded like Carey, right down to the wasting of water. Eva called Carey's friends. She discovered that Carey had left them at the festival, telling them he would catch up with them at the airlock. After waiting for him, they had gone out without him, expecting that he'd meet them on Shiva Ridge.

Carey's pressure suit was not in his locker at the north airlock. Eva tried not to panic. She alerted colony security. Hundreds of volunteers joined in a search of the surface. With the assistance of Carey's friends they found the footprints of the party, but none for Carey. Lunar Positioning Satellites could not raise his suit's locator. Parties scanned the prominent landmarks, but came up empty.

The next days became a nightmare. Eva spent all of her waking hours out on the surface with the search parties, coming inside only to recharge her air supply and catch an hour or two of sleep. Her eyes fell into a permanent squint from the brightness of the surface. For the first twenty-four hours Eva still hoped Carey might be found alive. He had fallen unconscious in the shadow of some rock, she told herself; hypothermia would keep his metabolism low so he wouldn't exhaust his oxygen.

As the hours passed she kept despair at bay by driving herself even harder. The third day found her a part of a line of twenty cousins, at hundred-meter intervals, sweeping Shiva ridge for the fourth time. Something was wrong with her faceplate: it was breaking all the gray landscape into particles, no piece of the moon connected to any other piece, and all of it was dead. The voices of the other searchers calling to each other sounded in her ear button. "Nothing here." "Where's here?" "I'm on the east end of the ridge, below Black Rock."

Eva felt numb. She came to the edge of a lava tube whose roof had fallen in. It was fifty meters to the shadowed bottom. Even in lunar gravity a fall would be fatal. She swayed on the edge, having trouble breathing. Her mouth was dry, and her eyes itched.

Someone grabbed her arm and pulled her away. "No," his voice came over her ear button, as close as her own thoughts. It was Jack. He wrapped her in a bear hug, drew her back. He made her return with him to Fowler, to eat a meal, to take some pills and sleep for fourteen hours.

After that Eva no longer tormented herself with impossibilities. Jack stayed with her every minute of her time on the surface. Despite her heartache, she still hoped Carey's body would turn up so she could figure out what had happened. But when a further week of searches still brought nothing, she asked that they be called off. The official inquest ruled Carey missing, presumed dead by hazard of fortune.

She turned to her work. The project was her only hope now. It was more than a matter of demonstrating the value of Cousins' science. Over the next months, the first assemblies using scans of organic compounds were completed. They produced edible soy protein and worked their way up toward applesauce.

At meetings in the boardroom that looked out over the green fields of Fowler basin, the other matrons watched her out of the corners of their eyes. Eva controlled her voice, operated her body as if by remote. Everything is normal, she told herself. Some mornings she would wake and listen for Carey thumping around the apartment, only to hear silence. She hid his pictures. Though she would not empty his room, she closed its door and never went inside. She went to watch the hockey team play. Other Cousins sat beside her and made a show of treating her normally.

Hockey was such a violent game—a boy's game. Had the cousins adopted it for that very reason, to go against the perception that women were soft? Eva watched Roz throw herself around the ice like a demon. What would drive such a shy girl to compete so hard?

At night she lay awake and thought about Carey. She imagined him out there on the surface, running out of air. What was it about boys and men that they always took such big risks? You couldn't protect them. If you tried to, they got sulky and depressed. She had never questioned the place the Cousins had prepared for boys in their world, how their aggression and desire for dominance had been thwarted and channeled. *Keep your son close; let your daughter go*, the homily went. Had she been fair to Carey? If she had him back with her this minute, could she keep herself from smothering him?

Jack went back to his own work: his team planted a copse of junipers, piñon, sage, and wildflowers on the east slopes of Fowler, hauling loads of their new soil that promised a better growth rate than the chemically prepared soils. He came home each night with dirt under his fingernails, scrubbed himself raw in the shower, and fell into bed exhausted. Jack and Eva had not made love after that night Carey disappeared. At first Eva had no desire, and then, after her need returned and she might have felt it a comfort to have Jack hold her in his arms, he seemed so depressed by Carey's loss that he would not touch her. Eva saw that worrying about her had taken Jack away from Roz.

"I'm sorry," she vowed to Jack's sleeping form one night. "I can do better."

Since Carey's disappearance, Roz spent less time at home. Eva saw the pain in Jack's eyes as he watched Roz. She wondered what it must be like for Roz, to have this single strong male presence always there in her life. She owed Roz and Jack better than she had been giving, and the effort to engage them would help her stop thinking about Carey.

She arranged for Roz to spend her second-semester practicum in the colony's materials co-operatives. What to do about Jack's relationship to Roz was harder to figure out. Eva was a physicist, and had never paid much attention to the theories of Nora Sobieski and the other founders. It wasn't as though a man taking an interest in his daughter's upbringing was necessarily unnatural. But Eva realized that, just like her with Carey, out of his fear of losing Roz, Jack ran the risk of smothering her. *Keep your son close; let your daughter go*: whether Jack could see it or not, it was time for Roz to begin to find her own place in the world.

Jack had taken to bringing home chard, romaine lettuce, and carrots from the gardens. He brought a potted juniper for the balcony where they ate their meals. There one night at dinner Eva suggested to Jack that Roz move out.

Jack looked frightened. "She's only fourteen, Eva."

"If she doesn't begin to break free now she will have a much harder time later."

"I understand that. It's just—it's not the way she grew up. She and I haven't been here that long. And with—with Carey gone . . ." his voice trailed off.

Eva watched him. "Jack, I know I've been distant. I know it's been hard for you. If you don't want to be alone with me, I'll understand. I just hope you won't live with Roz."

"For pity's, Eva! Don't you believe in love?"

She was taken aback. "Of course I do." She poked her fork at her salad.

"Well, I love Roz. I love . . . I love you."

Eva felt out of her depth. What did he mean when he said the word love? She looked into Jack's handsome face: blue eyes, curly bronze hair, square jaw. How much, when he looked so hurt, he reminded her of Carey. Jack watched her intently. He was trying to communicate something, but she had no idea what it was.

"I know you love us," Eva said. "That's not the question. But if Roz is ever going to fit in here, she needs to begin to network . . . I might even say the same for you."

"Network." He sat still as a stone.

He acted so wounded; he was putting her on the spot. Was this about sex? "I'm not trying to push you away, Jack. It's not me who's been turning away every night in bed."

"I realize that," he said defensively. "I thought that you were still grieving for Carey."

God, she was no good at this interpersonal stuff. She looked away. She tried the salad grown from the gardens he and his team had planted. "Let me handle my grief in my own way," she said.

He said nothing. He seemed more sad than angry. They ate in silence. After a while he asked her, "How's the salad?"

"The best I've ever tasted. And the pine nuts—are they from the new trees?"

"Yes," he said.

"The juniper smells wonderful."

"It's yours," he said. "I grew it for you."

Transformation

When Roz told Jack about Carey's plans to meet the First Imprints Club, Jack picked up Carey's pressure suit. He laid the suit on the floor, adjusted it so that the locator lay flat against the concrete, and ground his heel into it until the chip snapped. "Okay," Jack said. "You take his things and lose them some place on the surface where they'll never be found."

Roz knew that Jack's real reason for rushing her out was to keep her from seeing him dispose of Carey's body. She did not object. She stuffed Carey's clothes into the suit, sealed it up and, while her father turned back to the body, headed for the airlock.

"Wait," Jack said. "Take this."

Fearfully, she turned. Jack had taken something from Carey's hand. It was Carey's ring.

She shoved the ring inside her own suit, then hurried through the airlock onto the lunar surface.

The shadows of lunar afternoon lay precisely as they had when she had entered the lab an hour before, a girl seeking to apologize to her dad. Between then and now, something had broken.

Jack had looked so surprised, so guilty—so old. The skin beneath his eyes was dark and papery, as if he hadn't slept in a week. Had he looked this tired when she had argued with him in the plaza? It made her wonder just what had been going on all this time. How could Jack kill Carey? Had he been so near to breaking all along? As she shuffled across the humped, dusty surface, Roz fought to keep from crying again at the awfulness of Carey's death and the precariousness of their situation.

For most of her life, it had been just her and her father. Roz's mother Helen had been a graduate student in plant pathology when Jack met her at Purdue. Roz's first memory was of sitting in the bathtub as her mom taught her to count on her toes. When Roz was six, her mother's increasing bouts of depression broke up the marriage. Helen had custody of Roz for more than a year before Jack rescued her, and Roz remembered that year vividly: afternoons hanging out with the kids in the neighboring apartment, suppers of corn flakes, Helen coming back from her classes unhappy, Roz trying to wake Helen to get her to work in the mornings, Helen shouting at Jack every time he came to pick Roz up for visits. When Jack had stolen Roz away, though he never said anything bad about Helen, Roz felt that she would never miss her mother again.

Now Roz wished she knew where Helen was, what she was doing at just that moment. What had *she* gone through when she was fourteen? Nothing as bad as this.

As she moved away from Fowler across the lunar surface, Roz tried to stay to the shadows. But there was little chance of anyone spotting her. What she needed to do was lose Carey's suit somewhere that nobody was likely to find it for thirty or forty years.

It should not be so hard. These were the rumpled highlands, a landscape of hills, ridges, craters, and ejecta. Around the colony the ground was scuffed with a million bootprints. Roz hid hers among them, bouncing along below the eastern rim of Fowler.

She then struck off along a side track of footprints that aimed northeast. A couple of kilometers along, she broke off from the path and made a long leap to a rock scarp uncovered with dust. She landed clumsily but safe, and left no boot marks. She proceeded in this direction for some distance, aiming herself from rock to rock to leave as few footprints as possible. The short horizon made Roz feel as if she was a bug on a plate, nearing the edge of the world. She kept her bearings by periodically noting some point ahead and behind so that she would not get lost. That was the biggest danger of surface hopping, and the source of the rule against ever doing it alone. It would be easy to explain Carey's disappearance as an intoxicated boy getting lost and running out of air. A broken radio, a faulty locator.

A kilometer on, Roz found a pit behind a group of ejecta boulders. Deep in the shadow on the north side of the largest, she dug away the top layer of regolith and stuffed the suit into the pit. She shoved the dirt back over the suit. By the time she was done, her hands were freezing. She stood back on a boulder and inspected the spot. She had kept most of the scuffs she'd created to the shadows, which would not change much for some time in the slow lunar day. Roz headed back along the path she had come, rock to rock, taking long strides in the low gravity until she met the traveled path again. Up above her, a third of the way across the black sky from the sun, angry Mars gleamed beside Jupiter like an orange eye.

Her air supply was in the red when she reached Fowler's north lock. She was able to pass through without seeing anyone; the festival was still going strong.

Roz stowed her suit in an empty locker, set the combination, and walked back around the rim road toward Eva's apartment—the long way, making a three-quarter circuit of the crater. On the southeast slope she stopped and watched the lights of the festival. When she finally got home, she found an empty glass sitting on the living room floor, and the door to Jack and Eva's room was closed. She went to her own room, closed her door, undressed. There she found Carey's ring in her pocket, warm from the heat of her own body.

Through all of Eva's quizzing of Roz the next morning, Jack sat drinking juice, ignoring them both. Roz was stunned by how calm he looked. What went on inside? She had never thought that there might be things going on inside her father that were not apparent on the surface.

Then the searches began. Over and over Roz had to retell her story of parting with Carey at the festival. At just what time had she last seen Carey? What had Carey said? In what direction had Carey gone? Jack threw himself into the "search"—but whenever Roz looked at him, she saw that he was watching her.

As the search stretched beyond the first days, Carey's friends came up and sympathized with Roz. For the first time kids who had held her at arms' length confided in her. They shared their shock and grief. Roz supposed that, from the outside, her own terror looked like shock. Colony security used volunteers from the school in the searches, and Roz took part, though never in the northeast quadrant. Every time one of the parties returned she was petrified that they would have Carey's pressure suit.

Near the end of the third day, Roz was sitting in the apartment, clutching Carey's ring in her hand, when Jack brought Eva back with him. Eva was so sick Jack almost had to prop her up. Jack fed Eva, made her take some pills and go to sleep. He came out of their room and shut the door.

"What happened?" Roz asked.

Jack pulled Roz away from the door. "I caught Eva on the edge of a precipice. I think she was about to jump off."

"Oh, Jesus! What are we going to do?"

"She'll be okay after she gets some rest. We need to take care of her."

"Take care of her! We killed her son!"

"Keep your voice down. Nobody killed anyone. It was an accident."

"I don't think I can stand this, Dad."

"You're doing fine, Roz. I need you to be my strong girl. Just act normal."

Just act normal. Roz tried to focus on school. The hockey game against Shackleton was postponed, but the practices continued. When it became obvious that Carey wasn't coming back, Maryjane moved up to take Carey's place in Roz's line. At night Roz squeezed her eyes shut, pressed her palms against them to drive thoughts of Carey's body from her imagination. She would not talk to Jack about it, and in his few hurried words with her he never spoke of that night.

Roz hated hearing the sound of Jack's voice when he talked to Eva or anyone else, so casually modulated, so *sane*. Just act normal. When he

spoke with Roz his voice was edged with panic. Roz vowed that she would
never in her life have two voices.

Maybe Eva had two voices, too. After the searches were ended, Eva
seemed distressingly normal. Roz could tell Eva was upset only by the
firmness with which she spoke, as if she were thinking everything over
two or three times, and by the absolute quality of her silences.

At first Roz was afraid to be around Eva, she seemed so in control.
Yet Roz could tell that at some level Eva was deeply wounded in a way
she could not see in Jack. The only word Roz could think of to describe
Eva was a word so absurdly old fashioned that she would have been
embarrassed to say it aloud: noble. Eva was the strongest person Roz had
ever met. It made Roz want to comfort her—but Roz was too afraid.

The weeks passed, and they resumed a simulation of ordinary life.
Eva took an interest in Roz that she had not while Carey was still alive.
For Roz's second-semester practicum, Eva arranged for Roz to work
successive months in the colony's four materials co-operatives, Air, Water,
Agriculture, and Fabrication. Roz was glad to spend more time out of
the apartment.

With Air, Roz worked outside in the southwest industrial area, helping
move lunar regolith to the grinder. Various trace elements, including the
H_3 used in fusion reactors, were drawn off and saved. After grinding,
the regolith was put in a reduction chamber with powdered graphite
and heated to produce carbon monoxide, which was reintroduced to
the regolith in a second chamber to produce CO_2. The carbon dioxide
was separated by a solar-powered electrochemical cell. The carbon was
recycled as graphite, and the O_2 liquefied. The excess was sold to other
lunar colonies or traded for nitrogen.

With Water, she worked at the far end of the ice cavern, where the
ice was crushed, vaporized, distilled, and refrozen. Some of the water was
electrolyzed to provide oxygen and carbon, a rare element on the moon.

With Agriculture she shoveled sheep and guinea-pig shit, and moved
chicken wastes to recycling for fertilizer.

With Fabrication she did quality control for the anhydrous production
of fiberglass cables coated with iron. Any contamination of the fiberglass
with water would compromise its strength and durability. Structural
materials were one of the colony's other major exports.

Everything she learned during her practicum was so logical. Everything she felt when she was in the apartment with Eva and her father was insane. While she worked, when she could forget the expression on Jack's face when she'd found him standing above Carey's naked body, the colony felt like home. But the minute she thought about the place that was supposed to be her home, she felt lost. Looking down from the balcony of their apartment on the interior of the crater, she saw the spire that supported the dome as a great tree spreading over the Cousins' lives. Behind her she heard Jack and Eva's voices, so human, so mysterious.

Eva quizzed Roz every few days about the practicum. Because they spoke only about the practical issues of running the Society, these conversations were a relief to Roz. She thought they were a relief for Eva as well. Roz could ask any question, as long as it was about engineering. Eva would lean next to Roz over the tablet and click through diagrams of chemical syntheses, twisting the ends of her hair in her fingers.

One evening as they were going through one of these sessions, Jack got mad at them, complaining about noise or something. Afraid that he might say something that would make Eva suspicious, Roz went with him for a walk to talk over what was bothering him. When she told him she was thinking of moving out, he threatened to tell Eva what had happened to Carey. His paranoia was so sharp in the air that she could smell it. She begged him to be quiet.

Roz realized that she was trapped. It would be safer for her and Jack both if she moved out of the apartment. Raisa was still looking for a roommate, and it would only be the matter of a few days for her to make the arrangements and move her things. But there was nothing she could do.

One day late in Roz's practicum, Eva called her to the Fabrication research lab. Roz realized that it was not an accident that the last stop on her practicum tour was Fabrication, and the last stop at Fabrication was research, Eva's own area. Roz had a sudden dread that Eva knew something, that ever since the festival she had been setting a trap, which was about to spring.

Like the biotech lab that her father worked in, in the interests of preventing contamination the nanotech lab was separated from the colony.

At the end of the northwest lava tube, Roz suited up and passed through a lock onto the surface. It was months since Carey's disappearance, and full night now. Mars and Jupiter were no longer visible; Venus shone brightly on the horizon. She followed a string of lights to the lab, entered, and pulled off her suit.

Eva met her at the check-in. "Thank you for coming, Roz. Follow me. I want to show you the Quantum Non-destructive Scanner Array."

The QNSA lab was the largest in the facility. The scanner looked like nothing so much as a huge blue marble, the size of an elephant, divided at the equator. Eva had the technicians lift the upper hemisphere to expose the target area. "What we do here is pull a fast one on the universe. We bypass the uncertainty principle on the subatomic level by measuring test subjects at below the Planck-Wheeler length."

"I don't know that much physics," Roz said.

Eva put her hand on Roz's shoulder. Despite the affectionate gesture, she was not smiling. "We've made huge strides in the last six months."

"What's it for?"

"There are a hundred purposes—some of them quite revolutionary. On the most basic level, if we can scan to sufficient accuracy, and if the assembler team can succeed in producing a programmable assembler that can use the scan—then we will have created the most flexible manufacturing system in history. Any object we scan could be duplicated in the assembler."

"Isn't that expensive?"

"Smart girl. Yes, it is very expensive—of technology, energy, and time. It doesn't make economic sense to use a system like this to manufacture simple things, like, say, an electric motor. That would be like running an MRI to check whether there's gum in your pocket. But for more complicated things—organic compounds, for instance—it holds fascinating possibilities. Let me show you something."

She took Roz into a side room separated by a large window from the lab. In the corner was a refrigerator. From it Eva took out two apples. She handed them to Roz. "What do you think of these?"

Roz looked them over. They were the same size, the same shape. Both felt cool in her palms. In fact, they felt exactly alike. She looked at them more closely. There was a spray of freckles near the stem of the apple in her right hand. She held the other next to it, turned it until they were in the same position. An identical spray of freckles marked the second apple.

"They're the same."

"Yes. Now compare this." Eva pulled a third apple from the refrigerator. This one was past its prime; its skin was darker and softer, and it smelled sweet. Yet it had exactly the same pattern of freckles as the other two.

"All three of these apples were assembled from the same quantum scan. We scanned the original apple six months ago. These two apples were assembled from the QNS yesterday, the other a week ago. If we load the right raw materials into the assembler, we can create as many identical apples as we like."

"That's amazing!"

"Yes. Though it's too expensive a way to make apples. In fact, there aren't many things that would justify the expense of reproduction by QNSA."

Eva took the apples back. She put the old one and one of the new ones back into the refrigerator. Then she polished the third on her sleeve and took a bite of it. Chewing, she handed it to Roz. "Try it."

Roz took a bite. It tasted crisp and tart. Another lab worker came in and got a squeeze bottle out of the refrigerator. He nodded to Eva, smiled at Roz, and went out.

"I hoped at first that I might get over the loss of Carey," Eva said. She looked through the window at the big blue marble. "I told myself that he was only one person, that we all die eventually, that it was his recklessness that had killed him, and I never wanted him to be other than he was." She brushed the back of her hand against her eye. "But a son is not supposed to die before his mother. Everything looks different afterward. It's all just a collection of atoms."

Eva turned to Roz. "How does the apple taste?"

"Good."

"I'm glad. Now, Roz, I want to tell you what I'm going to do. It's something that no one's ever done before. Because of that it's not a crime yet, but if it doesn't become so common as to be ordinary in the future, I'm sure it will become a crime."

"What are you talking about?"

"Some months ago, the project had reached a stage where we could scan a living organism. We scanned several guinea pigs, even a sheep. One night, while the lab was empty, I brought Carey here and scanned him.

"I've been waiting until we worked the bugs out of the assembler. Three days ago we recreated one of the guinea pigs from a four-month-old scan. Do you know what that means?"

Roz held her breath. "I think so."

"If that guinea pig suffers no aftereffects, I am going to reconstitute Carey. I want you to help me."

The sky opened up and a torrent of pure joy shot down to fill Roz up. She could not believe it. She hugged Eva, buried her head against the tall woman's breast. It was a miracle. It was the way out.

Fire

Nematodes made up most of the animal life on Earth, by mass, Jack reminded himself. They were everywhere. The number of parasitic varieties was minuscule compared to the beneficial ones. Nothing to worry about.

But his hands itched. And his skin burned.

It had not taken Jack long to cut up Carey's body, run it through the reduction chamber, mince the remains in the crusher, and mix them into the project soil. He had hosed down the crusher and the floor of the lab. Fire, earth, water. Within a week there was nothing left of Carey but his elemental chemicals in the dirt.

Still, images of Carey were imprinted on the inside of Jack's eyelids. I'm a freakshow, he thought a dozen times each day, climbing down the slope to the crater floor, pruning seedlings in the greenhouse, sitting on the edge of the pool in Sobieski Park. Lying in bed with Eva. I'm a lethal male in a society constructed to prevent males from going lethal. I didn't even know it was happening. I'm a fucking maniac and no one can tell.

No one had noticed anything—at least he didn't think they had. He had a tough afternoon the day they transferred the test soil to the pilot project site on Fowler's east slope. He insisted that he amend the soil himself, plant the junipers with his own hands. He wore protective gloves.

When Amravati said something about it, he replied quickly, "Don't want to take a chance with these new bugs."

"If there are any bugs we don't know about, then we're all in trouble," she said.

The seedlings flourished. Growth rates were elevated as much as fifteen percent. Within three months the project had progressed enough to schedule a tour by the Board of Matrons. Eva and the others strolled over the slopes among the low, fragrant growth. As Eva walked over the ground that contained all that was left of her only son, a wave of heat swept over Jack. His face felt flushed; his forehead burned.

The Board approved the project. The next week they voted Amravati a commendation, with special notice of Jack's contribution. "If you don't watch out, Jack, you're going to get stuck here," Hal Keikosson said.

"What?" he said.

Hal smiled at him. "I mean you're becoming a Cousin, cousin."

A Cousin on the outside, a stranger within. There were lots of difficult aspects to the aftermath of Carey's death, among them the problem of Eva. For example, despite the fact that, during the search, he had saved Eva's life out on the edge of the precipice, it was impossible for him to touch her in bed. He had discovered how much her eyes were like Carey's. Lying beside her at night, hands burning, pretending to sleep until he heard Eva's faint snore, and pretending to sleep after that for fear of waking her, Jack felt more alone than he had since he was five years old. One night he heard Eva stir beside him, rise up on one elbow, and watch him. He heard her whisper, "I'm sorry. I can do better." What did she have to feel sorry about? How could she possibly be asking his forgiveness?

The colony clinic prescribed a salve for his skin that did nothing but make him smell like sulfur. I'm the lunar Mephistopheles, he thought. He resorted to magic: if some part of Carey was coming back to torment Jack, maybe bringing Carey home would mollify his ghost. Jack potted one of the junipers and set it up on their balcony. He fed Eva lettuce from the greenhouse to see what effect it would have on her. It made her suggest that Roz should move out.

Roz. That was the worst thing, the absolute worst. Jack was stunned that Roz had so readily put herself at risk to save him. Though it was, at some level he had difficulty admitting, immensely gratifying, and removed any doubt he had ever had that she loved him, now he could not look at Roz the same way. He was in debt to his daughter, and like a boulder that they were both chained to, that debt both united and stood between them at every moment.

When Roz started her practicum in Fabrication, she began to spend more time with Eva. Jack watched them joke together as they sat in the apartment and went over the steps in the manufacture of building glass. Their heads were so close together, Roz's red hair and Eva's brown. The skirl of Roz's silly, high-pitched giggle, for some reason, made him want to cry.

"You laugh too much," he said.

They looked up at him, dead silent, identical astonishment on their faces.

"Can't you keep quiet?" he said.

"Sorry, Dad," Roz muttered. "I didn't know I wasn't allowed to laugh." She pushed the tablet away from her. "I have something I need to tell you."

Jack tried to keep the panic out of his voice. "What's that?"

"I think I'm going to move out. There's an apartment that Raisa and I can move into opening up in the old section of the south wall."

"Raisa? I thought you didn't even like her."

"I think I was just projecting; she's really a good person. She's never mean."

Jack wanted to argue, but was intimidated by Eva's presence. Eva had put this idea in Roz's head. "Come with me," he said to Roz. "We'll take a walk. Do you mind, Eva? We need to talk this over father to daughter."

"Go right ahead."

Roz looked sullen, but she came with him. They descended from the apartment, down the pathway toward the crater floor. The inside of the dome was a brilliant cloudless sky. On the field below them a harvester sprayed soybeans into a hopper truck. "Is this because of Carey?" Jack asked.

Roz crossed her arms over her chest and looked at her feet. "I don't want to talk about Carey," she said.

"You know it was an accident, Roz, I—"

She bounced on her toes and leapt five feet into the air, coming down well ahead of him. A woman going the other way looked at her and smiled. Jack hurried to catch up.

Roz still wouldn't look at him. "I will not talk about Carey, Dad. This isn't about him. I'm fourteen, and a Cousins girl at fourteen who won't leave home is sick." She bounced again.

He didn't know what to say. He knew she was lying, that it had to have something to do with Carey. But he wasn't going to beg.

"You're going to tell Eva the truth," he said when he caught up.

"Don't be stupid!" Roz said. "I've given up too much for this. I don't want to move again."

Stupid. The stupid thing was deciding to come here. "I brought you here to keep us from drifting apart."

"Dad, did you think I was going to be with you forever?"

He rubbed his palms up and down his forearms, but that only made the itching worse. "Will you call me?"

"I'll see you every day."

Jack stopped following her. Roz continued down the path toward Sobieski Park, and did not look back.

"What do you think, Carey?" he whispered aloud as he watched his daughter walk away. "Is this one of those Earth things? One of those sexual ownership practices?"

Jack tried to imagine what it would be like to be alone with Eva in one of the largest apartments in the colony. Perhaps it would not be so bad. He could plant a dozen junipers on the balcony. He could prepare all their meals. Hell, he could bring in a bed of Carey's soil and sleep in it.

He began meeting Jamira Tamlasdaughter in the sauna at the gym. They would claim one of the private alcoves and fuck. The heat of the sauna made him forget his burning skin. There was nothing wrong with it. There was nothing right about it. Roz was always out. Eva stayed away even longer at the labs, sometimes not coming back at night until he was asleep. The mysterious absences grew until one night it had been a full twenty-four hours since Jack had last seen either Eva or Roz. It was fertile ground for worry. Someone had found Carey's pressure suit. Roz had not hidden it well enough, and now she was in trouble. Or Eva had tricked her into an admission. She had broken down, given in to guilt.

His phone rang. He touched the contact on his wristward.

"Dad? Can you meet me at Fabrication Research?"

Roz's voice was charged with excitement. He hadn't heard her sound so young in months. "What is it, Roz?"

"You won't believe it. All our troubles are over! We're resurrecting Carey!"

"What?"

"The assembler. I can't tell you more now, someone might hear. Come at 0300. If anyone asks, tell them that you're going somewhere else."

"Is Eva there?"

"Yes. I've got to go now. See you at 0300."

"Roz—"

He felt sick. Resurrecting Carey? Roz must have told Eva what had happened.

Still, what could he do but go? Jack paced the rooms for hours. He left after somatic midnight. The perimeter road to the north airlock was quiet; there was a slight breeze, a hum of insects around the lights. He told the lock attendant that he was going to biotech.

When he sealed up his suit he felt he could not breathe. He checked the readouts repeatedly, but despite the evidence that nothing was wrong, he felt stifled. Sweat trickled down his neck into his collar.

Outside the sun hammered down and the glare of the baked surface hid the stars. He upped the polarization on his faceplate, but still his eyes hurt. He followed the road from the airlock, between the fields of solar collectors, to the ramp entrance to the Fabrication Research Lab. He passed through the radiation maze, opened the outer door of the lab airlock. When he stripped off his suit his shirt was soaked with sweat. He wiped his arm across his brow, ran his fingers through his sweaty hair. He waited. He did not open the inner door.

And if, by some miracle, they did recreate Carey? Roz said that all their troubles would be over. They could go back to who they were.

Fat chance. He had hoped that coming to the Society would offer Roz a freedom that he could not earn for her on Earth. No one on the moon knew him. And even if he did fail again, among the cousins a father's faults would not determine how others saw his daughter. Roz could be herself, not some reflection of him.

As he stood there, poised before the inner lock door, he had a sudden memory of Helen, on their honeymoon. On the beach at St. Kitts. Helen had surprised him by wearing a new bikini, so small that when she pulled off her shorts and T-shirt she was clearly self-conscious. But proud, in some way. He remembered feeling protective of her, and puzzled, and a little sorry. It hit him for the first time that she was fighting her body for his attention, and how sad that must be for her—on the one hand to know she had this power over him that came simply from her sexuality, and on the other that she, Helen, was someone completely apart from that body that drew him like a magnet. For a moment he had seen himself from outside. He'd been ashamed of his own sexuality, and the way it threatened to deform their relationship. Who was she, really? Who was he?

At the time he had taken her in his arms, smiled, complimented her. He had felt sure that with time, they would know each other completely. How pathetic. After the breakup, he had at least thought that he could know his daughter. That was why he needed Roz—so he could love someone without sex coming in the way. To love someone without caring about himself.

How stupid he had been. Whether they'd come here or not, inevitably she would have seen him differently, or been destroyed by trying not to. Whether he'd killed Carey or not, Roz would have to fight to escape the mirror he held up to her.

With a sick feeling in his gut, he realized he had lost his daughter.

He was so hot. He was burning up. He shut his eyes and tried not to see or hear anything, but there was a roaring in his ears like a turbulent storm, and his eyes burned and flashed like lightning.

He would feel better if he went outside. Instead of opening the inner airlock door, he put his pressure suit back on and opened the outside door. It was bright and hot out on the surface—but in the shadows of the rocks it would be cool. He stepped out of the shadow of the radiation baffle, up the ramp to the dusty surface. Instead of following the path back to the colony, he struck off between the rows of solar collectors toward a giant boulder that loomed on the horizon. As he walked, on his sleeve keyboard he punched in the override code for his suit's pressure fail-safes.

By the time he had reached the chill shadow of the rock, all that remained between him and relief was the manual helmet release. He reached up to his neck and felt for the latch. He was so hot. He was burning up. But soon he would be cool again.

Happy Ending

When the indicators showed the airlock was occupied, they waited for Jack to enter the lab. Instead, after a few minutes the outer door of the airlock re-opened and he left again. Roz was worried.

"I'm going to see what he's up to," she told Eva.

She pulled on her pressure suit and waited the maddening few minutes it took the lock to recycle. As soon as pressure was equalized she slid open the outer door and ran up the ramp. There was no sign of her father on the path back to Fowler. But as she followed the footprints away from the ramp, she spotted a figure in the distance heading out toward the hills.

Roz hurried after, skipping as fast as she could without lurching off onto the solar collectors.

When she caught up, he was on his knees in the shadow of a big rock, jerking about spasmodically. The strangeness of his motion alarmed her. She had never seen anyone move like that. Before she could reach him he slowed, stopped, and fell, slowly, onto his side. Calmly, quietly. Less like a fall, more like the drift of a feather. She rushed to his side, and saw that he had broken the seal on his helmet.

"No!" she screamed, and the sound of her voice echoed in her ears. Jack's face was purple with broken blood vessels, his eyes bloody. He was dead.

High-G they called her, because she was so strong, and it was a good thing, as she carried her father's body back to the fabrication lab.

It was Roz's idea to put Jack's corpse into the assembler, to add the materials of his body to the atoms used to recreate Carey. There would be hell to pay with security, but Eva agreed to do it.

The assembly took seven days. When the others at the colony discovered what Eva was doing, there was some debate, but they let the process continue. At the end of the week the fluid supporting the nanomachines was drained off, revealing Carey's perfect body. Carey shuddered and coughed, and they helped him out of the assembler.

To him it was six months earlier, and his mother had just completed his scan. It took him a long time to accept that he had not fallen into some dream only seconds after he had been placed in the marble, to awaken in this vat of warm fluid. He thought he was the original, not the copy. For all practical purposes he was right.

Later, as they were finding a pressure suit they could adapt to Carey's size to take him home, he asked Roz, "Where's Jack?"

The Juniper Tree

All this happened a long time ago.

Nora Sobieski founded the Society of Cousins to free girls like Roz of the feeling that they must depend on their fathers or boyfriends for their sense of self, and incidentally to free boys like Carey of the need to prove themselves superior to other boys by owning girls like Roz. Girls still go through infatuations, still fall in love, still feel the influence of men as well as of women. But Roz and Eva in the end are actually in the same boat—a boat that does not contain Jack, or even Carey.

The young junipers stand ghostly gray in the night. The air is fragrant with piñon. In the thin, clear starlight Roz can see wildflowers blooming beneath the trees—columbine, pennyroyal, groundsel. She sits on the slope and pulls Carey's ring from her pocket. The ring is fashioned into the image of two vines that twine around each other, each with no beginning and no end, each eternally separate from the other.

Roz holds the ring in the middle of her palm, wondering if she should get rid of it at last, knowing that she can never give it back and keep her father's secret.

Stories for Men

One

Erno couldn't get to the club until an hour after it opened, so of course the place was crowded and he got stuck in the back behind three queens whose loud, aimless conversation made him edgy.

He was never less than edgy anyway, Erno—a seventeen-year-old biotech apprentice known for the clumsy, earnest intensity with which he propositioned almost every girl he met.

It was more people than Erno had ever seen in the Oxygen Warehouse. Even though Tyler Durden had not yet taken the stage, every table was filled, and people stood three deep at the bar. Rosamund, the owner, bustled back and forth providing drinks, her face glistening with sweat. The crush of people only irritated Erno. He had been one of the first to catch on to Durden, and the roomful of others, some of whom had probably come on his own recommendation, struck him as usurpers.

Erno forced his way to the bar and bought a tincture. Tyrus and Sid, friends of his, nodded at him from across the room. Erno sipped the cool, licorice-flavored drink and eavesdropped, and gradually his thoughts took on an architectural, intricate intellectuality.

A friend of his mother sat with a couple of sons who anticipated for her what she was going to see. "He's not just a comedian, he's a philosopher," said the skinny one. His foot, crossed over his knee, bounced in rhythm to the jazz playing in the background. Erno recognized him from a party he'd attended a few months back.

"We have philosophers," the matron said. "We even have comedians."

"Not like Tyler Durden," said the other boy.

"Tyler Durden—who gave him that name?"

"I think it's historical," the first boy said.

"Not any history I ever heard," the woman said. "Who's his mother?"

Erno noticed that there were more women in the room than there had been at any performance he had seen. Already the matrons were homing in. You could not escape their sisterly curiosity, their motherly tyranny. He realized that his shoulders were cramped; he rolled his head to try to loosen the spring-tight muscles.

The Oxygen Warehouse was located in what had been a shop in the commercial district of the northwest lava tube. It was a free-enterprise zone, and no one had objected to the addition of a tinctures bar, though some eyebrows had been raised when it was discovered that one of the tinctures sold was alcohol. The stage was merely a raised platform in one corner. Around the room were small tables with chairs. The bar spanned one end, and the other featured a false window that showed a nighttime cityscape of Old New York.

Rosamund Demisdaughter, who'd started the club, at first booked local jazz musicians. Her idea was to present as close to a retro Earth atmosphere as could be managed on the far side of the moon, where few of the inhabitants had ever even seen the Earth. Her clientele consisted of a few immigrants and a larger group of rebellious young cousins who were looking for an avant-garde. Erno knew his mother would not approve his going to the Warehouse, so he was there immediately.

He pulled his pack of fireless cigarettes from the inside pocket of his black twentieth-century suit, shook out a fag, inhaled it into life and imagined himself living back on Earth a hundred years ago. Exhaling a plume of cool, rancid smoke, he caught a glimpse of his razor haircut in the mirror behind the bar, then adjusted the knot of his narrow tie.

After some minutes the door beside the bar opened and Tyler Durden came out. He leaned over and exchanged a few words with Rosamund. Some of the men whistled and cheered. Rosamund flipped a brandy snifter high into the air, where it caught the ceiling lights as it spun in the low G, then slowly fell back to her hand. Having attracted the attention of the audience, she hopped over the bar and onto the small stage.

"Don't you people have anything better to do?" she shouted.

A chorus of rude remarks.

"Welcome to The Oxygen Warehouse," she said. "I want to say, before

I bring him out, that I take no responsibility for the opinions expressed by
Tyler Durden. He's not my boy."

Durden stepped onto the stage. The audience was quiet, a little
nervous. He ran his hand over his shaved head, gave a boyish grin. He was
a big man, in his thirties, wearing the blue coveralls of an environmental
technician. Around his waist he wore a belt with tools hanging from it, as
if he'd just come off shift.

"'Make love, not war!'" Durden said. "Remember that one? You got
that from your mother, in the school? I never liked that one. 'Make love,
not war,' they'll tell you. I hate that. I want to make love *and* war. I don't
want my dick just to be a dick. I want it to stand for something!"

A heckler from the audience shouted, "Can't it stand on its own?"

Durden grinned. "Let's ask it." He addressed his crotch. "Hey, son!"
He called down. "Don't you like screwing?"

Durden looked up at the ceiling, his face went simple, and he became
his dick talking back to him. "Hiya dad!" he squeaked. "Sure, I like
screwing!"

Durden winked at a couple of guys in makeup and lace in the front
row, then looked down again: "Boys or girls?"

His dick: "What day of the week is it?"

"Thursday."

"Doesn't matter, then. Thursday's guest mammal day."

"Outstanding, son."

"I'm a Good Partner."

The queers laughed. Erno did, too.

"You want I should show you?"

"Not now, son," Tyler told his dick. "You keep quiet for a minute,
and let me explain to the people, okay?"

"Sure. I'm here whenever you need me."

"I'm aware of that." Durden addressed the audience again. "Remember
what Mama says, folks: *Keep your son close, let your semen go.*" He recited
the slogan with exaggerated rhythm, wagging his finger at them, sober as
a scolding grandmother. The audience loved it. Some of them chanted
along with the catchphrase.

Durden was warming up. "But is screwing all there is to a dick? I
say no!

"A dick is a sign of power. It's a tower of strength. It's the tree of life. It's a weapon. It's an incisive tool of logic. It's the seeker of truth.

"Mama says that being male is nothing more than a performance. You know what I say to that? Perform this, baby!" He grabbed his imaginary cock with both of his hands, made a stupid face.

Cheers.

"But of course, *they* can't perform this! I don't care how you plank the genes, Mama don't have the *machinery*. Not only that, she don't have the *programming*. But mama wants to program *us* with *her* half-baked scheme of what women want a man to be. This whole place is about fucking up our *hardware* with their *software*."

He was laughing himself, now. Beads of sweat stood out on his scalp in the bright light.

"Mama says, 'Don't confuse your penis with a phallus.'" He assumed a female sway of his hips, lifted his chin and narrowed his eyes: just like that, he was an archetypal matron, his voice transmuted into a fruity contralto. "'Yes, you boys do have those nice little dicks, but we're living in a *post-phallic* society. A penis is merely a biological appendage.'"

Now he was her son, responding: "'Like a foot, Mom?'"

Mama: "'Yes, son. Exactly like a foot.'"

Quick as a spark, back to his own voice: "How many of you in the audience here have named your foot?"

Laughter, a show of hands.

"But Mama says the penis is designed solely for the propagation of the species. Sex gives pleasure in order to encourage procreation. A phallus, on the other hand—whichever hand you like—I prefer the left—"

More laughter.

"—a phallus is an idea, a cultural creation of the dead patriarchy, a symbolic sheath applied over the penis to give it meanings that have nothing to do with biology. . . ."

Durden seized his invisible dick again. "Apply my symbolic sheath, baby . . . oohhh, yes, I like it. . . ."

Erno had heard Tyler talk about his symbolic sheath before. Though there were variations, he watched the audience instead. Did they get it? Most of the men seemed to be engaged and laughing. A drunk in the first row leaned forward, hands on his knees, howling at Tyler's every word.

Queers leaned their heads together and smirked. Faces gleamed in the close air. But a lot of the men's laughter was nervous, and some did not laugh at all.

A few of the women, mostly the younger ones, were laughing. Some of them seemed mildly amused. Puzzled. Some looked bored. Others sat stonily with expressions that could only indicate anger.

Erno did not know how he felt about the women who were laughing. He felt hostility toward those who looked bored: why did you come here, he wanted to ask them. Who do you think you are? He preferred those who looked angry. That was what he wanted from them.

Then he noticed those who looked calm, interested, alert yet unamused. These women scared him.

In the back of the room stood some green-uniformed constables, male and female, carrying batons, red lights gleaming in the corner of their mirror spex, recording. Looking around the room, Erno located at least a half dozen of them. One, he saw with a start, was his mother.

He ducked behind a tall man beside him. She might not have seen him yet, but she would see him sooner or later. For a moment he considered confronting her, but then he sidled behind a row of watchers toward the back rooms. Another constable, her slender lunar physique distorted by the bulging muscles of a genetically engineered testosterone girl, stood beside the doorway. She did not look at Erno: she was watching Tyler, who was back to conversing with his dick.

"I'm tired of being confined," Tyler's dick was saying.

"You feel constricted?" Tyler asked.

He looked up in dumb appeal. "I'm stuck in your pants all day!"

Looking down: "I can let you out, but first tell me, are you a penis or a phallus?"

"That's a distinction without a difference."

"*Au contraire*, little man! You haven't been listening."

"I'm not noted for my listening ability."

"Sounds like you're a phallus to me," Tyler told his dick. "We have lots of room for penises, but Mama don't allow no phalluses 'round here."

"Let my people go!"

"Nice try, but wrong color. Look, son. It's risky when you come

out. You could get damaged. The phallic liberation movement is in its
infancy."

"I thought you Cousins were *all about* freedom."

"In theory. In practice, free phalluses are dangerous."

"Who says?"

"Well, Debra does, and so does Mary, and Sue, and Jamina most
every time I see her, and there was this lecture in We-Whine-You-Listen
class last week, and Ramona says so, too, and of course most emphatically
Baba, and then there's that bitch Nora . . ."

Erno spotted his mother moving toward his side of the room. He
slipped past the constable into the hall. There was the restroom, and a
couple of other doors. A gale of laughter washed in from the club behind
him at the climax of Tyler's story; cursing his mother, Erno went into the
restroom.

No one was there. He could still hear the laughter, but not the cause
of it. His mother's presence had cut him out of the community of male
watchers as neatly as if she had used a baton. Erno felt murderously angry.
He switched on a urinal and took a piss.

Over the urinal, a window played a scene in Central Park, on Earth,
of a hundred years ago. A night scene of a pathway beneath some trees,
trees as large as the largest in Sobieski Park. A line of electric lights on
poles threw pools of light along the path, and through the pools of light
strolled a man and a woman. They were talking, but Erno could not hear
what they were saying.

The woman wore a dress cinched tight at the waist, whose skirt flared
out stiffly, ending halfway down her calves. The top of her dress had a
low neckline that showed off her breasts. The man wore a dark suit like
Erno's. They were completely differentiated by their dress, as if they were
from different cultures, even species. Erno wondered where Rosamund
had gotten the image.

As Erno watched, the man nudged the woman to the side of the path,
beneath one of the trees. He slid his hands around her waist and pressed
his body against hers. She yielded softly to his embrace. Erno could not
see their faces in the shadows, but they were inches apart. He felt his dick
getting hard in his hand.

He stepped back from the urinal, turned it off, and closed his pants.

As the hum of the recycler died, the restroom door swung open and a woman came in. She glanced at Erno and headed for one of the toilets. Erno went over to the counter and stuck his hands into the cleaner. The woman's presence sparked his anger.

Without turning to face her, but watching in the mirror, he said, "Why are you here tonight?"

The woman looked up (she had been studying her fingernails) and her eyes locked on his. She was younger than his mother and had a pretty, heart-shaped face. "I was curious. People are talking about him."

"Do you think men want you here?"

"I don't know what the men want."

"Yes. That's the point, isn't it? Are you learning anything?"

"Perhaps." The woman looked back at her hands. "Aren't you Pamela Megsdaughter's son?"

"So she tells me." Erno pulled his tingling hands out of the cleaner.

The woman used the bidet, and dried herself. She had a great ass. "Did she bring you or did you bring her?" she asked.

"We brought ourselves," Erno said. He left the restroom. He looked out into the club again, listening to the noise. The crowd was rowdier, and more raucous. The men's shouts of encouragement were like barks, their laughter edged with anger. His mother was still there. He did not want to see her, or to have her see him.

He went back past the restroom to the end of the hallway. The hall made a right angle into a dead end, but when Erno stepped into the bend he saw, behind a stack of plastic crates, an old door. He wedged the crates to one side and opened the door enough to slip through.

The door opened into a dark, dimly lit space. His steps echoed. As his eyes adjusted to the dim light he saw it was a very large room hewn out of the rock, empty except for some racks that must have held liquid-oxygen cylinders back in the early days of the colony, when this place had been an actual oxygen warehouse. The light came from ancient bioluminescent units on the walls. The club must have been set up in this space years before.

The tincture still lent Erno an edge of aggression, and he called out: "I'm Erno, King of the Moon!"

"—ooo—ooo—ooon!" the echoes came back, fading to stillness. He kicked an empty cylinder, which rolled forlornly a few meters before it stopped. He wandered around the chill vastness. At the far wall, one of the darker shadows turned out to be an alcove in the stone. Set in the back, barely visible in the dim light, was an ancient pressure door.

Erno decided not to mess with it—it could open onto vacuum. He went back to the club door and slid into the hallway.

Around the corner, two men were just coming out of the restroom, and Erno followed them as if he were just returning as well. The club was more crowded than ever. Every open space was filled with standing men, and others sat cross-legged up front. His mother and another constable had moved to the edge of the stage.

"—the problem with getting laid all the time is, you can't think!" Tyler was saying. "I mean, there's only so much blood in the human body. That's why those old Catholics back on Earth put the lock on the Pope's dick. He had an empire to run: the more time he spent taking care of John Thomas the less he spent thinking up ways of getting money out of peasants. The secret of our moms is that, if they keep that blood flowing below the belt, it ain't never gonna flow back above the shirt collar. Keeps the frequency of radical male ideas down!"

Tyler leaned over toward the drunk in the first row. "You know what I'm talking about, soldier?"

"You bet," the man said. He tried to stand, wobbled, sat down, tried to stand again.

"Where do you work?"

"Lunox." The man found his balance. "You're *right*, you—"

Tyler patted him on the shoulder. "An oxygen boy. You know what I mean, you're out there on the processing line, and you're thinking about how maybe if you were to add a little more graphite to the reduction chamber you could increase efficiency by 15 percent, and just then Mary Ellen Swivelhips walks by in her skintight and—bam!" Tyler made the face of a man who'd been poleaxed. "Uh—what was I thinking of?"

The audience howled.

"Forty I.Q. points down the oubliette. And nothing, NOTHING's gonna change until we get a handle on this! Am I right, brothers?"

More howls, spiked with anger.

Tyler was sweating, laughing, trembling as if charged with electricity. "Keep your son close! *Penis, no! Phallus, si!*"

Cheers now. Men stood and raised their fists. The drunk saw Erno's mother at the edge of the stage and took a step toward her. He said something, and while she and her partner stood irresolute, he put his big hand on her chest and shoved her away.

The other constable discharged his electric club against the man. The drunk's arms flew back, striking a bystander, and two other men surged forward and knocked down the constable. Erno's mother raised her own baton. More constables pushed toward the stage, using their batons, and other men rose to stop them. A table was upended, shouts echoed, the room was hot as hell and turning into a riot, the first riot in the Society of Cousins in fifty years.

As the crowd surged toward the exits or toward the constables, Erno ducked back to the hallway. He hesitated, and then Tyler Durden came stumbling out of the melee. He took a quick look at Erno. "What now, kid?"

"Come with me," Erno said. He grabbed Tyler's arm and pulled him around the bend in the end of the hall, past the crates to the warehouse door. He slammed the door behind them and propped an empty oxygen cylinder against it. "We can hide here until the thing dies down."

"Who are you?"

"My name is Erno."

"Well, Erno, are we sure we want to hide? Out there is more interesting."

Erno decided not to tell Tyler that one of the constables was his mother. "Are you serious?"

"I'm always serious." Durden wandered back from the door into the gloom of the cavern. He kicked a piece of rubble, which soared across the room and skidded up against the wall thirty meters away. "This place must have been here since the beginning. I'm surprised they're wasting the space. Probably full of toxics."

"You think so?" Erno said.

"Who knows?" Durden went toward the back of the warehouse, and Erno followed. It was cold, and their breath steamed the air. "Who would have figured the lights would still be growing?" Durden said.

"A well-established colony can last for fifty years or more," Erno said. "As long as there's enough moisture in the air. They break down the rock."

"You know all about it."

"I work in biotech," Erno said. "I'm a gene hacker."

Durden said nothing, and Erno felt the awkwardness of his boast.

They reached the far wall. Durden found the pressure door set into the dark alcove. He pulled a flashlight from his belt. The triangular yellow warning signs around the door were faded. He felt around the door seam.

"We probably ought to leave that alone," Erno said.

Durden handed Erno the flashlight, took a pry bar from his belt, and shoved it into the edge of the door. The door resisted, then with a grating squeak jerked open a couple of centimeters. Erno jumped at the sound.

"Help me out here, Erno," Durden said.

Erno got his fingers around the door's edge, and the two of them braced themselves. Durden put his feet up on the wall and used his legs and back to get leverage. When the door suddenly shot open Erno fell back and whacked his head. Durden lost his grip, shot sideways out of the alcove, bounced once, and skidded across the dusty floor. While Erno shook his head to clear his vision, Durden sat spread-legged, laughing. "Bingo!" he said. He bounced up. "You okay, Erno?"

Erno felt the back of his skull. He wasn't bleeding. "I'm fine," he said.

"Let's see what we've got, then."

Beyond the door a dark corridor cut through the basalt. Durden stepped into the path marked by his light. Erno wanted to go back to the club—by now things must have died down—but instead he followed.

Shortly past the door the corridor turned into a cramped lava tube. Early settlers had leveled the floor of the erratic tube formed by the draining away of cooling lava several billion years ago. Between walls that had been erected to form rooms ran a path of red volcanic gravel much like tailings from the oxygen factory. Foamy irregular pebbles kicked up by their shoes rattled off the walls. Dead light fixtures broke the ceiling at intervals. Tyler stopped to shine his light into a couple of the doorways, and at the third he went inside.

"This must be from the start of the colony," Erno said. "I wonder why it's been abandoned."

"Kind of claustrophobic." Durden shone the light around the small room.

The light fell on a small rectangular object in the corner. From his belt Durden pulled another tool, which he extended into a probe.

"Do you always carry this equipment?" Erno asked.

"Be prepared," Durden said. He set down the light and crouched over the object. It looked like a small box, a few centimeters thick. "You ever hear of the Boy Scouts, Erno?"

"Some early lunar colony?"

"Nope. Sort of like the Men's House, only different." Durden forced the probe under an edge, and one side lifted as if to come off. "Well, well!"

He put down the probe, picked up the object. He held it end-on, put his thumbs against the long side, and opened it. It divided neatly into flat sheets attached at the other long side.

"What is it?" Erno asked.

"It's a book."

"Is it still working?"

"This is an unpowered book. The words are printed right on these leaves. They're made of paper."

Erno had seen such old-fashioned books in vids. "It must be very old. What is it?"

Durden carefully turned the pages. "It's a book of stories." Durden stood up and handed the book to Erno. "Here. You keep it. Let me know what it's about."

Erno tried to make out the writing, but without Tyler's flashlight it was too dim.

Durden folded up his probe and hung it on his belt. He ran his hand over his head, smearing a line of dust over his scalp. "Are you cold? I suppose we ought to find our way out of here." Immediately he headed out of the room and back down the corridor.

Erno felt he was getting left behind in more ways than one. Clutching the book, he followed after Durden and his bobbing light. Rather than heading back to the Oxygen Warehouse, the comedian continued down the lava tube.

Eventually the tube ended in another old pressure door. When Durden touched the key panel at its side, amazingly, it lit.

"What do you think?" Durden said.

"We should go back," Erno said. "We can't know whether the lock door on the other side is still airtight. The fail-safes could be broken. We could open the door onto vacuum." He held the book under his armpit and blew on his cold hands.

"How old are you, Erno?"

"Seventeen."

"Seventeen?" Durden's eyes glinted in shadowed eye sockets. "Seventeen is no age to be cautious."

Erno couldn't help but grin. "You're right. Let's open it."

"My man, Erno!" Durden slapped him on the shoulder. He keyed the door open. They heard the whine of a long-unused electric motor. Erno could feel his heart beat, the blood running swiftly in his veins. At first nothing happened, then the door began to slide open. There was a chuff of air escaping from the lava tube, and dust kicked up. But the wind stopped as soon as it started, and the door opened completely on the old airlock, filled floor to ceiling with crates and bundles of fiberglass building struts.

It took them half an hour to shift boxes and burrow their way through the airlock, to emerge at the other end into another warehouse, this one still in use. They crept by racks of construction materials until they reached the entrance, and sneaked out into the colony corridor beyond.

They were at the far end of North Six, the giant lava tube that served the industrial wing of the colony. The few workers they encountered on the late shift might have noticed Erno's suit, but said nothing.

Erno and Tyler made their way back home. Tyler cracked jokes about the constables until they emerged into the vast open space of the domed crater that formed the center of the colony. Above, on the huge dome, was projected a night starfield. In the distance, down the rimwall slopes covered with junipers, across the crater floor, lights glinted among the trees in Sobieski Park. Erno took a huge breath of air, fragrant with piñon.

"The world our ancestors gave us," Tyler said, waving his arm as if offering it to Erno.

As Tyler turned to leave, Erno called out impulsively, "That was an adventure!"

"The first of many, Erno." Tyler said, and jogged away.

Celibacy Day

On Celibacy Day, everyone gets a day off from sex.

Some protest this practice, but they are relatively few. Most men take it as an opportunity to retreat to the informal Men's Houses that, though they have no statutory sanction, sprang up in the first generation of settlers.

In the Men's House, men and boys talk about what it is to be a man, a lover of other men and women, a father in a world where fatherhood is no more than a biological concept. They complain about their lot. They tell vile jokes and sing songs. They wrestle. They gossip. Heteros and queers and everyone in between compare speculations on what they think women really want, and whether it matters. They try to figure out what a true man is.

As a boy Erno would go to the Men's House with his mother's current partner or one of the other men involved in the household. Some of the men taught him things. He learned about masturbation, and cross-checks, and Micro Language Theory.

But no matter how welcoming the men were supposed to be to each other—and they talked about brotherhood all the time—there was always that little edge when you met another boy there, or that necessary wariness when you talked to an adult. Men came to the Men's House to spend time together and remind themselves of certain congruencies, but only a crazy person would want to live solely in the company of men.

Two

The founders of the Society of Cousins had a vision of women as independent agents, freethinkers forming alliances with other women to create a social bond so strong that men could not overwhelm them. Solidarity, sisterhood, motherhood. But Erno's mother was not like those women. Those women existed only in history vids, sitting in meeting circles, laughing, making plans, sure of themselves and complete.

Erno's mother was a cop. She had a cop's squinty eyes and a cop's suspicion of anyone who stepped outside of the norm. She had a cop's lack of imagination, except as she could imagine what people would do wrong.

Erno and his mother and his sister Celeste and his Aunt Sophie and his cousins Lena and Aphra, and various men, some of whom may have been fathers, some of them Good Partners, and others just men, lived in an apartment in Sanger, on the third level of the northeast quadrant, a small place looking down on the farms that filled the floor of the crater they called Fowler, though the real Fowler was a much larger crater five kilometers distant.

Erno had his own room. He thought nothing of the fact that the girls had to share a room, and would be forced to move out when they turned fourteen. *Keep your son close, let your daughter go*, went the aphorism Tyler had mocked. Erno's mother was not about to challenge any aphorisms. Erno remembered her expression as she had stepped forward to arrest the drunk: sad that this man had forced her to this, and determined to do it. She was comfortable in the world; she saw no need for alternatives. Her cronies came by the apartment and shared coffee and gossip, and they were just like all the other mothers and sisters and aunts. None of them were extraordinary.

Not that any of the men Erno knew were extraordinary, either. Except Tyler Durden. And now Erno knew Durden, and they had spent a night breaking rules and getting away with it.

Celeste and Aphra were dishing up oatmeal when Erno returned to the apartment that morning. "Where were you?" his mother asked. She looked up from the table, more curious than upset, and Erno noticed a bruise on her temple.

"What happened to your forehead?" Erno asked.

His mother touched a hand to her forehead, as if she had forgotten it. She waved the hand in dismissal.

"There was trouble at a club in the enterprise district," Aunt Sophie said. "The constables had to step in, and your mother was assaulted."

"It was a riot!" Lena said eagerly. "There's going to be a big meeting about it in the park today." Lena was a month from turning fourteen, and looking forward to voting.

Erno sat down at the table. As he did so he felt the book, which he had tucked into his belt at the small of his back beneath his now rumpled suit jacket. He leaned forward, pulled a bowl of oatmeal toward him, and took up a spoon. Looking down into the bowl to avoid anyone's eyes, he idly asked, "What's the meeting for?"

"One of the rioters was knocked into a coma," Lena said. "The social order committee wants this comedian Tyler Durden to be made invisible."

Erno concentrated on his spoon. "Why?"

"You know about him?" his mother asked.

Before he had to think of an answer, Nick Farahsson, his mother's partner, shambled into the kitchen. "Lord, Pam, don't you pay attention? Erno's one of his biggest fans."

His mother turned on Erno. "Is that so?"

Erno looked up from his bowl and met her eyes. She looked hurt. "I've heard of him."

"Heard of him?" Nick said. "Erno, I bet you were there last night."

"I bet *you* weren't there," Erno said.

Nick stretched. "I don't need to hear him. I have no complaints." He came up behind Erno's mother, nuzzled the nape of her neck, and cupped her breast in his hand.

She turned her face up and kissed him on the cheek. "I should hope not."

Lena made a face. "Heteros. I can't wait until I get out of here." She had recently declared herself a lesbian and was quite judgmental about it.

"You'd better get to your practicum, Lena," Aunt Sophie said. "Let your aunt take care of her own sex life."

"This guy Durden is setting himself up for a major fall," said Nick. "Smells like a case of abnormal development. Who's his mother?"

Erno couldn't keep quiet. "He doesn't have a mother. He doesn't need one."

"Parthenogenesis," Aunt Sophie said. "I didn't think it had been perfected yet."

"If they ever do, what happens to me?" Nick said.

"You have your uses." Erno's mother nudged her shoulder against his hip.

"You two can go back to your room," Aunt Sophie said. "We'll take care of things for you."

"No need." Nick grabbed a bowl of oatmeal and sat down. "Thank you, sweetheart," he said to Aphra. "I can't see what this guy's problem is."

"Doesn't it bother you that you can't vote?" Erno said. "What's fair about that?"

"I don't want to vote," Nick said.

"You're a complete drone."

His mother frowned at him. Erno pushed his bowl away and left for his room.

"You're the one with special tutoring!" Lena called. "The nice clothes. What work do you do?"

"Shut up," Erno said softly, but his ears burned.

He had nothing to do until his 1100 biotech tutorial, and he didn't even have to go if he didn't want to. Lena was right about that, anyway. He threw the book on his bed, undressed, and switched on his screen. On the front page was a report of solar activity approaching its eleven-year peak, with radiation warnings issued for all surface activity. Erno called up the calendar. There it was: a discussion on Tyler Durden was scheduled in the amphitheater at 1600. Linked was a vid of the riot and a forum for open citizen comment. A cousin named Tashi Yokiosson had been clubbed in the fight and was in a coma, undergoing nanorepair.

Erno didn't know him, but that didn't prevent his anger. He considered calling up Tyrus or Sid, finding out what had happened to them, and telling them about his adventure with Tyler. But that would spoil the secret, and it might get around to his mother. Yet he couldn't let his night with Tyler go uncelebrated. He opened his journal, and wrote a poem:

> *Going outside the crater*
> *finding the lost tunnels*
> *of freedom*
> *and male strength.*
> *Searching with your brother*
> *shoulder to shoulder*
> *like men.*

> *Getting below the surface*
> *of a stifling society*
> *sounding your XY shout.*

Flashing your colors
like an ancient Spartan bird
proud, erect, never to be softened
by the silent embrace of woman

No females aloud.

Not bad. It had some of the raw honesty of the Beats. He would read it at the next meeting of the Poets' Club. He saved it with the four hundred other poems he had written in the last year: Erno prided himself on being the most prolific poet in his class. He had already won four Laurel Awards, one for best Lyric, one for best Sonnet, and two for best Villanelle—plus a Snappie for best limerick of 2097. He was sure to make Bard at an earlier age than anyone since Patrick Maurasson.

Erno switched off the screen, lay on his bed, and remembered the book. He dug it out from under his discarded clothes. It had a blue cover, faded to purple near the binding, made of some sort of fabric. Embossed on the front was a torch encircled by a laurel wreath. He opened the book to its title page: *Stories for Men*, "An Anthology by Charles Grayson." Published in August 1936, in the United States of America.

As a fan of Earth culture, Erno knew that most Earth societies used the patronymic, so that Gray, Grayson's naming parent, would be a man, not a woman.

Stories for men. The authors on the contents page were all men—except perhaps for odd names like "Dashiell." Despite Erno's interest in twentieth-century popular art, only a couple were familiar. William Faulkner he knew was considered a major Earth writer, and he had seen the name Hemingway before, though he had associated it only with a style of furniture. But even assuming the stories were all written by men, the title said the book was stories *for* men, not stories *by* men.

How did a story for a man differ from a story for a woman? Erno had never considered the idea before. He had heard storytellers in the park, and read books in school—Murasaki, Chopin, Cather, Ellison, Morrison, Ferenc, Sabinsdaughter. As a child, he had loved the Alice books, and *Flatland*, and Maria Hidalgo's kids' stories, and Seuss. None seemed particularly male or female.

He supposed the Cousins did have their own stories for men. Nick loved interactive serials, tortured romantic tales of interpersonal angst set in the patriarchal world, where men struggled against injustice until they found the right women and were taken care of. Erno stuck to poetry. His favorite novel was Tawanda Tamikasdaughter's *The Dark Blood*—the story of a misunderstood young Cousin's struggles against his overbearing mother, climaxed when his father miraculously reveals himself and brings the mother to heel. At the Men's House, he had also seen his share of porn—thrillers set on Earth where men forced women to do whatever the men wanted, and like it.

But this book did not look like porn. A note at the beginning promised the book contained material to "interest, or alarm, or amuse, or instruct, or—and possibly most important of all—entertain you." Erno wondered that Tyler had found this particular 160-year-old book in the lava tube. It seemed too unlikely to be coincidence.

What sort of things would entertain an Earthman of 1936? Erno turned to the first story, "The Ambassador of Poker" by "Achmed Abdullah."

But the archaic text was frustratingly passive—nothing more than black type physically impressed on the pages, without links or explanations. After a paragraph or so rife with obscure cultural references—"cordovan brogues," "knickerbockers," "County Sligo," "a four-in-hand"—Erno's night without sleep caught up with him, and he dozed off.

Heroes

Why does a man remain in the Society of Cousins, when he would have much more authority outside of it, in one of the other lunar colonies, or on Earth?

For one thing, the sex is great.

Men are valued for their sexuality, praised for their potency, competed for by women. From before puberty, a boy is schooled by both men and women on how to give pleasure. A man who can give such pleasure has high status. He is recognized and respected throughout the colony. He is welcome in any bed. He is admired and envied by other men.

Three

Erno woke suddenly, sweaty and disoriented, trailing the wisps of a dream that faded before he could call it back. He looked at his clock: 1530. He was going to miss the meeting.

He washed his face, applied personal hygiene bacteria, threw on his embroidered jumpsuit, and rushed out of the apartment.

The amphitheater in Sobieski Park was filling as Erno arrived. Five or six hundred people were already there; other Cousins would be watching on the link. The dome presented a clear blue sky, and the ring of heliotropes around its zenith flooded the air with sunlight. A slight breeze rustled the old oaks, hovering over the semicircular ranks of seats like aged grandmothers. People came in twos and threes, adults and children, along the paths that led down from the colony perimeter road through the farmlands to the park. Others emerged from the doors at the base of the central spire that supported the dome. Erno found a seat in the top row, far from the stage, off to one side where the seats gave way to grass.

Chairing the meeting was Debra Debrasdaughter. Debrasdaughter was a tiny sixty-year-old woman who, though she had held public office infrequently and never for long, was one of the most respected Cousins. She had been Erno's teacher when he was six, and he remembered how she'd sat with him and worked through his feud with Bill Grettasson. She taught him how to play forward on the soccer team. On the soccer field she had been fast and sudden as a bug. She had a warm laugh and sharp brown eyes.

Down on the stage, Debrasdaughter was hugging the secretary. Then the sound person hugged Debrasdaughter. They both hugged the secretary again. A troubled-looking old man sat down in the front row, and all three of them got down off the platform and hugged him. He brushed his hand along Debrasdaughter's thigh, but it was plain that his heart wasn't in it. She kissed his cheek and went back up on the stage.

A flyer wearing red wings swooped over the amphitheater and soared back up again, slowly beating the air. Another pair of flyers was racing around the perimeter of the crater, silhouetted against the clusters of apartments built into the crater walls. A thousand meters above his head Erno could spy a couple of others on the edge of the launch platform at the top of the spire. As he watched, squinting against the sunlight, one of the tiny figures spread its wings and pushed off, diving down, at first ever so slowly, gaining speed, then, with a flip of wings, soaring out level. Erno could feel it in his own shoulders, the stress that maneuver put on your arms. He didn't like flying. Even in lunar gravity, the chances of a fall were too big.

The amplified voice of Debrasdaughter drew him back to the amphitheater. "Thank you, Cousins, for coming," she said. "Please come to order."

Erno saw that Tyler Durden had taken a seat off to one side of the stage. He wore flaming red coveralls, like a shout.

"A motion has been made to impose a decree of invisibility against Thomas Marysson, otherwise known as Tyler Durden, for a period of one year. We are met here for the first of two discussions over this matter, prior to holding a colony-wide vote."

Short of banishment, invisibility was the colony's maximum social sanction. Should the motion carry, Tyler would be formally ostracized. Tagged by an AI, continuously monitored, he would not be acknowledged by other Cousins. Should he attempt to harm anyone, the AI would trigger receptors in his brain stem to put him to sleep.

"This motion was prompted by the disturbances that have ensued as a result of public performances of Thomas Marysson. The floor is now open for discussion."

A very tall woman who had been waiting anxiously stood, and as if by prearrangement, Debrasdaughter recognized her. The hovering mikes picked up her high voice. "I am Yokio Kumiosdaughter. My son is in the hospital as a result of this shameful episode. He is a good boy. He is the kind of boy we all want, and I don't understand how he came to be in that place. I pray that he recovers and lives to become the good man I know he can be.

"We must not let this happen to anyone else's son. At the very least, invisibility will give Thomas Marysson the opportunity to reflect on his actions before he provokes another such tragedy."

Another woman rose. Erno saw it was Rosamund Demisdaughter.

"With due respect to Cousin Kumiosdaughter, I don't believe the riot in my club was Tyler's fault. Her son brought this on himself. Tyler is not responsible for the actions of the patrons. Since when do we punish people for the misbehavior of others?

"The real mistake was sending constables," Rosamund continued. "Whether or not the grievances Tyler gives vent to are real or only perceived, we must allow any Cousins to speak their mind. The founders understood that men and women are different. By sending armed officers into that club, we threatened the right of those men who came to see Tyler Durden to be different."

"It was stupid strategy!" someone interrupted. "They could have arrested Durden easily after the show."

"Arrested him? On what grounds?" another woman asked.

Rosamund continued. "Adil Al-Hafez said it when he helped Nora Sobieski raise the money for this colony: 'The Cousins are a new start for men as much as women. We do not seek to change men, but to offer them the opportunity to be other than they have been.'"

A man Erno recognized from the biotech factory took the floor. "It's all very well to quote the founders back at us, but they were realists too. Men *are* different. Personalized male power has made the history of Earth one long tale of slaughter, oppression, rape, and war. Sobieski and Al-Hafez and the rest knew that, too: the California massacre sent them here. Durden's incitements will inevitably cause trouble. This kid wouldn't have gotten hurt without him. We can't stand by while the seeds of institutionalized male aggression are planted."

"This is a free-speech issue!" a young woman shouted.

"It's not about speech," the man countered. "It's about violence."

Debrasdaughter called for order. The man looked sheepish and sat down. A middle-aged woman with a worried expression stood. "What about organizing a new round of games? Let them work it out on the rink, the flying drome, the playing field."

"We have games of every description," another woman responded. "You think we can make Durden join the hockey team?"

The old man in the front row croaked out, "Did you see that game last week against Aristarchus? They could use a little more organized male aggression!" That drew a chorus of laughter from the crowd.

When the noise died down, an elderly woman took the floor. "I have been a Cousin for seventy years," she said. "I've seen troublemakers.

There will always be troublemakers. But what's happened to the Good Partners? I remember the North tube blowout of '32. Sixty people died. Life here was brutal and dangerous. But men and women worked together shoulder to shoulder; we shared each other's joys and sorrows. We were good bedmates then. Where is that spirit now?"

Erno had heard such tiresome sermonettes about the old days a hundred times. The discussion turned into a cacophony of voices.

"What are we going to do?" said another woman. "Deprive men of the right to speak?"

"Men are already deprived of the vote! How many voters are men?"

"By living on the colony stipend, men *choose* not to vote. Nobody is stopping you from going to work."

"We work already! How much basic science do men do? Look at the work Laurasson did on free energy. And most of the artists are men."

"—they have the time to devote to science and art *because of* the material support of the community. They have the luxury of intellectual pursuit."

"And all decisions about what to do with their work are made by women."

"The decisions, which will affect the lives of everyone in the society, are made not by women, but by voters."

"And most voters are women."

"Back to beginning of argument!" someone shouted. "Reload program and repeat."

A smattering of laughter greeted the sarcasm. Debrasdaughter smiled. "These are general issues, and to a certain degree I am content to let them be aired. But do they bear directly on the motion? What, if anything, are we to do about Thomas Marysson?"

She looked over at Tyler, who looked back at her coolly, his legs crossed.

A woman in a constable's uniform rose. "The problem with Thomas Marysson is that he claims the privileges of artistic expression, but he's not really an artist. He's a provocateur."

"Most of the artists in history have been provocateurs," shot back a small, dark man.

"He makes *me* laugh," said another.

"He's smart. Instead of competing with other men, he wants to organize them. He encourages them to band together."

The back-and-forth rambled on. Despite Debrasdaughter's attempt to keep order, the discussion ran into irrelevant byways, circular arguments, vague calls for comity, and general statements of male and female grievance. Erno had debated all this stuff a million times with the guys at the gym. It annoyed him that Debrasdaughter did not force the speakers to stay on point. But that was typical of a Cousins' meeting—they would talk endlessly, letting every nitwit have her say, before actually getting around to deciding anything.

A young woman stood to speak, and Erno saw it was Alicia Keikosdaughter. Alicia and he had shared a tutorial in math, and she had been the second girl he had ever had sex with.

"Of course Durden wants to be seen as an artist," Alicia said. "There's no mystique about the guy who works next to you in the factory. Who wants to sleep with him? The truth—"

"I will!" a good-looking woman interrupted Alicia.

The assembly laughed.

"The truth—" Alicia tried to continue.

The woman ignored her. She stood, her hand on the head of the little girl at her side, and addressed Tyler Durden directly. "I think you need to get laid!" She turned to the others. "Send him around to me! I'll take care of any revolutionary impulses he might have." More laughter.

Erno could see Alicia's shoulders slump, and she sat down. It was a typical case of a matron ignoring a young woman. He got up, moved down the aisle, and slid into a spot next to her.

Alicia turned to him. "Erno. Hello."

"It's not your fault they won't listen," he said. Alicia was wearing a tight satin shirt and Erno could not help but notice her breasts.

She kissed him on the cheek. She turned to the meeting, then back to him. "What do you think they're going to do?"

"They're going to ostracize him, I'll bet."

"I saw him on link. Have you seen him?"

"I was there last night."

Alicia leaned closer. "Really?" she said. Her breath was fragrant, and her lips full. There was a tactile quality to Alicia that Erno found deeply sexy—when she talked to you she would touch your shoulder or bump her knee against yours, as if to reassure herself that you were really there. "Did you get in the fight?"

A woman on the other side of Alicia leaned over. "If you two aren't going to pay attention, at least be quiet so the rest of us can."

Erno started to say something, but Alicia put her hand on his arm. "Let's go for a walk."

Erno was torn. Boring or not, he didn't want to miss the meeting, but it was hard to ignore Alicia. She was a year younger than Erno yet was already on her own, living with Sharon Yasminsdaughter while studying environmental social work. One time Erno had heard her argue with Sharon whether it was true that women on Earth could not use elevators because if they did they would inevitably be raped.

They left the amphitheater and walked through the park. Erno told Alicia his version of the riot at the club, leaving out his exploring the deserted lava tube with Tyler.

"Even if they don't make him invisible," Alicia said, "you know that somebody is going to make sure he gets the message."

"He hasn't hurt anyone. Why aren't we having a meeting about the constable who clubbed Yokiosson?"

"The constable was attacked. A lot of cousins feel threatened. I'm not even sure how I feel."

"The Unwritten Law," Erno muttered.

"The what?"

"Tyler does a bit about it. It was an Earth custom, in most of the patriarchies. The 'unwritten law' said that, if a wife had sex with anyone other than her husband, the husband had the right to kill her and her lover, and no court would hold him guilty."

"That's because men had all the power."

"But you just said somebody would send Tyler a message. Up here, if a man abuses a woman, even threatens to, then the abused woman's friends take revenge. When was the last time anyone did anything about that?"

"I get it, Erno. That must seem unfair."

"Men don't abuse women here."

"Maybe that's why."

"It doesn't make it right."

"You're right, Erno. It doesn't. I'm on your side."

Erno sat down on the ledge of the pool surrounding the fountains. The fountains were the pride of the colony: in a conspicuous show of water consumption the pools surrounded the central spire and wandered beneath the park's trees. Genetically altered carp swam in their green depths, and the air was more humid here than anywhere else under the dome.

Alicia sat next to him. "Remind me why we broke up," Erno said.

"Things got complicated." She had said the same thing the night she told him they shouldn't sleep together anymore. He still didn't know what that meant, and he suspected she said it only to keep from saying something that might wound him deeply. Much as he wanted to insist that he would prefer her honesty, he wasn't sure he could stand it.

"I'm going crazy at home," he told Alicia. "Mother treats me like a child. Lena is starting to act like she's better than me. I do real work at Biotech, but that doesn't matter."

"You'll be in university soon. You're a premium gene hacker."

"Who says?" Erno asked.

"People."

"Yeah, right. And if I am, I still live at home. I'm going to end up just like Nick," he said, "the pet male in a household full of females."

"Maybe something will come of this. Things can change."

"If only," Erno said morosely. But he was surprised and gratified to have Alicia's encouragement. Maybe she cared for him after all. "There's one thing, Alicia . . . I could move in with you."

Alicia raised an eyebrow. He pressed on. "Like you say, I'll be studying at the university next session. . . ."

She put her hand on his leg. "There's not much space, with Sharon and me. We couldn't give you your own room."

"I'm not afraid of sharing a bed. I can alternate between you."

"You're so manly, Erno!" she teased.

"I aim to please," he said, and struck a pose. Inside he cringed. It was a stupid thing to say, so much a boy trying to talk big.

Alicia did a generous thing—she laughed. There was affection and understanding in it. It made him feel they were part of some club together.

Erno hadn't realized how afraid he was that she would mock him. Neither said anything for a moment. A finch landed on the branch above them, turned its head sideways, and inspected them. "You know, you could be just like Tyler Durden, Erno."

Erno started—what did she mean by that? He looked her in the face. Alicia's eyes were calm and green, flecked with gold. He hadn't looked into her eyes since they had been lovers.

She kissed him. Then she touched his lips with her finger. "Don't say anything. I'll talk to Sharon."

He put his arm around her. She melted into him.

In the distance the sounds of the debate were broken by a burst of laughter. "Let's go back," she said.

"All right," he said reluctantly.

They walked back to the amphitheater and found seats in the top row, beside two women in their twenties who joked with each other.

"This guy is no Derek Silviasson," one of them said.

"If he could fuck like Derek, now *that* would be comedy," said her blond partner.

Debrasdaughter was calling for order.

"We cannot compel any cousin to indulge in sex against his will. If he chooses to be celibate, and encourages his followers to be celibate, we can't prevent that without undermining the very freedoms we came here to establish."

Nick Farahsson, his face red and his voice contorted, shouted out, "You just said the key word—followers! We don't need followers here. Followers have ceded their autonomy to a hierarchy. Followers are the tool of phallocracy. Followers started the riot." Erno saw his mother, sitting next to Nick, try to calm him.

Another man spoke. "What a joke! We're all a bunch of followers! Cousins follow customs as slavishly as any Earth patriarch."

"What I don't understand," someone called out directly to Tyler, "is, if you hate it here so much, why don't you just leave? Don't let the airlock door clip your ass on the way out."

"This is my home, too," Tyler said.

He stood and turned to Debrasdaughter. "If you don't mind, I would like to speak."

"We'd be pleased to hear what you have to say," Debrasdaughter said. The trace of a smile on her pale face made her look girlish despite her gray hair. "Speaking for myself, I've been waiting."

Tyler ran his hand over his shaved scalp, came to the front of the platform. He looked up at his fellow citizens, and smiled. "I think you've outlined all the positions pretty clearly so far. I note that Tashi Yokiosson didn't say anything, but maybe he'll get back to us later. It's been a revealing discussion, and now I'd just like to ask you to help me out with a demonstration. Will you do this little thing for me?

"I'd like you all to put your hand over your eyes. Like this—" He covered his own eyes with his palm, peeked out. Most of the assembly did as he asked. "All of you got your eyes covered? Good!

"Because, sweethearts, this is the closest I am going to get to invisibility."

Tyler threw his arms wide, and laughed.

"Make me invisible? You can't see me now! You don't recognize a man whose word is steel, whose reality is not dependent on rules. Men have fought and bled and died for you. Men put their lives on the line for every microscopic step forward our pitiful race has made. Nothing's more visible than the sacrifices men have made for the good of their wives and daughters. Yes, women died, too—but they were *real* women, women not threatened by the existence of masculinity.

"You see that tower?" Tyler pointed to the thousand-meter spire looming over their heads. "I can climb that tower! I can fuck every real woman in this amphitheater. I eat a lot of food, drink a lot of alcohol, and take a lot of drugs. I'm *bigger* than you are. I sweat more. I howl like a dog. I make noise. You think anyone can make more noise than me?

"One way or another, Mama, I'm going to keep you awake all night! And *you* think you're the girl that can stop me?

"My Uncle Dick told me when I was a boy, son, don't take it out unless you intend to use it! Well, it's out and it's in use! Rim ram god damn, sonafabitch fuck! It is to laugh. This whole discussion's been a waste of oxygen. I'm real, I'm here, get used to it.

"Invisible? Just *try* not to see me."

Then Tyler crouched and leapt three meters into the air, tucked, did a roll. Coming down, he landed on his hands and did a handspring. The second his feet touched the platform, he shot off the side and ran, taking long, loping strides out of the park and through the cornfields.

A confused murmur rippled through the assembly, broken by a few angry calls. Many puzzled glances. Some people stood.

Debrasdaughter called for order. "I'll ask the assembly to calm down," she said.

Gradually, quiet came.

"I'm sure we are all stimulated by that very original statement. I don't think we are going to get any farther today, and I note that it is coming on time for the swing-shifters to leave, so unless there are serious objections I would like to call this meeting to a close.

"The laws call for a second open meeting a week from today, followed by a polling period of three days, at the end of which the will of the colony will be made public and enacted. Do I hear any further discussion?"

There was none.

"Then I hereby adjourn this meeting. We will meet again one week from today at 1600 hours. Anyone who wishes to post a statement in regard to this matter may do so at the colony site, where a room will be open continuously for debate. Thank you for your participation."

People began to break up, talking. The two women beside Erno, joking, left the theater.

Alicia stood. "Was that one of his routines?"

Tyler's speech had stirred something in Erno that made him want to shout. He was grinning from ear to ear. "It is to laugh," he murmured.

Alicia grabbed Erno's wrist. She pulled a pen from her pocket, turned his hand so the palm lay open, and on it wrote "Gilman 334."

"Before you do anything stupid, Erno," she said, "call me."

"Define stupid," he said.

But Alicia had turned away. He felt the tingle of the writing on his hand as he watched her go.

Work

Men are encouraged to apply for an exemption from the mita: the compulsory weekly labor that each cousin devotes to the support of the colony. The cost of this exemption is forfeiture of the right to vote. As artists, writers, artisans, athletes, performers, and especially as scientists, men have an easier path than women. Their interests are supported to the limits of the cousins' resources. But this is not accorded the designation of work, and all practical decisions as to what to do with any creations of their art or discoveries they might make are left to voters, who are overwhelmingly women.

Men who choose such careers are praised as public-spirited volunteers, sacrificing for the sake of the community. At the same time, they live a life of relative ease, pursuing their interests. They compete with each other for the attentions of women. They may exert influence, but have no legal responsibilities, and no other responsibilities except as they choose them. They live like sultans, but without power. Or like gigolos. Peacocks, and studs.

And those who choose to do work? Work—ah, work is different. Work is mundane labor directed toward support of the colony. Male workers earn no honors, accumulate no status. And because men are always outnumbered by women on such jobs, they have little chance of advancement to a position of authority. They just can't get the votes.

"Twenty-Five Bucks"

Erno began to puzzle out some of the *Stories for Men*. One was about a "prize-fighter"—a man who fought another man with his fists for money. This aging fighter agrees with a promoter to fight a younger, stronger man for "twenty-five bucks," which from context Erno gathered was a small sum of money. The boxer spends his time in the ring avoiding getting beaten up. During a pause between the "rounds" of the fight, the promoter comes to him and complains that he is not fighting hard enough, and swears he will not pay the boxer if he "takes a dive." So in the next round the boxer truly engages in the brutal battle, and within a minute gets beaten unconscious.

But because this happens immediately after the promoter spoke to him, in the sight of the audience, the audience assumes the boxer was *told* by the promoter to take a dive. They protest. Rather than defend the boxer, the promoter denies him the twenty-five bucks anyway.

The boxer, unconscious while the promoter and audience argue, dies of a brain hemorrhage.

The story infuriated Erno. It felt so *wrong*. Why did the boxer take on the fight? Why did he allow himself to be beaten so badly? Why did the promoter betray the boxer? What was the point of the boxer's dying in the end? Why did the writer—someone named James T. Farrell—invent this grim tale?

Four

A week after the meeting, when Erno logged onto school, he found a message for him from "Ethan Edwards." It read:

> I saw you with that girl. Cute. But no sex, Erno. I'm counting on men like you.

Erno sent a reply: "You promised me another adventure. When?"

Then he did biochemistry ("Delineate the steps in the synthesis of human growth hormone") and read Gender & Art for three hours until he had to get to his practicum at Biotech.

In order to reduce the risk of stray bugs getting loose in the colony, the biotech factories were located in a bunker separate from the main crater. Workers had to don pressure suits and ride a bus for a couple of kilometers across the lunar surface. A crowd of other biotech workers already filled the locker room at the north airlock when Erno arrived.

"Tyrus told me you're fucking Alicia Keikosdaughter, Erno," said Paul Gwynethsson, whose locker was next to Erno's. "He was out flying. He saw you in the park."

"So? Who are you fucking?" Erno asked. He pulled on his skintight. The fabric, webbed with thermoregulators, sealed itself, the suit's environment system powered up, and Erno locked down his helmet. The helmet's heads-up display was green. He and Paul went to the airlock, passed their IDs through the reader, and entered with the others. The exit sign posted the solar storm warning. Paul teased Erno about Alicia as the air was cycled through the lock and they walked out through the radiation maze to the surface.

They got on the bus that dropped off the previous biotech shift. The bus bumped away in slow motion down the graded road. It was late in the lunar afternoon, probably only a day or so of light before the two-week night. If a storm should be detected and the alert sounded, they would have maybe twenty minutes to find shelter before the radiation flux hit the exposed surface. But the ride to the lab went uneventfully.

A man right off the cable train from Tsander was doing a practicum in the lab. His name was Cluny. Like so many Earthmen, he was short and impressively muscled, and spoke slowly, with an odd accent. Cluny was not yet a citizen and had not taken a Cousins name. He was still going through training before qualifying to apply for exemption from the *mita*.

Erno interrupted Cluny as he carried several racks of micro-environment bulbs to the sterilizer. He asked Cluny what he thought of Tyler Durden.

Cluny was closemouthed; perhaps he thought Erno was testing him: "I think if he doesn't like it up here, I can show him lots of places on Earth happy to take him."

Erno let him get on with his work. Cluny was going to have a hard time over the next six months. The culture shock would be nothing next to the genetic manipulation he would have to undergo to adjust him for low-G. The life expectancy of an unmodified human on the moon was forty-eight. No exercise regimen or drugs could prevent the cardiovascular atrophy and loss of bone mass that humans evolved for Earth would suffer.

But the retroviruses could alter the human genome to produce solid fibrolaminar bones in 1/6 G, prevent plaque buildup in arteries, ensure pulmonary health, and prevent a dozen other fatal low-G syndromes.

At the same time, licensing biotech discoveries was the colony's major source of foreign exchange, so research was under tight security. Erno pressed his thumb against the gene scanner. He had to go through three levels of clearances to access the experiment he had been working on. Alicia was right—Erno was getting strokes for his rapid learning in gene techniques, and already had a rep. Even better, he liked it. He could spend hours brainstorming synergistic combinations of alterations in mice, adapting Earth genotypes for exploitation.

Right now he was assigned to the ecological design section under Lemmy Odillesson, the premiere agricultural genobotanist. Lemmy was working on giant plane trees. He had a vision of underground bioengineered forests, entire ecosystems introduced to newly opened lava tubes that would transform dead, airless immensities into habitable biospheres. He wanted to live in a city of underground lunar tree houses.

Too soon Erno's six-hour shift was over. He suited up, climbed to the surface, and took the bus back to the north airlock. As the shift got off, a figure came up to Erno from the shadows of the radiation maze.

It was a big man in a tiger-striped skintight, his faceplate opaqued. Erno shied away from him, but the man held his hands, palms up, in front of him to indicate no threat. He came closer, leaned forward. Erno flinched. The man took Erno's shoulder, gently, and pulled him forward until the black faceplate of his helmet kissed Erno's own.

"Howdy, Erno." Tyler Durden's voice, carried by conduction from a face he could not see, echoed like Erno's own thought.

Erno tried to regain his cool. "Mr. Durden, I presume."

"Switch your suit to Channel Six," Tyler said. "Encrypted." He pulled away and touched the pad on his arm, and pointed to Erno's. When Erno did the same, his radio found Tyler's wavelength, and he heard Tyler's voice in his ear.

"I thought I might catch you out here."

The other workers had all passed by; they were alone. "What are you doing here?"

"You want adventure? We got adventure."

"What adventure?"

"Come along with me."

Instead of heading in through the maze, Tyler led Erno back out to the surface. The fan of concrete was deserted, the shuttle bus already gone back to the lab and factories. From around a corner, Tyler hauled out a backpack, settled it over his shoulders, and struck off east, along the graded road that encircled Fowler. The mountainous rim rose to their right, topped by the beginnings of the dome; to their left was the rubble of the broken highlands. Tyler moved along at a quick pace, taking long strides in the low G with a minimum of effort.

After a while Tyler asked him, "So, how about the book? Have you read it?"

"Some. It's a collection of stories, all about men."

"Learning anything?"

"They seem so primitive. I guess it was a different world back then."

"What's so different?"

Erno told him the story about the prize-fighter. "Did they really do that?"

"Yes. Men have always engaged in combat."

"For money?"

"The money is just an excuse. They do it anyway."

"But why did the writer tell that story? What's the point?"

"It's about elemental manhood. The fighters were men. The promoter was not."

"Because he didn't pay the boxer?"

"Because he knew the boxer had fought his heart out, but he pretended that the boxer was a coward in order to keep the audience from getting mad at him. The promoter preserved his own credibility by trashing the boxer's. The author wants you to be like the boxer, not the promoter."

"But the boxer dies—for twenty-five bucks."

"He died a man. Nobody can take that away from him."

"But nobody knows that. In fact, they all think he died a coward."

"The promoter knows he wasn't. The other fighter knows, probably. And thanks to the story, now you know, too."

Erno still had trouble grasping exactly the metaphor Tyler intended when he used the term "man." It had nothing to do with genetics. But before he could quiz Tyler, the older man stopped. By this time they had circled a quarter of the colony and were in the shadow of the crater wall. Tyler switched on his helmet light and Erno did likewise. Erno's thermoregulator pumped heat along the microfibers buried in his suit's skin, compensating for the sudden shift from the brutal heat of lunar sunlight to the brutal cold of lunar darkness.

"Here we are," Tyler said, looking up the crater wall. "See that path?"

It wasn't much of a path, just a jumble of rocks leading up the side of the crater, but once they reached it Erno could see that, by following patches of luminescent paint on boulders, you could climb the rim mountain to the top. "Where are we going?" Erno asked.

"To the top of the world," Tyler said. "From up there I'll show you the empire I'll give you if you follow me."

"You're kidding."

Tyler said nothing.

It was a hard climb to the crater's lip, where a concrete rim formed the foundation of the dome. From here, the dome looked like an unnaturally swollen stretch of *mare*, absurdly regular, covered in lunar regolith. Once the dome had been constructed over the crater, about six meters of lunar soil had been spread evenly over its surface to provide a radiation shield for the interior. Concentric rings every ten meters kept the soil from sliding down the pitch of the dome. It was easier climbing here, but surreal. The horizon of the dome moved ahead of them as they progressed, and it was hard to judge distances.

"There's a solar storm warning," Erno said. "Aren't you worried?"

"We're not going to be out long."

"I was at the meeting," Erno said.

"I saw you," Tyler said. "Cute girl, the dark-skinned one. Watch out. You know what they used to say on Earth?"

"What?"

"If women didn't have control of all the pussy, they'd have bounties on their heads."

Erno laughed. "How can you say that? They're our sisters, our mothers."

"And they still have control of all the pussy."

They climbed the outside of the dome.

"What are you going to do to keep from being made invisible?" Erno asked.

"What makes you think they're going to try?"

"I don't think your speech changed anybody's mind."

"So? No matter what they teach you, my visibility is not socially constructed. That's the lesson for today."

"What are we doing out here?"

"We're going to demonstrate this fact."

Ahead of them a structure hove into sight. At the apex of the dome, just above the central spire, stood a maintenance airlock. Normally, this would be the way workers would exit to inspect or repair the dome's exterior—not the way Erno and Tyler had come. This was not a public airlock, and the entrance code would be encrypted.

Tyler led them up to the door. From his belt pouch he took a key card and stuck it into the reader. Erno could hear him humming a song over his earphones. After a moment, the door slid open.

"In we go, Erno," Tyler said.

They entered the airlock and waited for the air to recycle. "This could get us into trouble," Erno said.

"Yes, it could."

"If you can break into the airlock you can sabotage it. An airlock breach could kill hundreds of people."

"You're absolutely right, Erno. That's why only completely responsible people like us should break into airlocks."

The interior door opened into a small chamber facing an elevator. Tyler put down his backpack, cracked the seal on his helmet, and began stripping off his garish suit. Underneath he wore only briefs. Rust-colored pubic hair curled from around the edges of the briefs. Tyler's skin was pale, the muscles in his arms and chest well developed, but his belly soft. His skin was crisscrossed with a web of pink lines where the thermoregulator system of the suit had marked him.

Feeling self-conscious, Erno took off his own suit. They were the same height, but Tyler outweighed him by twenty kilos. "What's in the backpack?" Erno asked.

"Rappelling equipment." Tyler gathered up his suit and the pack and, ignoring the elevator, opened the door beside it to a stairwell. "Leave your suit here," he said, ditching his own in a corner.

The stairwell was steep and the cold air tasted stale; it raised goose bumps on Erno's skin. Clutching the pack to his chest, Tyler hopped down the stairs to the next level. The wall beside them was sprayed with gray insulation. The light from bioluminescents turned their skin greenish yellow.

Instead of continuing down the well all the way to the top of the spire, Tyler stopped at a door on the side of the stairwell. He punched in a code. The door opened into a vast darkness, the space between the exterior and interior shells of the dome. Tyler shone his light inside: Three meters high, broken by reinforcing struts, the cavity stretched out from them into the darkness, curving slightly as it fell away. Tyler closed the door behind them and, in the light of his flash, pulled a notebook from the pack and called up a map. He studied it for a minute, and then led Erno into the darkness.

To the right about ten meters, an impenetrable wall was one of the great cermet ribs of the dome that stretched like the frame of an umbrella from the central spire to the distant crater rim.

Before long Tyler stopped, shining his light on the floor. "Here it is."

"What?"

"Maintenance port. Periodically they have to inspect the interior of the dome, repair the fiberoptics." Tyler squatted down and began to open the lock.

"What are you going to do?"

"We're going to hang from the roof like little spiders, Erno, and leave a gift for our cousins."

The port opened and Erno got a glimpse of the space that yawned below. A thousand meters below them the semicircular ranks of seats of the Sobieski Park amphitheater glowed ghostly white in the lights of the artificial night. Tyler drew ropes and carabiners from his pack, and from the bottom, an oblong device, perhaps fifty centimeters square, wrapped in fiber-optic cloth that glinted in the light of the flashlight. At one end was a timer. The object gave off an aura of threat that was both frightening and instantly attractive.

"What is that thing? Is it a bomb?"

"A bomb, Erno? Are you crazy?" Tyler snapped one of the lines around a reinforcing strut. He donned a harness and handed an identical one to Erno. "Put this on."

"I'm afraid of heights."

"Don't be silly. This is safe as a kiss. Safer, maybe."

"What are we trying to accomplish?"

"That's something of a metaphysical question."

"That thing doesn't look metaphysical to me."

"Nonetheless, it is. Call it the Philosopher's Stone. We're going to attach it to the inside of the dome."

"I'm not going to blow any hole in the dome."

"Erno, I couldn't blow a hole in the dome without killing myself. I guarantee you that, as a result of what we do here, I will suffer whatever consequences anyone else suffers. More than anyone else, even. Do I look suicidal to you, Erno?"

"To tell the truth, I don't know. You sure do some risky things. Why don't you tell me what you intend?"

"This is a test. I want to see whether you trust me."

"You don't trust *me* enough to tell me anything."

"Trust isn't about being persuaded. Trust is when you do something because your brother asks you to. I didn't have to ask you along on this adventure, Erno. I trusted you." Tyler crouched there, calmly watching Erno. "So, do you have the balls for this?"

The moment stretched. Erno pulled on the climbing harness.

Tyler ran the ropes through the harness, gave him a pair of gloves, and showed Erno how to brake the rope behind his back. Then, with the maybe-bomb Philosopher's Stone slung over his shoulder, Tyler dropped through the port. Feeling like he was about to take a step he could never take back, Erno edged out after him.

Tyler helped him let out three or four meters of rope. Erno's weight made the rope twist, and the world began to spin dizzily. They were so close to the dome's inner surface that the "stars" shining there were huge fuzzy patches of light in the braided fiberglass surface. The farmlands of the crater floor were swathed in shadow, but around the crater's rim, oddly twisted from this god's-eye perspective, the lights of apartment districts cast fans of illumination on the hanging gardens and switchbacked perimeter road. Erno could make out a few microscopic figures down there. Not far from Tyler and him, the top of the central spire obscured their view to the west. The flying stage, thirty meters down from where the spire met the roof, was closed for the night, but an owl nesting underneath flew out at their appearance and circled below them.

Tyler began to swing himself back and forth at the end of his line, gradually picking up amplitude until, at the apex of one of his swings, he latched himself onto the dome's inner surface. "C'mon, Erno! Time's wasting!"

Erno steeled himself to copy Tyler's performance. It took effort to get himself swinging, and once he did the arcs were ponderous and slow. He had trouble orienting himself so that one end of his oscillation left him close to Tyler. At the top of every swing gravity disappeared and his stomach lurched. Finally, after what seemed an eternity of trying, Erno swung close enough for Tyler to reach out and snag his leg.

He pulled Erno up beside him and attached Erno's belt line to a ringbolt in the dome's surface. Erno's heart beat fast.

"Now you know you're alive," Tyler said.

"If anyone catches us up here, our asses are fried."

"Our asses are everywhere and always fried. That's the human condition. Let's work."

While Tyler pulled the device out of the bag he had Erno spread glue onto the dome's surface. When the glue was set, the two of them pressed the Philosopher's Stone into it until it was firmly fixed. Because of its reflective surface it would be invisible from the crater floor. "Now, what time did Debra Debrasdaughter say that meeting was tomorrow?"

"1600," Erno said. "You knew that."

Tyler flipped open the lid over the Stone's timer and punched some keys. "Yes, I did."

"And you didn't need my help to do this. Why did you make me come?"

The timer beeped; the digital readout began counting down. Tyler flipped the lid closed. "To give you the opportunity to betray me. And if you want to, you still have"—he looked at his wristward—"fourteen hours and thirteen minutes."

Male Dominance Behavior

Erno had begun building his store of resentment when he was twelve, in Eva Evasdaughter's molecular biotechnology class. Eva Evasdaughter came from an illustrious family: her mother had been the longest serving member of the colony council. Her grandmother, Eva Kabatsumi, jailed with Nora Sobieski in California, had originated the matronymic system.

It took Erno a while to figure out that that didn't make Evasdaughter a good teacher. He was the brightest boy in the class. He believed in the cousins, respected authority, and worshipped women like his mother and Evasdaughter.

Evasdaughter was a tall woman who wore tight short-sleeved tunics that emphasized her small breasts. Erno had begun to notice such things; sex play was everyone's interest that semester, and he had recently had several erotic fondling sessions with girls in the class.

One day they were studying protein engineering. Erno loved it. He liked how you could make a gene jump through hoops if you were clever enough. He got ahead in the reading. That day he asked Eva Evasdaughter about directed protein mutagenesis, a topic they were not due to study until next semester.

"Can you make macro-modifications in proteins—I mean replace entire sequences to get new enzymes?" He was genuinely curious, but at some level he also was seeking Evasdaughter's approval of his doing extra work.

She turned on him coolly. "Are you talking about using site-directed mutagenesis, or chemical synthesis of oligonucleotides?"

He had never heard of site-directed mutagenesis. "I mean using oligonucleotides to change the genes."

"I can't answer unless I know if we're talking about site-directed or synthesized oligonucleotides. Which is it?"

Erno felt his face color. The other students were watching him. "I—I don't know."

"Yes, you don't," Evasdaughter said cheerfully. And instead of explaining, she turned back to the lesson.

Erno didn't remember another thing for the rest of that class, except looking at his shoes. Why had she treated him like that? She made him feel stupid. Yes, she knew more biotech than he did, but she was the teacher! Of course she knew more! Did that mean she had to put him down?

When he complained to his mother, she only said that he needed to listen to the teacher.

Only slowly did he realize that Evasdaughter had exhibited what he had always been taught was male dominance behavior. He had presented a challenge to her superiority, and she had smashed him flat. After he was smashed, she could afford to treat him kindly. But she would teach him only after he admitted that he was her inferior.

Now that his eyes were opened, he saw this behavior everywhere. Every day Cousins asserted their superiority in order to hurt others. He had been lied to, and his elders were hypocrites.

Yet when he tried to show his superiority, he was told to behave himself. Superior/ inferior is wrong, they said. Difference is all.

Five

One thing Tyler had said was undoubtedly true: this was a test. How devoted was Erno to the Society of Cousins? How good a judge was he of Tyler's character? How eager was he to see his mother and the rest of his world made uncomfortable, and how large a discomfort did he think was justified? Just how angry was Erno?

After Erno got back to his room, he lay awake, unable to sleep. He ran every moment of his night with Tyler over in his mind, parsed every sentence, and examined every ambiguous word. Tyler had never denied that the Philosopher's Stone was a bomb. Erno looked up the term in the dictionary: a philosopher's stone was "an imaginary substance sought by alchemists in the belief that it would change base metals into gold or silver."

He did not think the change that Tyler's stone would bring had anything to do with gold or silver.

He looked at his palm, long since washed clean, where Alicia had written her number. She'd asked him to call her before he did anything stupid.

At 1545 the next day Erno was seated in the amphitheater among the crowds of cousins. More people were here than had come the previous week, and the buzz of their conversation, broken by occasional laughter, filled the air. He squinted up at the dome to try to figure out just where they had placed the stone. The dome had automatic safety devices to seal any minor air leak. But it couldn't survive a hole blasted in it. Against the artificial blue sky Erno watched a couple of flyers circling like hawks.

1552. Tyler arrived, trailing a gaggle of followers, mostly young men trying to look insolent. He'd showed up—what did that mean? Erno noted that this time, Tyler wore black. He seemed as calm as he had before, and he chatted easily with the others, then left them to take a seat on the stage.

At 1559 Debra Debrasdaughter took her place. Erno looked at his watch.

1600.

Nothing happened.

Was that the test? To see whether Erno would panic and fall for a ruse? He tried to catch Tyler's eye, but got nothing.

Debrasdaughter rapped for order. The ranks of cousins began to quiet, to sit up straighter. Near silence had fallen, and Debrasdaughter began to speak.

"Our second meeting to discuss—"

A flash of light seared the air high above them, followed a second later by a concussion. Shouts, a few screams.

Erno looked up. A cloud of black smoke shot rapidly from a point against the blue. One flyer tumbled, trying to regain his balance; the other had dived a hundred meters seeking a landing place. People pointed and shouted. The blue sky flickered twice, went to white as the imaging system struggled, then recovered.

People boiled out of the amphitheater, headed for pressurized shelter. Erno could not see if the dome had been breached. The smoke, instead of dissipating, spread out in an arc, then flattened up against the dome. It formed tendrils, shapes. He stood there, frozen. It was not smoke at all, he realized, but smart paint.

The nanodevices spread the black paint onto the interior of the dome. The paint crawled and shaped itself, forming letters. The letters, like a message from God, made a huge sign on the inside of the clear blue sky:

"BANG! YOU'RE DEAD!"

"You're Dead!"

One of the other *Stories for Men* was about Harry Rodney and Little Bert, two petty criminals on an ocean liner that has struck an iceberg and is sinking, with not enough lifeboats for all the passengers. The patriarchal custom was that women and children had precedence for spaces in the boats. Harry gives up his space in a boat in favor of some girl. Bert strips a coat and scarf from an injured woman, steals her jewelry, abandons her belowdecks, and uses her clothes to sneak into a lifeboat.

As it happens, both men survive. But Harry is so disgusted by Bert's crime that he persuades him to run away and pretend he is dead. For years, whenever Bert contacts Harry, Harry tells him to stay away or else the police might discover him. Bert never returns home for fear of being found out.

Six

In the panic and confusion, Tyler Durden disappeared. On his seat at the meeting lay a note: "I did it."

As a first step in responding to the threat to the colony, the Board of Matrons immediately called the question of ostracism, and by evening the population had voted: Tyler Durden was declared invisible.

As if that mattered. He could not be found.

Seven

It took several days for the writing to be erased from the dome.

A manhunt did not turn up Tyler. Nerves were on edge. Rumors arose, circulated, were denied. Tyler Durden was still in the colony, in disguise. A cabal of followers was hiding him. No, he and his confederates had a secret outpost ten kilometers north of the colony. Durden was in the employ of the government of California. He had stockpiled weapons and was planning an attack. He had an atomic bomb.

At the gym entrance, AIs checked DNA prints, and Erno was conscious, as never before, of the cameras in every room. He wondered if any monitors had picked up his excursion with Tyler. Every moment he expected a summons on his wristward to come to the assembly offices.

When Erno entered the workout room, he found Tyrus and a number of others wearing white T-shirts that said, "BANG! YOU'RE DEAD!"

Erno took the unoccupied rowing machine next to Ty. Ty was talking to Sid on the other side of him.

A woman came across the room to use the machines. She was tightly muscled, and her dark hair was pulled back from her sweaty neck. As she approached, the young men went silent and turned to look at her. She hesitated. Erno saw something on her face he had rarely seen on a woman's face before: fear. The woman turned and left the gym.

None of the boys said anything. If the others had recognized what had just happened, they did not let it show.

Erno pulled on his machine. He felt the muscles in his legs knot. "Cool shirt," he said.

"Tyrus wants to be invisible, too," said Sid. Sid wasn't wearing one of the shirts.

"Eventually someone will check the vids of Tyler's performances, and see me there," said Ty between strokes. "I'm not ashamed to be Tyler's fan." At thirteen, Erno and Ty had been fumbling lovers, testing out their sexuality. Now Ty was a blunt overmuscled guy who laughed like a hyena. He didn't laugh now.

"It was a rush to judgment," one of the other boys said. "Tyler didn't harm a single Cousin. It was free expression."

"He could just as easily have blown a hole in the dome," said Erno. "Do they need any more justification for force?"

Ty stopped rowing and turned toward Erno. Where he had sweated through the fabric, the "Bang!" on his shirt had turned bloodred. "Maybe it will come to force. We do as much work, and we're second-class citizens." He started rowing again, pulled furiously at the machine, fifty reps a minute, drawing quick breaths.

"That Durden has a pair, doesn't he?" Sid said. Sid was a popular stud-boy. His thick chestnut hair dipped below one eye. "You should have seen the look on Rebecca's face when that explosion went off."

"I hear, if they catch him, the council's not going to stop at invisibility," Erno said. "They'll kick him out."

"Invisibility won't slow Tyler down," Ty said. "Would you obey the decree?" he asked Sid.

"Me? I'm too beautiful to let myself get booted. If Tyler Durden likes masculinists so much, let him go to one of the other colonies, or to Earth. I'm getting laid too often."

Erno's gut tightened. "They will kick him out. My mother would vote for it in a second."

"Let 'em try," Ty grunted, still rowing.

"Is that why you're working out so much lately, Ty?" Sid said. "*Planning to move to Earth?*"

"No. I'm just planning to bust your ass."

"I suspect it's not busting you want to do to my ass."

"Yeah. Your ass has better uses."

"My mother says Tyler's broken the social contract," Erno said.

"Does your mother"—Ty said, still rowing—"keep your balls under her pillow?"

Sid laughed.

Erno wanted to grab Ty and tell him, *I was there. I helped him do it!* But he said nothing. He pulled on the machine. His face burned.

After a minute Erno picked up his towel and went to the weight machine. No one paid him any attention. Twenty minutes later he hit the sauna. Sweating in the heat, sullen, resentful. He had *been* there, had taken a bigger risk than any of these fan-boys.

Coming out of the sauna he saw Sid heading for the sex rooms, where any woman who was interested could find a male partner who was willing. Erno considered posting himself to one of the rooms. But he wasn't a stud; he was just an anonymous minor male. He had no following. It would be humiliating to sit there waiting for someone, or worse, to be selected by some old bag.

A day later Erno got himself one of the T-shirts. Wearing it didn't make him feel any better.

It came to him that maybe this was the test Tyler intended: not whether Erno would tell about the Philosopher's Stone before it happened, but whether he would admit he'd helped set it after he saw the uproar it caused in the colony.

If that was the test, Erno was failing. He thought about calling Tyler's apartment, but the constables were sure to be monitoring that number. A new rumor had it Tyler had been captured and was being held in protective custody—threats had been made against his life—until the Board of Matrons could decide when and how to impose the invisibility. Erno imagined Tyler in some bare white room, his brain injected with nanoprobes, his neck fitted with a collar.

At Biotech, Erno became aware of something he had never noticed before: how the women assumed first pick of the desserts in the cafeteria. Then, later, when he walked by their table, four women burst into laughter. He turned and stared at them, but they never glanced at him.

Another day he was talking with a group of engineers on break: three women, another man, and Erno. Hana from materials told a joke: "What do you have when you have two little balls in your hand?"

The other women grinned. Erno watched the other man. He stood as if on a trapdoor, a tentative smile on his face. The man was getting ready to laugh, because that was what you did when people told jokes, whether or not they were funny. It was part of the social contract—somebody went into joke-telling mode, and you went into joke-listening mode.

"A man's undivided attention," Hana said.

The women laughed. The man grinned.

"How can you tell when a man is aroused?" Pearl said. "—He's breathing."

"That isn't funny," Erno said.

"Really? I think it is," Hana said.

"It's objectification. Men are just like women. They have emotions, too."

"Cool off, Erno," said Pearl. "This isn't gender-equity class."

"There is no gender equity here."

"Someone get Erno a T-shirt."

"Erno wants to be invisible."

"We're already invisible!" Erno said, and stalked off. He left the lab, put on his suit, and took the next bus back to the dome. He quit going to his practicum: he would not let himself be used anymore. He was damned if he would go back there again.

A meeting to discuss what to do about the missing comedian was disrupted by a group of young men marching and chanting outside the meeting room. Constables were stationed in public places, carrying clubs. In online discussion rooms, people openly advocated closing the Men's Houses for fear conspiracies were being hatched in them.

And Erno received another message. This one was from "Harry Callahan."

> Are you watching, Erno? If you think our gender situation
> is GROSS, you can change it. Check exposition.

Crimes of Violence

The incidence of crimes of violence among the Cousins is vanishingly small. Colony archives record eight murders in sixty years. Five of them were man against man, two man against woman, and one woman against woman.

This does not count vigilante acts of women against men, but despite the lack of official statistics, such incidents, too, are rare.

Eight

"It's no trick to be celibate when you don't like sex."

"That's the point," Erno insisted. "He does like sex. He likes sex fine. But he's making a sacrifice in order to establish his point: He's not going to be a prisoner of his dick."

Erno was sitting out on the ledge of the terrace in front of their apartment, chucking pebbles at the recycling bin at the corner and arguing with his cousin Lena. He had been arguing with a lot of people lately, and not getting anywhere. Every morning he still left as if he were going to Biotech, but instead he hung out in the park or gym. It would take some time for his mother to realize he had dropped out.

Lena launched into a tirade, and Erno was suddenly very tired of it all. Before she could gain any momentum, he threw a last pebble that whanged off the bin, got up and, without a word, retreated into the apartment. He could hear Lena's squawk behind him.

He went to his room and opened a screen on his wall. The latest news was that Tashi Yokiosson had regained consciousness, but that he had suffered neurological damage that might take a year or more to repair. Debate on the situation raged on the net. Erno opened his documents locker and fiddled with a melancholy sonnet he was working on, but he wasn't in the mood.

He switched back to Tyler's cryptic message. *You can change it. Check exposition.* It had something to do with Biotech, Erno was pretty sure. He had tried the public databases, but had not come up with anything. There were databases accessible only through the biotech labs, but he would have to return to his practicum to view them, and that would mean he would have to explain his absence. He wasn't ready for that yet.

On impulse, Erno looked up Tyler in the colony's genome database. What was the name Debrasdaughter had called him?—Marysson, Thomas Marysson. He found Tyler's genome. Nothing about it stood out.

Debaters had linked Tyler's bio to the genome. Marysson had been born thirty-six years ago. His mother was a second-generation Cousin; his grandmother had arrived with the third colonization contingent, in 2038. He had received a general education, neither excelling nor failing anything. His mother had died when he was twenty. He had moved out into the dorms, had worked uneventfully in construction and repair for fourteen years, showing no sign of rebelliousness before reinventing himself as Tyler Durden, the comedian.

Until two years ago, absolutely nothing had distinguished him from any of a thousand male Cousins.

Bored, Erno looked up his own genome.

There he lay in rows of base pairs, neat as a tile floor. Over at Biotech, some insisted that everything you were was fixed in those sequences in black-and-white. Erno didn't buy it. Where was the gene for desire there, or hope, or despair, or frustration? Where was the gene that said he would sit in front of a computer screen at the age of seventeen, boiling with rage?

He called up his mother's genome. There were her sequences. Some were the same as his. Of course there was no information about his father. To prevent dire social consequences, his father must remain a blank spot in his history, as far as the Society of Cousins was concerned. Maybe some families kept track of such things, but nowhere in the databases were fathers and children linked.

Of course they couldn't stop him from finding out. He knew others who had done it. His father's genome was somewhere in the database, for medical purposes. If he removed from his own those sequences that belonged to his mother, then what was left—at least the sequences she had not altered when she had planned him—belonged to his father. He could cross-check those against the genomes of all the colony's men.

From his chart, he stripped those genes that matched his mother's. Using what remained, he prepared a search engine to sort through the colony's males.

The result was a list of six names. Three were brothers: Stuart, Simon, and Josef Bettesson. He checked the available public information on them. They were all in their nineties, forty years older than Erno's mother. Of the remaining men, two were of about her age: Sidney Orindasson and Micah Avasson. Of those two, Micah Avasson had the higher correlation with Erno's genome.

He read the public records for Micah Avasson. Born in 2042, he would be fifty-six years old. A physical address: men's dormitory, East Five lava tube. He keyed it into his notebook.

Without knocking, his mother came into the room. Though he had no reason to be ashamed of his search, Erno shoved the notebook into his pocket.

She did not notice. "Erno, we need to talk."

"By talk do you mean interrogate, or lecture?"

His mother's face stiffened. For the first time he noticed the crow's feet at the corners of her eyes. She moved around his room, picking up his clothes, sorting, putting them away. "You should keep your room cleaner. Your room is a reflection of your mind."

"Please, mother."

She held one of his shirts to her nose, sniffed, and made a face. "Did I ever tell you about the time I got arrested? I was thirteen, and Derek Silviasson and I were screwing backstage in the middle of a performance of *A Doll's House*. We got a little carried away. When Nora opened the door to leave at the end of the second act, she tripped over Derek and me in our second act."

"They arrested you? Why?"

"The head of the Board was a prude. It wouldn't have mattered so much but *A Doll's House* was her favorite play."

"You and Derek Silviasson were lovers?"

She sat down on his bed, a meter from him, and leaned forward. "After the paint bombing, Erno, they went back to examine the recordings from the spex of the officers at the Oxygen Warehouse riot. Who do you suppose, to my surprise, they found there?"

Erno swiveled in his chair to avoid her eyes. "Nick already told you I went there."

"But you didn't. Not only were you there, but at one point you were together with Durden."

"What was I doing?"

"Don't be difficult. I'm trying to protect you, Erno. The only reason I know about this is that Harald Gundasson let me know on the sly. Another report says Durden met you outside the North airlock one day. You're likely to be called in for questioning. I want to know what's going on. Are you involved in some conspiracy?"

His mother looked so forlorn he found it hard to be hostile. "As far as I know there is no conspiracy."

"Did you have something to do with the paint bomb?"

"No. Of course not."

"I found out you haven't been to your practicum. What have you been doing?"

"I've been going to the gym."

"Are you planning a trip to Earth?"

"Don't be stupid, mother."

"Honestly, Erno, I can't guess what you are thinking. You're acting like a spy."

"Maybe I am a spy."

His mother laughed.

"Don't laugh at me!"

"I'm not laughing because you're funny. I'm laughing because I'm scared! This is an ugly business, Erno."

"Stop it, mother. Please."

She stared at him. He tried not to look away. "I want you to listen. Tyler Durden is a destroyer. I've been to Aristarchus, to Tycho. I've seen the patriarchy. Do you want that here?"

"How would I know? I've never been there!" His eyes fell on the copy of *Stories for Men*. "Don't tell me stories about rape and carnage," he said, looking at the book's cover. "I've heard them all before. You crammed them down my throat with my baby food."

"They're true. Do you deny them?"

Erno clenched his jaw, tried to think. Did she have to browbeat him? "I don't know!"

"It's not just carnage. It's waste and insanity. You want to know what they're like—one time I had a talk with this security man at Shackleton. They were mining lunar ice for reaction mass in the shuttles.

"I put it to him that using lunar ice for rocket fuel was criminally wasteful. Water is the most precious commodity on the moon, and here they are blowing it into space.

"He told me it was cheaper to use lunar ice than haul water from Earth. My argument wasn't with him, he said, it was with the laws of the marketplace. Like most of them, he condescended to me, as if I were a child or idiot. He thought that invoking the free market settled the issue, as if to go against the market were to go against the laws of nature. The goal of conquering space justified the expenditure, he said—that they'd get more water somewhere else when they used up the lunar ice."

"He's got an argument."

"The market as a law of nature? 'Conquering space?' How do you conquer space? That's not a goal, it's a disease."

"What does this have to do with Tyler Durden?"

"Durden is bringing the disease here!"

"He's fighting oppression! Men have no power here; they are stifled and ignored. There are no real male Cousins."

"There are plenty of male Cousins. There are lots of role models. Think of Adil Al-Hafaz, of Peter Sarahsson—of Nick, for pity's sake!"

"Nick? Nick?" Erno laughed. He stood. "You might as well leave now, officer."

His mother looked hurt. "Officer?"

"That's why you're here, isn't it?"

"Erno, I know you don't like me. I'm dull and conventional. But being unconventional, by itself, isn't a virtue. I'm your mother."

"And you're a cop."

That stopped her for a moment. She took a deep breath. "I dearly love you, Erno, but if you think—"

That tone of voice. He'd heard it all his life: all the personal anecdotes are over, now. We're done with persuasion, and it's time for you to do what I say.

"You dearly love nothing!" Erno shouted. "All you want is to control me!"

She started to get up. "I've given you every chance—"

Erno threw *Stories for Men* at her. His mother flinched, and the book struck her in the chest and fell slowly to the floor. She looked more startled than hurt, watching the book fall, tumbling, leaves open; she looked as if she were trying to understand what it was—but when she faced him again, her eyes clouded. Trembling, livid, she stood, and started to speak. Before she could say a word Erno ran from the room.

Property

A man on his own is completely isolated. Other men might be his friends or lovers, but if he has a legal connection to anyone, it is to his mother.

Beyond a certain point, property among the Cousins is the possession of the community. Private property passes down from woman to woman, but only outside of the second degree of blood relation. A woman never inherits from her biological mother. A woman chooses her friends and mates, and in the event of her death, her property goes to them. If a woman dies without naming an heir, her property goes to the community.

A man's property is typically confined to personal possessions. Of course, in most families he is petted, and has access to more resources than any female, but the possessions are gotten for him by his mother or his mate, and they belong to her. What property he might hold beyond that belongs to his mother. If he has no mother, then it belongs to his oldest sister. If he has no sister, then it goes to the community.

A man who forsakes his family has nowhere to go.

Nine

The great jazzmen were all persecuted minorities. Black men like Armstrong, Ellington, Coltrane, Parker. And the comedians were all Jews and black men. Leaving his mother's apartment, Erno saw himself the latest in history's long story of abused fighters for expressive freedom.

Erno stalked around the perimeter road, head down. To his left, beyond the parapet, the crater's inner slope, planted with groundsel, wildflowers, and hardy low-G modifications of desert scrub, fell away down to the agricultural fields, the park, and two kilometers distant, clear through the low-moisture air, the aspen-forested opposite slopes. To his right rose the ranks of apartments, refectories, dorms, public buildings and labs, clusters of oblong boxes growing higgledy-piggledy, planted with vines and hanging gardens, divided by ramps and stairs and walkways, a high-tech cliff city in pastel concrete glittering with ilemenite crystals. A small green lizard scuttled across the pebbled composite of the roadway and disappeared among some ground cover.

Erno ignored the people on their way to work and back, talking or playing. He felt like smashing something. But smashing things was not appropriate Cousins behavior.

In the southwest quad he turned up a ramp into a residential district. These were newer structures, products of the last decade's planned expansion of living quarters, occupied for the most part by new families.

He moved upward by steady leaps, feeling the tension on his legs, enjoying the burn it generated.

Near the top of the rimwall he found Gilman 334. He pressed the door button. The screen remained blank, but after a moment Alicia's voice came from the speaker. "Erno. Come on in."

The door opened and he entered the apartment. It consisted mostly of an open lounge, furnished in woven furniture, with a couple of small rooms adjoining. Six young women were sitting around inhaling mood enhancers, listening to music. The music was Monk, "Brilliant Corners." Erno had given it to Alicia; she would never have encountered twentieth-century jazz otherwise.

There was something wrong with Monk in this context. These girls ought to be listening to some lunar music—one of the airy mixed choral groups, or Shari Cloudsdaughter's "Sunlight or Rock." In this circle of females, the tossed-off lines of Sonny Rollins' sax, the splayed rhythms of Monk's piano, seemed as if they were being stolen. Or worse still, studied—by a crew of aliens for whom they could not mean what they meant to Erno.

"Hello," Erno said. "Am I crashing your party?"

"You're not crashing." Alicia took him by the arm. "This is Erno," she said to the others. "Some of you know him."

Sharon was there, one of the hottest women in Alicia's cohort at school—he had heard Sid talk about her. He recognized Betty Sarahsdaughter, Liz Bethsdaughter, both of them, like Alicia, studying social work, both of whom had turned him down at one time or another. Erno liked women as individuals, but in a group, their intimate laughter, gossip, and private jokes—as completely innocent as they might be—made him feel like he knew nothing about them. He drew Alicia aside. "Can we talk—in private?"

"Sure." She took Erno to one of the bedrooms. She sat on the bed, gestured to a chair. "What's the matter?"

"I had a fight with my mother."

"That's what mothers are for, as far as I can tell."

"And the constables are going to call me in for questioning. They think I may be involved in some conspiracy with Tyler Durden."

"Do you know where he is?"

Erno's defenses came up. "Do you care?"

"I don't want to know where he is. If you know, keep it to yourself. I'm *not* your mother."

"I could be in trouble."

"A lot of us will stand behind you on this, Erno. Sharon and I would." She reached out to touch his arm. "I'll go down to the center with you."

Erno moved to the bed beside her. He slid his hand to her waist, closed his eyes, and rubbed his cheek against her hair. To his surprise, he felt her hand between his shoulder blades. He kissed her, and she leaned back. He looked into her face: her green eyes, troubled, searched his. Her bottom lip was full. He kissed her again, slid his hand to her breast, and felt the nipple taut beneath her shirt.

Leave aside the clumsiness—struggling out of their clothes, the distraction of "Straight, No Chaser" from the other room, Erno's momentary thought of the women out there wondering what was going on in here—and it was the easiest thing in the world. He slid into Alicia as if he were coming home. Though his head swirled with desire, he tried to hold himself back, to give her what she wanted. He kissed her all over. She giggled and teased him and twisted her fingers in his hair to pull him down to her, biting his lip. For fifteen or twenty minutes, the Society of Cousins disappeared.

Erno watched her face, watched her closed eyes and parted lips, as she concentrated on her pleasure. It gave him a feeling of power. Her skin flushed, she gasped, shuddered, and he came.

He rested his head upon her breast, eyes closed, breathing deeply, tasting the salt of her sweat. Her chest rose and fell, and he could hear her heart beating fast, then slower. He held her tight. Neither said anything for a long time.

After a while he asked her, quietly, "Can I stay here?"

Alicia stroked his shoulder, slid out from beneath him, and began to pull on her shirt. "I'll talk to Sharon."

Sharon. Erno wondered how many of the other women in the next room Alicia was sleeping with. Alicia was a part of that whole scene, young men and women playing complex mating games that Erno was no good at. He had no idea what "talking to Sharon" might involve. But Alicia acted as if the thought of him moving in was a complete surprise.

"Don't pull a muscle or anything stretching to grasp the concept," Erno said softly.

Alicia reacted immediately. "Erno, we've never exchanged two words about partnering. What do you expect me to say?"

"We did talk about it—in the park. You said you would talk to Sharon then. Why didn't you?"

"Please, Erno." She drew up her pants and the fabric seamed itself closed over her lovely, long legs. "When you're quiet, you're so sweet."

Sweet. Erno felt vulnerable, lying there naked with the semen drying on his belly. He reached for his clothes. "That's right," he muttered, "I forgot. Sex is the social glue. Fuck him so he doesn't cause any trouble."

"Everything isn't about your penis, Erno. Durden is turning you into some self-destructive *boy*. Grow up."

"Grow up?" Erno tugged on his pants. "You don't want me grown up. You want the sweet boy, forever. I've figured it out now—you're never even there with me, except maybe your body. At least I think it was you."

Alicia stared at him. Erno recognized that complete exasperation: he had seen it on his mother. From the next room drifted the sound of "Blue Monk," and women laughing.

"Sharon was right," Alicia said, shaking her head. And she chuckled, a little rueful gasp, as if to say, *I can't believe I'm talking with this guy.*

Erno took a step forward and slapped her face. "You bitch," he breathed. "You fucking bitch."

Alicia fell back, her eyes wide with shock. Erno's head spun. He fled the room, ran through the party and out of the apartment.

It was full night now, the dome sprinkled with stars. He stalked down the switchback ramps toward the perimeter road, through the light thrown by successive lampposts, in a straight-legged gait that kicked him off the pavement with every stride. He hoped that anyone who saw him would see his fury and think him dangerous. Down on the road he stood at the parapet, breathing through his mouth and listening to the hum of insects in the fields below.

In the lamplight far to his left, a person in a green uniform appeared. On impulse Erno hopped over the parapet to the slope. Rather than wait for the constable to pass, he bounced off down toward the crater's floor, skidding where it was steep, his shoes kicking up dust. He picked up speed, making headlong four- or five-meter leaps, risking a fall every time his feet touched.

It was too fast. Thirty meters above the floor he stumbled and went flying face forward. He came down sideways, rolled, and slammed his head as he flipped and skidded to a halt. He lay trying to catch his breath. He felt for broken limbs. His shirt was torn and his shoulder ached. He pulled himself up and went down the last few meters to the crater floor, then limped through the fields for Sobieski Park.

In a few minutes he was there, out of breath and sweating. At the fountain he splashed water on his face. He felt his shoulder gingerly, then made his way to the amphitheater. At first he thought the theater was deserted, but then he saw, down on the stage, a couple of women necking, oblivious of him.

He stood in the row where he had spotted Alicia some weeks before. He had hit her. He couldn't believe he had hit her.

Ten

Erno slept in the park and in the morning headed for his biotech shift as if he had never stopped going. No one at the airlock questioned him. Apparently, even though his mind was chaos, he looked perfectly normal. The radiation warning had been renewed; solar monitors reported conditions ripe for a coronal mass ejection. Cousins obliged to go out on the surface were being advised to keep within range of a radiation shelter.

When Erno arrived at the bunker he went to Lemmy Odilleson's lab. Lemmy had not arrived yet. He sat down at his workstation, signed onto the system, pressed his thumb against the gene scanner and accessed the database.

He tried the general index. There was no file named "exposition." Following Tyler's reference to "gross," he looked for any references to the number 144. Nothing. Nothing on the gross structures of nucleotides, either. He tried coming at it from the virus index. Dozens of viruses had been engineered by the Cousins to deal with problems from soil microbes to cellular breakdowns caused by exposure to surface radiation. There was no virus called "exposition."

While he sat there Lemmy showed up. He said nothing of Erno's sudden appearance after his extended absence. "We're making progress on integrating the morphological growth genes into the prototypes," he said excitedly. "The sequences for extracting silicon from the soil are falling into place."

"That's good," Erno said. He busied himself cleaning up the chaos Lemmy typically left in his notes. After a while, he asked casually, "Lemmy, have you ever heard about a virus called 'exposition'?"

"X-position?" Lemmy said vaguely, not looking up from a rack of test bulbs. "Those prefixes go with female sex-linked factors. The Y-position are the male."

"Oh, right."

As soon as Erno was sure Lemmy was caught up in his lab work, he turned back to the archives. First he went to Gendersites, a database he knew mostly for its concentration of anticancer modifications. X-position led him to an encyclopedia of information on the X chromosome. Erno called up a number of files, but he saw no point in digging through gene libraries at random. He located a file of experiments on female-linked syndromes from osteoporosis to postmenopausal cardiac conditions.

On a whim, he did a search on "gross."

Up popped a file labeled Nucleotide Repeats. When Erno opened the file, the heading read:

Get
Rid
Of
Slimy
girlS

The sounds of the lab around him faded as he read the paper.

It described a method for increasing the number of unstable trinucleotide repeats on the X chromosome. All humans had repeat sequences, the presence of which were associated with various diseases: spinal and bulbar muscular atrophy, fragile X mental retardation, myotonic dystrophy, Huntington disease, spinocerebrellar ataxia, dentatorubral-pallidoluysian atrophy, and Machado-Joseph disease. All well understood neurological disorders.

In normal DNA, the repeats were below the level of expression of disease. Standard tests of the zygote assured this. The GROSS paper told how to construct two viruses: the first would plant a time bomb in the egg. At a particular stage of embryonic development the repetition of trinucleotides would explode. The second virus would plant compensating sequences on the Y chromosome.

Creating the viruses would be a tricky but not impossible problem in plasmid engineering. Their effect, however, would be devastating. In males the Y chromosome would suppress the X-linked diseases, but in females the trinucleotide syndromes would be expressed. When the repeats kicked in, the child would develop any one of a host of debilitating or fatal neurological disorders.

Of course once the disorder was recognized, other gene engineers would go to work curing it, or at least identifying possessors prenatally. The GROSS virus would not destroy the human race—but it could burden a generation of females with disease and early death.

Tyler had led Erno to this monstrosity. What was he supposed to do with it?

Nonetheless, Erno downloaded the file into his notebook. He had just finished when Cluny came into the lab.

"Hello, Professor Odillesson," Cluny said to Lemmy. He saw Erno and did a double take. Erno stared back at him.

"I'm not a professor, Michael," Lemmy said.

Cluny pointed at Erno. "You know the constables are looking for him?"

"They are? Why?"

Erno got up. "Don't bother explaining. I'll go."

Cluny moved to stop him. "Wait a minute."

Erno put his hand on Cluny's shoulder to push him aside. Cluny grabbed Erno's arm.

"What's going on?" Lemmy asked.

Erno tried to free himself from Cluny, but the Earthman's grip was firm. Cluny pulled him, and pain shot through the shoulder Erno had hurt in yesterday's spill. Erno hit Cluny in the face.

Cluny's head jerked back, but he didn't let go. His jaw clenched and his expression hardened into animal determination. He wrestled with

Erno; they lost their balance, and in slow motion stumbled against a lab bench. Lemmy shouted and two women ran in from the next lab. Before Erno knew it he was pinned against the floor.

"Dead Man"

Many of the stories for men were about murder. The old Earth writers seemed fascinated by murder, and wrote about it from a dozen perspectives.

In one of the stories, a detective whose job it is to throw illegal riders off cargo trains finds a destitute man—a "hobo"—hiding on the train. While being brutally beaten by the detective, the hobo strikes back and unintentionally kills him.

The punishment for such a killing, even an accidental one, is death. Terrified, knowing that he has to hide his guilt, the hobo hurries back to the city. He pretends he never left the "flophouse" where he spent the previous night. He disposes of his clothes, dirty with coal dust from the train.

Then he reads a newspaper report. The detective's body has been found, but the investigators assume that he fell off the train and was killed by accident, and are not seeking anyone. The hobo is completely free from suspicion. His immediate reaction is to go to the nearest police station and confess.

Eleven

Erno waited in a small white room at the constabulary headquarters. As a child Erno had come here many times with his mother, but now everything seemed different. He was subject to the force of the state. That fucking cow Cluny. The constables had taken his notebook. Was that pro forma, or would they search it until they found the GROSS file?

He wondered what Alicia had done after he'd left the day before. What had she told her friends?

The door opened and two women came in. One of them was tall and good-looking. The other was small, with a narrow face and close-cropped blond hair. She looked to be a little younger than his mother. She sat down across from him; the tall woman remained standing.

"This can be simple, Erno, if you let it," the small woman said. She had an odd drawl that, combined with her short stature, made Erno wonder if she was from Earth. "Tell us where Tyler Durden is. And about the conspiracy."

Erno folded his arms across his chest. "I don't know where he is. There is no conspiracy."

"Do we have to show you images of you and him together during the Oxygen Warehouse riot?"

"I never saw him before that, or since. We were just hiding in the back room."

"You had nothing to do with the smartpaint explosion?"

"No."

The tall woman, who still had not spoken, looked worried. The blond interrogator leaned forward, resting her forearms on the table. "Your DNA was found at the access portal where the device was set."

Erno squirmed. He imagined a sequence of unstable nucleotide triplets multiplying in the woman's cells. "He asked me to help him. I had no idea what it was."

"No idea. So it could have been a bomb big enough to blow a hole in the dome. Yet you told no one about it."

"I knew he wasn't going to kill anyone. I could tell."

The interrogator leaned back. "I hope you will excuse the rest of us if we question your judgment."

"Believe me, I would never do anything to hurt a cousin. Ask my mother."

The tall woman finally spoke. "We have. She does say that. But you have to help us out, Erno. I'm sure you can understand how upset all this has made the polity."

"Forget it, Kim," the other said. "Erno here's not going to betray his lover."

"Tyler's not my lover," Erno said.

The blond interrogator smirked. "Right."

The tall one said, "There's nothing wrong with you being lovers, Erno."

"They why did this one bring it up?"

"No special reason," said the blond. "I'm just saying you wouldn't betray him."

"Well, we're not lovers."

"Too bad," the blond muttered.

"You need to help us, Erno," the tall one said. "Otherwise, even if we let you go, you're going to be at risk of violence from other cousins."

"Only if you tell everyone about me."

"So we should just let you go, and not inconvenience you by telling others the truth about you," said the blond.

"What truth? You don't know me."

She came out of her chair, leaning forward on her clenched fists. Her face was flushed. "Don't know you? I know all about you."

"Mona, calm down," the other woman said.

"Calm down? Earth history is full of this! Men sublimate their sexual attraction in claims of brotherhood—with the accompanying military fetishism, penis comparing, suicidal conquer-or-die movements. Durden is heading for one of those classic orgasmic armageddons: Masada, Hitler in the bunker, David Koresh, September 11, the California massacre."

The tall one grabbed her shoulder and tried to pull her back. "Mona."

Mona threw off the restraining hand, and pushed her face up close to Erno's. "If we let this little shit go, I guarantee you he'll be involved in some transcendent destructive act—suicidally brave, suicidally cowardly—aimed at all of us. The signs are all over him." Spittle flew in Erno's face.

"You're crazy," Erno said. "If I wanted to fuck him, I would just fuck him."

The tall one tried again. "Come away, officer."

Mona grabbed Erno by the neck. "Where is he!"

"Come away, now!" The tall cop yanked the small woman away, and she fell back. She glared at Erno. The other, tugging her by the arm, pulled her out of the room.

Erno tried to catch his breath. He wiped his sleeve across his sweating face. He sat there alone for a long time, touching the raw skin where she had gripped his neck. Then the door opened and his mother came in.

"Mom!"

She carried some things in her hands, put them on the table. It was the contents of his pockets, including his notebook. "Get up."

"What's going on?"

"Just shut up and come with me. We're letting you go."

Erno stumbled from the chair. "That officer is crazy."

"Never mind her. I'm not sure she isn't right. It's up to you to prove she isn't."

She hustled him out of the office and into the hall. In seconds Erno found himself, dizzy, in the plaza outside the headquarters. "You are not out of trouble. Go home, and stay there," his mother said, and hurried back inside.

Passersby in North Six watched him as he straightened his clothes. He went to sit on the bench beneath the acacia trees at the lava tube's center. He caught his breath.

Erno wondered if the cop would follow through with her threat to tell about his helping with the explosion. He felt newly vulnerable. But it was not just vulnerability he felt. He had never seen a woman lose it as clearly as the interrogator had. He had gotten to her in a way he had never gotten to a matron in his life. She was actually *scared* of him!

Now what? He put his hand in his pocket, and felt the notebook.

He pulled it out. He switched it on. The GROSS file was still there, and so was the address he'd written earlier.

A Dream

Erno was ten when his youngest sister Celeste was born. After the birth, his mother fell into a severe depression. She snapped at Erno, fought with Aunt Sophie, and complained about one of the husbands until he moved out. Erno's way of coping was to disappear; his cousin Aphra coped by misbehaving.

One day Erno came back from school to find a fire in the middle of the kitchen floor, a flurry of safetybots stifling it with foam, his mother screaming, and Aphra—who had apparently started the fire—shouting back at her. Skidding on the foam, Erno stepped between the two of them, put his hands on Aphra's chest, and made her go to her room.

The whole time, his mother never stopped shouting. Erno was angrier at her than at Aphra. She was supposed to be the responsible one. When he returned from quieting Aphra, his mother ran off to her room and slammed the door. Erno cleaned the kitchen and waited for Aunt Sophie to come home.

The night of the fire he had a dream. He was alone in the kitchen, and then a man was there. The man drew him aside. Erno was unable to make out his face. "I am your father," the man said. "Let me show you something." He made Erno sit down and called up an image on the table. It was Erno's mother as a little girl. She sat, cross-legged, hunched over some blocks, her face screwed up in troubled introspection. "That's her second phase of work expression," Erno's father said.

With a shock, Erno recognized the expression on the little girl's face as one he had seen his mother make as she concentrated.

"She hates this photo," Erno's father said, as if to persuade Erno not to judge her: she still contained that innocence, that desire to struggle against a problem she could not solve. But Erno was mad. As he resisted, the father pressed on, and began to lose it too. He ended up screaming at Erno, "You can't take it? I'll make you see! I'll make you see!"

Erno put his hands over his ears. The faceless man's voice was twisted with rage. Eventually he stopped shouting. "There you go, there you go," he said quietly, stroking Erno's hair. "You're just the same."

Twelve

On his way to the East Five tube, Erno considered the officer's rant. Maybe Tyler did want to sleep with him. So what? The officer was some kind of homophobe and ought to be relieved. Raving about violence while locking him up in a room. And then trying to choke him. Yes, he had the GROSS file in his pocket, yes, he had hit Alicia—but he was no terrorist. The accusation was just a way for the cop to ignore men's legitimate grievances.

But they must not have checked the file, or understood it if they did. If they knew about GROSS, he would never have been freed.

Early in the colony's life, the East Five lava tube had been its major agricultural center. The yeast vats now produced only animal fodder, but the hydroponics rack farms still functioned, mostly for luxury items. The rote work of tending the racks fell to cousins who did not express ambition to do anything more challenging. They lived in the tube warrens on the colony's Minimum Living Standard.

A stylized painting of a centaur graced the entrance of the East Five men's warren. Since the artist had not likely ever studied a real horse, the stance of the creature looked deeply suspect to Erno. At the lobby interface Erno called up the AI attendant. The AI came onscreen as a dark brown woman wearing a glittery green shirt.

"I'm looking for Micah Avasson," Erno asked it.

"Who is calling?"

"Erno Pamelasson."

"He's on shift right now."

"Can I speak with him?"

"Knock yourself out." The avatar pointed offscreen toward a dimly lit passageway across the room. She appeared on the wall near the doorway, and called out to Erno, "Over here. Follow this corridor, third exit left to the Ag tube."

Outside of the lobby, the corridors and rooms here had the brutal utilitarian quality that marked the early colony, when survival had been the first concern and the idea of humane design had been to put a mirror at the end of a room to try to convince the eye that you weren't living in a cramped burrow some meters below the surface of a dead world. An environmental social worker would shudder.

The third exit on the left was covered with a clear permeable barrier. From the time he was a boy Erno had disliked passing through these permeable barriers; he hated the feel of the electrostatics brushing his face. He took a mask from the dispenser, fitted it over his nose and mouth, closed his eyes and passed through into the Ag tube. Above, layers of gray mastic sealed the tube roof; below, a concrete floor supported long rows of racks under light transmitted fiberoptically from the heliostats. A number of workers wearing coveralls and oxygen masks moved up and down the rows tending the racks. The high-CO_2 air was laden with humidity, and even through the mask smelled of phosphates.

Erno approached a man bent over a drawer of seedlings he had pulled out of a rack. The man held a meter from which wires dangled to a tube immersed in the hydroponics fluid. "Excuse me," Erno said. "I'm looking for Micah Avasson."

The man lifted his head, inspected Erno, then without speaking turned. "Micah!" He called down the row.

A tall man a little farther down the aisle looked up and peered at them. He had a full head of dark hair, a birdlike way of holding his shoulders. After a moment he said, "I'm Micah Avasson."

Erno walked down toward him. Erno was nonplussed—the man had pushed up his mask from his mouth and was smoking a cigarette, using real fire. No, not a cigarette—a joint.

"You can smoke in here? What about the fire regulations?"

"We in the depths are not held to as high a standard as you." Micah said this absolutely deadpan, as if there were not a hint of a joke. "Not enough O_2 to make a decent fire anyway. It takes practice just to get a good buzz off this thing in here without passing out."

Joint dangling from his lower lip, the man turned back to the rack. He wore yellow rubber gloves, and was pinching the buds off the tray of squat green leafy plants. Erno recognized them as a modified broadleaf sensamilla.

"You're using the colony facilities to grow pot."

"This is my personal crop. We each get a personal rack. Sparks initiative." Micah kept pinching buds. "Want to try some?"

Erno gathered himself. "My name is Erno Pamelasson. I came to see you because—"

"You're my son," Micah said, not looking at him.

Erno stared, at a loss for words. Up close the lines at the corners of the man's eyes were distinct, and there was a bit of sag to his chin. But the shape of Micah's face reminded Erno of his own reflection in the mirror.

"What did you want to see me about?" Micah pushed the rack drawer closed and looked at Erno. When Erno stood there dumb, he wheeled the stainless-steel cart beside him down to the next rack. He took a plastic bin from the cart, crouched, pulled open the bottom drawer of the rack, and began harvesting cherry tomatoes.

Finally, words came to Erno. "Why haven't I ever seen you before?"

"Lots of boys never meet their fathers."

"I'm not talking about other fathers. Why aren't you and my mother together?"

"You assume we were together. How do you know that we didn't meet in the sauna some night, one time only?"

"Is that how it was?"

Micah lifted a partially yellow tomato on his fingertips, then left it on the vine to ripen. He smiled. "No. Your mother and I were in love. We lived together for twenty-two months. And two days."

"So why did you split?"

"That I don't remember so well. We must have had our reasons. Everybody has reasons."

Erno touched his shoulder. "Don't give me that."

Micah stood, overbalancing a little. Erno caught his arm to steady him. "Thanks," Micah said. "The knees aren't what they used to be." He took a long drag on the joint, exhaled at the roof far overhead. "All right, then. The reason we broke up is that your mother is a cast-iron bitch. And I am a cast-iron bastard. The details of our breakup all derive from those simple facts, and I don't recall them. I do recall that we had good fun making you, though. I remember that well."

"I bet."

"You were a good baby, as babies go. Didn't cry too much. You had a sunny disposition." He took a final toke on the joint, and then dropped the butt into the bin of tomatoes. "Doesn't seem to have lasted."

"Were you there when I was born?"

"So we're going to have this conversation." Micah exhaled the last cloud of smoke, slipped his mask down, and finally fixed his watery brown eyes on Erno. "I was there. I was there until you were maybe six or seven months. Then I left."

"Did she make you leave?"

"Not really." His voice was muffled now. "She was taken with me at first because of the glamor—I was an acrobat, the *Cirque Jacinthe*? But her sister was in the marriage, and her friends. She had her mentor, her support group. I was just the father. It was okay while it was fun, and maybe I thought it was something more when we first got together, but after a while it wasn't fun anymore."

"You just didn't want the responsibility!"

"Erno, to tell you the truth, that didn't have much to do with it. I liked holding you on my lap and rubbing you with my beard. You would giggle. I would toss you up into the air and catch you. You liked that. Drove your mother crazy—you're going to hurt him, she kept saying."

Erno had a sudden memory of being thrown high, floating, tumbling. Laughing.

"So why did you leave?"

"Pam and I just didn't get along. I met another woman, that got hot, and Pam didn't seem to need me around anymore. I had filled my purpose."

Emotion worked in Erno. He shifted from foot to foot. "I don't understand men like you. They've stuck you down here in a dorm! You're old, and you've got nothing."

"I've got everything I need. I have friends."

"Women shit on you, and you don't care."

"There are women just like me. We have what we want. I work. I read. I grow my plants. I have no desire to change the world. The world works for me.

"The genius of the founders, Erno"—Micah opened another drawer and started on the next rack of tomatoes—"was that they minimized the contact of males and females. They made it purely voluntary. Do you realize how many centuries men and women tore themselves to pieces through forced intimacy? In every marriage, the decades of lying that paid for every week of pleasure? That the vast majority of men and women, when they spoke honestly, regretted the day they had ever married?"

"We have no power!"

Micah made a disgusted noise. "Nobody has any power. On Earth, for every privilege, men had six obligations. I'm sorry you feel that something has been taken from you. If you feel that way, I suggest you work on building your own relationships. Get married, for pity's sake. Nothing is stopping you."

Erno grabbed Micah's wrist. "Look at me!"

Micah looked. "Yes?"

"You knew I was your son. Doesn't that mean you've been paying attention to me?"

"From a distance. I wish you well, you understand."

"You know I was responsible for the explosion at the meeting! The constables arrested me!"

"No. Really? That sounds like trouble, Erno."

"Don't you want to ask me anything?"

"Give me your number. If I think of something, I'll call. Assuming you're not banished by then."

Erno turned away. He stalked down the row of hydroponics.

"Come by again, Erno!" Micah called after him. "Anytime. I mean it. Do you like music?"

The next man down was watching Erno now. He passed through the door out of the Ag tube, tore off the mask, and threw it down.

Some of the permeable barrier must have brushed Erno's face when he passed through, because as he left East Five he found he couldn't keep his eyes from tearing up.

"The Grandstand Complex"

Two motorcycle racers have been rivals for a long time. The one telling the story has been beating the other, Tony Lukatovich, in every race. Tony takes increasing risks to win the crowd's approval, without success. Finally he makes a bet with the narrator: whoever wins the next race, the loser will kill himself.

The narrator thinks Tony is crazy. He doesn't want to bet. But when Tony threatens to tell the public he is a coward, he agrees.

In the next race, Tony and another rider are ahead of the narrator until the last turn, where Tony's bike bumps the leader's and they both crash. The narrator wins, but Tony is killed in the crash.

Then the narrator finds out that, *before the race*, Tony told a newspaper reporter that the narrator had decided to retire after the next fatal crash. Did Tony deliberately get himself killed in order to make him retire?

Yet, despite the news report, the winner doesn't have to retire. He can say he changed his mind. Tony hasn't won anything, has he? If so, what?

Thirteen

Erno had not left the apartment in days. In the aftermath of his police interview, his mother had hovered over him like a bad mood, and it was all he could do to avoid her reproachful stare. Aunt Sophie and Lena and even Aphra acted like he had some terminal disease that might be catching. They intended to heap him with shame until he was crushed. He holed up in his room listening to an ancient recording, "Black and Blue," by Louis Armstrong. The long-dead jazzman growled, "What did I do, to feel so black and blue?"

A real man would get back at them. Tyler would. And they would know that they were being gotten, and they would be gotten in the heart of their assumption of superiority. Something that would show women permanently that men were not to be disregarded.

Erno opened his notebook and tried writing a poem.

> When you hit someone
> It changes their face.
>
> Your mother looks shocked and old.
> Alicia looks younger.
> Men named Cluny get even stupider than they are.
>
> It hurts your fist.
> It hurts your shoulder.
>
> The biggest surprise: you can do it.
> Your fist is there at the end of your arm
> Waiting
> At any and every moment
> Whether you are aware of it or not.
>
> Once you know this
> The world changes.

He stared at the lines for some minutes, then erased them. In their place he tried writing a joke.

Q: How many matrons does it take to screw in a lightbulb?
A: Lightbulbs don't care to be screwed by matrons.

He turned off his screen and lay on his bed, his hands behind his head, and stared at the ceiling. He could engineer the GROSS virus. He would not even need access to the biotech facilities; he knew where he could obtain almost everything required from warehouses within the colony. But he would need a place secret enough that nobody would find him out.

Suddenly he knew the place. And with it, he knew where Tyler was hiding.

The northwest lava tube was fairly busy when Erno arrived at 2300. Swing-shift Cousins wandered into the open clubs, and the free-enterprise shops were doing their heaviest business. The door to the Oxygen Warehouse was dark, and a public notice was posted on it. The door was locked, and Erno did not want to draw attention by trying to force it.

So he returned to the construction materials warehouse in North Six. Little traffic here, and Erno was able to slip inside without notice. He kept behind the farthest aisle until he reached the back wall and the deserted airlock that was being used for storage. It took him some minutes to move the building struts and slide through to the other end. The door opened and he was in the deserted lava tube.

It was completely dark. He used his flashlight to retrace their steps from weeks ago.

Before long, Erno heard a faint noise ahead. He extinguished the flash and saw, beyond several bends in the distance, a faint light. He crept along until he reached a section where light fell from a series of open doorways. He slid next to the first and listened.

The voices from inside stopped. After a moment one of them called, "Come in."

Nervous, Erno stepped into the light from the open door. He squinted and saw Tyler and a couple of other men in a room cluttered with tables, cases of dried food, oxygen packs, scattered clothes, blankets, surface suits. On the table were book readers, half-filled juice bulbs, constables' batons.

One of the younger men came up to Erno and slapped him on the back. "Erno. My man!" It was Sid.

The others watched Erno speculatively. Tyler leaned back against the table. He wore a surface skintight; beside him lay his utility belt. His hair had grown out into a centimeter of red bristle. He grinned. "I assume you've brought the goods, Erno."

Erno pulled his notebook from his pocket. "Yes."

Tyler took the notebook and, without moving his eyes from Erno's, put it on the table. "You can do this, right?"

"Erno's a wizard," Sid said. "He can do it in his sleep."

The other young men just watched Erno. They cared what he was going to say.

"I can do it."

Tyler scratched the corner of his nose with his index finger. "Will you?"

"I don't know."

"Why don't you know? Is this a hard decision?"

"Of course it is. A lot of children will die. Nothing will ever be the same."

"We're under the impression that's the point, Erno. Come with me," Tyler said, getting off the table. "We need to talk."

Tyler directed the others to go back to work and took Erno into another room. This one had a cot, a pile of clothes, and bulbs of alcohol lying around. On a wall screen was a schematic of the colony's substructure.

Tyler pushed a pile of clothes off a chair. "Sit down."

Erno sat. "You knew about this place before we came here the night of the riot."

Tyler said nothing.

"They asked me if there was a conspiracy," Erno continued. "I told them no. Is there?"

"Sure there is. You're part of it."

"I'm not part of anything."

"That's the trouble with men among the Cousins, Erno. We're not part of anything. If a man isn't part of something, then he's of no use to anybody."

"Help me out, Tyler. I don't get it."

"They say that men can't live only with other men. I don't believe that. Did you ever study the warrior culture?"

"No."

"Men banding together—for duty, honor, clan. That's what the warrior lived by throughout history. It was the definition of manhood.

"The matrons say men are extreme, that they'll do anything. They're right. A man will run into a collapsing building to rescue a complete stranger. That's why, for most of human history, the warrior was necessary for the survival of the clan—later the nation.

"But the twentieth century drained all the meaning out of it. First the great industrial nations exploited the warrior ethic, destroying the best of their sons for money, for material gain, for political ideology. Then the feminist movement, which did not understand the warrior, and feared and ridiculed him, grew. They even persuaded some men to reject masculinity.

"All this eventually erased the purpose from what was left of the warrior culture. Now, if the warrior ethic can exist at all, it must be personal. 'Duty, honor, self.'"

"Self?"

"Self. In some way it was always like that. Sacrifice for others is not about the others, it's the ultimate assertion of self. It's the self, after all, that decides to place value in the other. What's important is the *self* and the *sacrifice*, not the cause for which you sacrifice. In the final analysis, all sacrifices are in service of the self. The pure male assertion."

"You're not talking about running into a collapsing building, Tyler."

Tyler laughed. "Don't you get it yet, Erno? We're living in a collapsing building!"

"If we produce this virus, people are going to die."

"Living as a male among the Cousins is death. They destroy certain things, things that are good—only this society defines them as bad. Fatherhood. Protection of the weak by the strong. There's no *force* here, Erno. There's no *growth*. The Cousins are an evolutionary dead end. In time of peace it may look fine and dandy, but in time of war, it would be wiped out in a moment."

Erno didn't know what to say.

"This isn't some scheme for power, Erno. You think I'm in this out of some abstract theory? This is life's blood. This—"

Sid ran in from the hall. "Tyler," he said. "The warehouse door has cycled again!"

Tyler was up instantly. He grabbed Erno by the shirt. "Who did you tell?"

"Tell? No one!"

"Get the others!" Tyler told Sid. But as soon as Sid left the room an explosion rocked the hall, and the lights went out. Tyler still had hold of Erno's shirt, and dragged him to the floor. The air was full of stinging fumes.

"Follow me if you want to live!" Tyler whispered.

They crawled away from the hall door, toward the back of the room. In the light of the wall screen, Tyler upended the cot and yanked open a meter-square door set into the wall. When Erno hesitated, Tyler dragged him into the dark tunnel beyond.

They crawled on hands and knees for a long time. Erno's eyes teared from the gas, and he coughed until he vomited. Tyler pulled him along in the blackness until they reached a chamber, dimly lit in red, where they could stand. On the other side of the chamber was a pressure door.

"Put this on," Tyler said, shoving a surface suit into Erno's arms. "Quickly!"

Erno struggled to pull on the skintight, still gasping for breath. "I swear I had nothing to do with this," he said.

"I know," Tyler said. He sealed up his own suit and locked down his tiger-striped helmet.

"Brace yourself. This isn't an airlock," Tyler said, and hit the control on the exterior door.

The moment the door showed a gap, the air blew out of the chamber, almost knocking Erno off his feet. When it opened wide enough, they staggered through into a crevasse. The moisture in the escaping air froze and fell as frost in the vacuum around them. Erno wondered if their pursuers would be able to seal the tube or get back behind a pressure door before they passed out.

Tyler and Erno emerged from the crevasse into a sloping pit, half of which was lit by the glare of hard sunlight. They scrambled up the slope through six centimeters of dust and reached the surface.

"Now what?" Erno said.

Tyler shook his head and put his hand against Erno's faceplate. He leaned over and touched his helmet to Erno's. "Private six, encrypted."

Erno switched his suit radio.

"They won't be out after us for some time," Tyler said. "Since we left that Judas book of yours behind, they may not even know where we are."

"Judas book?"

"Your notebook—you must have had it with you when the constables questioned you."

"Yes. But they didn't know what the download meant or they wouldn't have returned it to me."

"Returned it to you? Dumbass. They put a tracer in it."

Erno could see Tyler's dark eyes dimly through the faceplate, inches from his own, yet separated by more than glass and vacuum. "I'm sorry."

"Forget it."

"When we go back, we'll be arrested. We might be banished."

"We're not going back just yet. Follow me."

"Where can we go?"

"There's a construction shack at an abandoned ilemenite mine south of here. It's a bit of a hike—two to three hours—but what else are we going to do on such a fine morning?"

Tyler turned and hopped off across the surface. Erno stood dumbly for a moment, then followed.

They headed south along the western side of the crater. The ground was much rockier, full of huge boulders and pits where ancient lava tubes had collapsed millennia ago. The suit Erno wore was too tight, and pinched him in the armpits and crotch. His thermoregulators struggled against the open sunlight, and he felt his body inside the skintight slick with sweat. The bind in his crotch became a stabbing pain with every stride.

Around to the south side of Fowler, they struck off to the south. Tyler followed a line of boot prints and tractor treads in the dust. The land rose to Adil's Ridge after a couple of kilometers, from which Erno looked back and saw, for the first time, all of the domed crater where he had spent his entire life.

"Is this construction shack habitable?" he asked.

"I've got it outfitted."

"What are we going to do? We can't stay out here forever."

"We won't. They'll calm down. You forget that we haven't done anything but spray a prank message on the dome. I'm a comedian. What do they expect from a comedian?"

Erno did not remind Tyler of the possible decompression injuries their escape might have caused. He tucked his head down and focused on keeping up with the big man's steady pace. He drew deep breaths. They skipped along without speaking for an hour or more. Off to their left, Erno noticed a line of distant pylons, with threads of cable strung between them. It was the cable train route from Fowler to Tsander several hundred kilometers south.

Tyler began to speak. "I'm working on some new material. For my comeback performance. It's about the difference between love and sex."

"Okay. So what's the difference?"

"Sex is like a fresh steak. It smells great, you salivate, you consume it in a couple of minutes, you're satisfied, you feel great, and you fall asleep."

"And love?"

"Love is completely different. Love is like flash-frozen food—it lasts forever. Cold as liquid hydrogen. You take it out when you need it, warm it up. You persuade yourself it's just as good as sex. People who promote love say it's even better, but that's a lie constructed out of necessity. The only thing it's better than is starving to death."

"Needs a little work," Erno said. After a moment he added, "There's a story in *Stories for Men* about love."

"I'd think the stories for men would be about sex."

"No. There's no sex in any of them. There's hardly any women at all. Most of them are about men competing with other men. But there's one about a rich man who bets a poor young man that hunger is stronger than love. He locks the poor man and his lover in separate rooms with a window between them, for seven days, without food. At the end of the seven days they're starving. Then he puts them together in a room with a single piece of bread."

"Who eats it?"

"The man grabs it, and is at the point of eating it when he looks over at the woman, almost unconscious from hunger. He gives it to her. She refuses it, says he should have it because he's more hungry than she is. So they win the bet."

Tyler laughed. "If it had been a steak, they would have lost." They continued hiking for a while. "That story isn't about love. It's about the poor man beating the rich man."

Erno considered it. "Maybe."

"So what have you learned from that book? Anything?"

"Well, there's a lot of killing—it's like the writers are obsessed with killing. The characters kill for fun, or sport, or money, or freedom, or to get respect. Or women."

"That's the way it was back then, Erno. Men—"

Tyler's voice was blotted out by a tone blaring over their earphones. After fifteen seconds an AI voice came on:

"SATELLITES REPORT A MAJOR SOLAR CORONAL MASS EJECTION. PARTICLE FLUX WILL BEGIN TO RISE IN TWENTY MINUTES, REACHING LETHAL LEVELS WITHIN THIRTY. ALL PERSONS ON THE SURFACE SHOULD IMMEDIATELY SEEK SHELTER. REFRAIN FROM EXPOSURE UNTIL THE ALL CLEAR SOUNDS.

"REPEAT: A MAJOR SOLAR RADIATION EVENT HAS OCCURRED. ALL PERSONS SHOULD IMMEDIATELY TAKE SHELTER."

Both of them stopped. Erno scanned the sky, frantic. Of course there was no difference. The sun threw the same harsh glare it always threw. His heart thudded in his ears. He heard Tyler's deep breaths in his earphones.

"How insulated is this shack?" he asked Tyler. "Can it stand a solar storm?"

Tyler didn't answer for a moment. "I doubt it."

"How about the mine? Is there a radiation shelter? Or a tunnel?"

"It was a strip mine. Besides," Tyler said calmly, "we couldn't get there in twenty minutes."

They were more than an hour south of the colony.

Erno scanned the horizon, looking for some sign of shelter. A crevasse, a lava tube—maybe they'd run out of air, but at least they would not fry. He saw, again, the threads of the cable towers to the east.

"The cable line!" Erno said. "It has radiation shelters for the cable cars all along it."

"If we can reach one in time."

Erno checked his clock readout. 0237. Figure they had until 0300. He leapt off due east, toward the cable towers. Tyler followed.

The next fifteen minutes passed in a trance, a surreal slow-motion broken-field race through the dust and boulders toward the pylons to the east. Erno pushed himself to the edge of his strength, until a haze of spots rose before his eyes. He seemed to move with agonizing slowness.

They were 500 meters from the cable pylon. 300 meters. 100 meters. They were beneath it.

When they reached the pylon, Erno scanned in both directions for a shelter. The cable line was designed to dip underground for radiation protection periodically all along the length of its route. The distance between the tunnels was determined by the top speed of the cable car and the amount of advance warning the passengers were likely to get of a solar event. There was no way of telling how far they were from a shelter, or in which direction the closest lay.

"South," Tyler said. "The colony is the next shelter north, and it's too far for us to run, so our only shot should be south."

It was 0251. They ran south, their leaps no longer strong and low, but with a weary desperation to them now. Erno kept his eyes fixed on the horizon. The twin cables stretched above them like strands of spiderweb, silver in the sunlight, disappearing far ahead where the next T pylon stood like the finish line in a race.

The T grew, and suddenly they were on it. Beyond, in its next arc, the cable swooped down to the horizon. They kept running, and as they drew closer, Erno saw that a tunnel opened in the distance, and the cable ran into it. He gasped out a moan that was all the shout he could make.

They were almost there when Erno realized that Tyler had slowed, and was no longer keeping up. He willed himself to stop, awkwardly, almost pitching facefirst into the regolith. He looked back. Tyler had slowed to a stroll.

"What's wrong?" Erno gasped.

"Nothing," Tyler said. Though Erno could hear Tyler's ragged breath, there was no hurry in his voice.

"Come on!" Erno shouted.

Tyler stopped completely. "Women and children first."

Erno tried to catch his breath. His clock read 0304. "What?"

"You go ahead. Save your pathetic life."

"Are you crazy? Do you want to die?"

"Of course not. I want you to go in first."

"Why?"

"If you can't figure it out by now, I can't explain it, Erno. It's a story for a man."

Erno stood dumbstruck.

"Come out here into the sunshine with me," Tyler said. "It's nice out here."

Erno laughed. He took a step back toward Tyler. He took another. They stood side by side.

"That's my man Erno. Now, how long can you stay out here?"

The sun beat brightly down. The tunnel mouth gaped five meters in front of them. 0307. 0309. Each watched the other, neither budged.

"My life isn't pathetic," Erno said.

"Depends on how you look at it," Tyler replied.

"Don't you think yours is worth saving?"

"What makes you think this is a real radiation alert, Erno? The broadcast could be a trick to make us come back."

"There have been warnings posted for weeks."

"That only makes it a more plausible trick."

"That's no reason for us to risk our lives—on the chance it is."

"I don't think it's a trick, Erno. I'll go into that tunnel. After you."

Erno stared at the dark tunnel ahead. 0311. A single leap from safety. Even now lethal levels of radiation might be sluicing through their bodies. A bead of sweat stung his eye.

"So this is what it means to be a man?" Erno said softly, as much to himself as to Tyler.

"This is it," Tyler said. "And I'm a better man than you are."

Erno felt an adrenaline surge. "You're not better than me."

"We'll find out."

"You haven't accomplished anything."

"I don't need you to tell me what I've accomplished. Go ahead, Erno. Back to your cave."

0312. 0313. Erno could feel the radiation. It was shattering proteins and DNA throughout his body, rupturing cell walls, turning the miraculously ordered organic molecules of his brain into sludge. He thought about Alicia, the curve of her breast, the light in her eyes. Had she told her friends that he had hit her? And his mother. He saw the shock and surprise in her face when the book hit her. How angry he had been. He wanted to explain to her why he had thrown it. It shouldn't be that hard to explain.

He saw his shadow reaching out beside him, sharp and steady, two arms, two legs and a head, an ape somehow transported to the moon. No, not an ape—a man. What a miracle that a man could keep himself alive in this harsh place—not just keep alive, but make a home of it. All the intellect and planning and work that had gone to put him here, standing out under the brutal sun, letting it exterminate him.

He looked at Tyler, fixed as stone.

"This is insane," Erno said—then ran for the tunnel.

A second after he sheltered inside, Tyler was there beside him.

Fourteen

They found the radiation shelter midway through the tunnel, closed themselves inside, stripped off their suits, drank some water, breathed the cool air. They crowded in the tiny stone room together, smelling each other's sweat. Erno started to get sick: he had chills, he felt nausea. Tyler made him sip water, put his arm around Erno's shoulders.

Tyler said it was radiation poisoning, but Erno said it was not. He sat wordless in the corner the nine hours it took until the all-clear came. Then, ignoring Tyler, he suited up and headed back to the colony.

Fifteen

So that is the story of how Erno discovered that he was not a man. That, indeed, Tyler was right, and there was no place for men in the Society of Cousins. And that he, Erno, despite his grievances and rage, was a cousin.

The cost of this discovery was Erno's own banishment, and one thing more.

When· Erno turned himself in at the constabulary headquarters, eager to tell them about GROSS and ready to help them find Tyler, he was surprised at their subdued reaction. They asked him no questions. They looked at him funny, eyes full of rage and something besides rage. Horror? Loathing? Pity? They put him in the same white room where he had sat before, and left him there alone. After a while the blond interrogator, Mona, came in and told him that three people had been injured when Tyler and Erno had blown the vacuum seal while escaping. One, who had insisted on crawling after them through the escape tunnel, had been caught in there and died: Erno's mother.

Erno and Tyler were given separate trials, and the colony voted: they were to be expelled. Tyler's banishment was permanent; Erno was free to apply for readmission in ten years.

The night before he left, Erno, accompanied by a constable, was allowed to visit his home. Knowing how completely inadequate it was, he apologized to his sister, his aunt, and his cousins. Aunt Sophie and Nick treated him with stiff rectitude. Celeste, who somehow did not feel the rage against him that he deserved, cried and embraced him. They let him pack a duffel with a number of items from his room.

After leaving, he asked the constable if he could stop a moment on the terrace outside the apartment before going back to jail. He took a last look at the vista of the domed crater from the place where he had lived every day of his life. He drew a deep breath and closed his eyes. His mother seemed everywhere around him. All he could see was her crawling, on hands and knees in the dark, desperately trying to save him from himself. How angry she must have been, and how afraid. What must she have thought, as the air flew away and she felt her coming death? Did she regret giving birth to him?

He opened his eyes. There on the terrace stood the recycler he had thrown pebbles at for years. He reached into his pack, pulled out *Stories for Men*, and stepped toward the bin.

Alicia came around a corner. "Hello, Erno," she said.

A step from the trash bin, Erno held the book awkwardly in his hand, trying to think of something to say. The constable watched them.

"I can't tell you how sorry I am," he told Alicia.

"I know you didn't mean this to happen," she said.

"It doesn't matter what I meant. It happened."

On impulse, he handed her the copy of *Stories for Men*. "I don't know what to do with this," he said. "Will you keep it for me?"

The next morning they put him on the cable car for Tsander. His exile had begun.

Under the Lunchbox Tree

On Monday they started the godawful retreat olympics with track and field at the biodrome, and Mira, with a leap of five meters, placed last in the broad jump, and that was it: she vowed to be out of there by the end of the week. The infirmary was Plan A, and wasn't working.

She sat on the examining table, her feet dangling, trying to look sick. The infirmary was only two rooms, an office and a treatment room that contained the table with a multi-scanner hovering over it like a big preying mantis. The scanner's boom was an off-white that must have been designed to reassure patients when it was new twenty years ago. The color reminded Mira of spoiled milk. One wall was tuned to a pix of a tropical paradise, probably Hawaii or the Philippines, if she knew her Earth landscapes. A cone-shaped green volcano in the distance hovered over a green field, bordered by a white fence, where horses stood about cropping grass or poised swag-bellied and sleepy-eyed with their heads down, their sweet faces thinking horsy thoughts, twitching a shoulder or haunch now and then to dislodge a fly. Even the horses did not improve Mira's state of mind.

"I don't see any sign of an infection," the nurse called from the other room. She came into the examining room and laid the diagnostic window down beside Mira on the table. "You see?"

The bar charts were all in the green.

"My stomach hurts," Mira insisted.

"There are no indications." The nurse was a pale matron wannabe with a ratty haircut.

"Maybe I'm feeling a little better," Mira admitted. "I guess I'll just go back to my group."

"Do you need me to take you?" the nurse asked in a way that made it entirely clear that the last thing she fancied was minding some malingering twelve-year-old for a moment longer than she had to.

"I'll be fine," Mira said. She hopped off the table. "Thanks."

"Don't mention it." The nurse retreated to the office. As Mira left the clinic she grabbed the diagnostic window, thumbed its release, crumpled it, and shoved it into her pocket.

She fled the clinic down the corridor. She acted as if she was going back to the playing fields that took up half of the volcanic bubble that contained Camp Swampy. But when she came to the archway that opened out onto the green fields and great overarching white roof, she hurried past it toward the experimental forest habitat, trying to come up with Plan B.

As she skipped along the hall she sang:

"My spacesuit has three holes in it.
My suit it has three holes.
If it didn't have three holes in it,
It wouldn't be my suit.

One hole for my head,
One hole used in bed,
The other hole means
Holy beans!
I'm dead!"

Past the sauna she veered left into the greenhouse. Beyond the semi-permeable barrier the air was humid and the thick-leafed trees towered over the paths. Bright sunlight from the heliotropes in the roof filtered down through their branches. She heard the buzz of insects and chirp of birds.

The thing she hated about retreat was the phony sisterhood. It wasn't that Mira didn't like some of the girls—Kara and Rita were even her friends—it was that you were supposed to pretend that you had some mystical connection to people you wouldn't be caught dead marrying.

Along the path she found a lunchbox tree. The boxes nearest the trunk were small and green, but the ones farthest out and high up, on the big limbs, were square, white, and ripe. Mira leaped up a couple of meters or more and managed to snatch one. She landed clumsily, cradling the box in her lap. Raised letters on the celluloid read "LUNCH": she pulled the top open. Inside were a sandwich, a cookie, a bladder of lemonade, and an apple. She broke the peanut-butter-and-jelly sandwich from its stem inside and took a bite. As she ate, she dug Comet out of her pocket. She turned him over in her fingers and ran her thumbnail along his frozen black mane.

Like Veronica—it was Veronica's trick at retreat to put on a big show of sisterhood, when back in the colony she was the biggest backstabber in school. She gave away secrets and told lies. When Mira had revealed her plans to get a horse, Veronica had blabbed it to everyone in the school. Mira could hardly show her face for a month.

Mira had more in common with her brother Marco than she would ever have with Veronica. But the counselors acted like you couldn't have that connection with a boy. Mira liked boys—and not just the sex part. Most boys, if they liked or didn't like you, they couldn't hide it. They didn't pretend to be your pal and then dirk you when you weren't around—or if a boy did try that, he wasn't any good at it. But in sharing circle Mira had to keep such thoughts to herself or they would accuse her of gender dysphoria.

And absolutely worst of all, retreat was boring.

Mira broke the lemonade bladder away from the side of the lunchbox and sucked on its stem. The lemonade was a little sour, but good.

She tucked Comet into one pocket and pulled the diagnostic window out of the other. She laid it flat, tugged the top corners to turn it rigid. It was a single-sheet display with a retractable pipette along the edge for taking blood samples.

She played with the controls. She took the pipette and stuck it into the lemonade; after a moment she stuck it into the ground next to her.

The temperature display went into the orange. The blood readouts turned various shades of red. Mira blew into the pipette and reattached it to the side of the window. She took a bite of her apple.

"What are you doing here?"

Startled, Mira looked up. It was a man. She didn't think there were any men at Camp Swampy.

The man wore green coveralls and carried a caddy filled with spray bottles and plastic gloves. "You retreat girls aren't supposed to come into the greenhouse. We got a lot of experiments going in here."

Mira bowed her head. "I'm sorry," she said.

"And you oughtn't to be taking lunches from the trees."

Mira blinked hard a couple of times and was gratified to generate a couple of tears. Eyes brimming, she looked up at the man. He was little, with white hair thinning on top, long enough on the sides to be pulled back and tied in a knot at the back of his neck. He had a round face and no chin. His eyes were innocent blue.

He saw her tears, and his tone changed. He put down the caddy. "What's the matter?"

"My—my mother," Mira said. She pointed to the diagnostic window. "She's dying."

"What?" He glanced at the window's readouts. "Where'd you get this?"

"The director called me down to the clinic. They didn't say what it was about, and when I got there, the doctor—the doctor"—Mira threw a little quaver into her voice—"she said mother had caught a retrovirus from the Aristarchans. They said she was under quarantine. I could only see her by remote, and they gave me this. They said it wouldn't do any good for me to go back home, I wouldn't be able to see her. So they're making me stay here for the rest of the retreat."

"No."

"Yes. And I couldn't go back to the meetings, so I ran away and hid in here. And I got hungry, and—"

The man knelt down next to her. "It's okay, girl. I get it."

"I can't go back to the retreat."

"There's really nothing else for you to do. Maybe if you ask the director."

"She's the one who says I have to stay here!"

"I don't know what to say."

"Can't you take me home?"

"Oh, no. I couldn't."

"Do you know where there's a rover?"

"Well—"

"You must, if you work around here. Please, will you take me home? Please?"

"Girl, that's not for me to decide. I'm just a tech."

Mira started to cry in earnest. It was almost as if her mother really were sick and dying. She imagined her, instead of being on vacation with Richard, floating in a tank of milky fluid being worked over desperately by nanomachines. Tiny telltales would wink red and green on monitors in the silent, dusky room. *"Please,"* she whispered.

The man sat back on his haunches and was quiet for a moment. Mira turned off the diagnostic and crumpled it—no use leaving it open for him to think about. He would have to be pretty simple to buy her story anyway. She looked at the ground and cried some more.

At last the man said, "Do you have a suit? Can you get it?"

"Yes," Mira said, looking into his guileless eyes.

"Okay. Meet me at the service airlock in twenty minutes; I think I can get one of the rovers. But I really think you should talk to the director again."

"Oh, thank you, thank you! You don't know how much this means to me."

"What's your name?"

"Mira. What's yours?"

"Theodore Dorasson. People call me Teddy."

"Thank you, Teddy. Thank you. I promise, you won't regret it."

"Can't regret a good deed."

Mira went back to the athletic fields. She circled the edge of the track, past the multiple bars where the gymnastics nerds were showing off their acrobatics, toward the locker room. Kara and Rita were in line by the high-jump pit, Rita gabbing away as usual and Kara standing with one hip thrust out, her hand on it. Kara saw Mira and her gaze moved a centimeter to follow her, but Mira shook her head and Kara turned back. Rita didn't even notice. Mira ran the gauntlet of the counselors without getting called.

Until she reached the locker room, where Counselor Leanne stopped her. "What are you doing in here?"

"Counselor Betty told me to change into my running shoes. She said I can't get out of it any longer."

"Okay, then. Hurry up." Leanne went out to the track.

They were supposed to go on a surface hike the next afternoon and had already been assigned skinsuits. Mira pulled hers from her locker, bundled it into a tote bag, tucked the helmet under her arm, and snuck out the back door of the locker room. She tried to look as if she was in complete control, but she had a bright orange helmet in her arms, her heart was racing like a bird's, and if anyone had tried to stop her she would have collapsed on the spot.

She left the dorm section and went down a level to the substructure. Down a hallway past rooms for environment systems, HVAC, storage, and power, Mira followed signs toward the maintenance airlocks.

She turned a corner and almost ran into Teddy. He grabbed her shoulder and put a finger to his lips. Teddy already wore a skinsuit, yellow with silver reflective stripes along the legs and arms. He held his helmet under his arm and looked up and down the corridor. He looked like he should have a caption over his head labeled, "I am breaking the rules—please stop me."

"Follow me," he whispered, and led her down a side way to a door marked "No Admittance." He unlocked it and hustled Mira inside. They were in a room that smelled of ozone, full of keening pipes. "Put your suit on," Teddy said.

He made no move to give her privacy. As if she'd ever consider sleeping with him! But still, aware of his presence, Mira stripped to her briefs and pulled on the boots, then rolled the suit up her legs and onto her belly. The fabric closed itself over her, tight as skin. She shrugged into the sleeves. The web of thermoregulators adjusted itself over her, squirming as if alive. She was transferring the contents of her pockets to the suit's belt pouch when Teddy touched her arm. She jumped.

"I'm just checking your suit's power," Teddy said. He pointed at her forearm readouts. "Do you have a fresh heat sink?"

"Yes," she said.

He handed her the helmet. "Let's go."

They passed down an aisle between machines and came out through a door in the back of the garage. Teddy led her along a row of crawlers and they climbed into the cab of a small surface rover.

He sealed the cab door. "Get down on the floor. Don't put on your helmet; we'll go shirtsleeves. But keep it next to you."

Mira curled into a ball on the floor and felt the slight vibration as

Teddy started the rover's engine. The vehicle lurched forward, turned once, twice, then paused. Teddy hit some switches, and from outside she heard the rumble of a cargo airlock door opening. The rover moved forward again, stopped, the door closed behind them, and the air cycled.

Mira looked up at Teddy behind the rover's controls. He stared intently ahead. She could not guess what he was thinking. Teddy had to be on Minimum Living Standard, a nonvoter working the mita. A man this old working the mita was a nobody. If he had even a scrap of talent or ambition, he could be an artist, a musician, a scientist. Instead he lived in a dorm and did scutwork.

Or else he had some tragic story in his past. Mira wondered what it could be. His wife had been killed in an accident. Or his mate had used him as a boytoy, and once he lost his looks she let him go. Though by the look of him he didn't seem like someone who would ever have made a boytoy.

Ten minutes later Mira felt a bump through the rover's floor as the outer airlock door opened. This time there was no sound. Teddy set the rover in drive and, as simple as that, they were out.

"Okay, you can get up now," he said. "Strap yourself in."

Teddy steered the rover through the radiation maze outside the airlock. The harsh lights of the maze made Mira squint. Near the end the amount of dust on the concrete increased, and then, suddenly, they were out on the surface.

It was mid-afternoon, not much different from when Mira had arrived at camp three days earlier. The sun blasted down, blotting out the contours of the landscape. They were on a ridge, with low hills in the distance, ejecta from the impacts that formed the craters to the north, including the colony's. The dust over the regolith was torn up here with rover tracks and bootprints. The road was a simple graded path four meters wide running straight north until it snaked off into the hills at the short horizon.

"Relax," Teddy said. "Two hours and you'll be home." He handed Mira a squeeze bottle of water. "Some music?" He touched a control on the panel and the sound of a piano throbbed from the speakers. The music was furious and dark.

"What is this?"

"Alkan. A French composer, back on Earth."

"I don't like it."

"Give it a try. A girl should try new things."

Two hours was much longer than it had taken her to get to retreat on the cable train. What would happen when the counselors found she had escaped?

"I'm sure your mother is going to be all right," Teddy said. He had switched to the onboard AI and let the rover drive itself.

"I guess."

"They should let you into the hospital when you get back. They won't care they told you don't come."

"How can you be so sure?"

"You're her girl. You love her."

Mira reminded herself of the image she had created of her mother in the nanorepair tank. She made it real in her mind. Richard was there, and Marco, watching from behind a window. The technicians were helpful and efficient. Marco wore the video tats their mother had given him on Founder's Day. Richard wore black, as usual.

"What does your mother do?"

"She's a plant geneticist. She invented the lunchbox tree."

"No."

"Really. That's why I went there when I found out she was sick. It made me feel like I was close to her."

"That makes sense. She must be on one of the teams of geneticists."

"She works alone. That's why they sent her to Aristarchus. They're having some kind of breakdown in the ecosystem there, and she was hired to fix it."

"Seems I might have heard of that."

Mira reached into her belt pouch and pulled out Comet. "Look at this," she said.

"What is that? Is it a horse?"

"While she was there, mother was going to arrange to get me a horse from Earth. I'm going to be the only girl on the moon to have a horse." It was the first true thing she had told Teddy. "At least I *was*," she added, trying to get a little crack into her voice. She thought it sounded pretty good.

Teddy must have thought so too. "Now, don't you think about that right now. Think about good thoughts. Have you ever seen a horse?"

"I've ridden one—in VR." She had downloaded "Beginning Horsemanship," from the library.

"What will you do when you get your horse?"

"I'll train him to jump! I'll school him down on the floor of Fowler, in Sobieski Park. We can get permission for a stable in the tower basement. Back on Earth, they even have horses in cities! It'll probably be hard for him to get used to low-G at first. I'll feed him the same fodder they give the sheep and pigs. I'll brush him every night, and pick his hooves. I'll braid his mane. I'll clean up after him—we can recycle his wastes. I won't let anyone else touch him, except maybe Marco. Can you imagine how high he'll be able to jump up here? I'll bet we'll clear the fountains in Sobieski without even getting wet! He's going to be named Comet."

"Sounds good. Sounds like you got it all planned."

The piano music rumbled on. Though trouble might be coming, with Teddy looking like a chinless baby it was all Mira could do to keep from busting out laughing.

It got hot in the cab. The rover already smelled sour, and Mira caught a strong whiff of Teddy's sweat. They had reached the crest of Adil's Ridge, and the road began a series of switchbacks descending to the plain. At the hairpin turns the dropoffs were 100 meters or more. Between breaks in the hills she could see, ahead of them, glittering fields of solar collectors, and in the distance the domed crater that was home.

Though the rover's brain, running off the LPS network, was quite adequate to negotiate the twisting road, Teddy hovered over the controls. A damp strand of hair had come undone from his ponytail and hung by his cheek.

A red light started blinking on the control panel. The piano music stopped and a voice began: "This is a constabulary alert. A child—"

Teddy touched a key on the board and the voice snuffed out, replaced again by the piano. Neither of them said anything.

After a while Mira said, "I don't care for this music. It's crippled. How come you like it?"

"There's a piano in the warren," Teddy said. "I play it sometimes."

"Are you any good?"

"I could never play any Alkan. On a good day I can play a slow rag with only a couple of mistakes."

"You live in the warren?"

"Yes."

"Don't you have any family?"

"My mother died a long time ago. I lived with my Aunt Sonia for a while. I've never been married."

"How old are you?"

"I'm sixty."

Mira pulled her feet up onto the seat and hugged her knees. "What a waste," she muttered.

"What?"

"Nothing. What happens to you when they find out you took this rover?"

"I can explain the situation. You'll tell them about your mother, won't you? They'll go easy once they hear that."

"You think so? They told me not to come home. I was in retreat."

"Some things are more important than retreat. Your director will understand, once she thinks about it."

"But if they don't understand—what will you do?"

"I suppose they'll bust me back to the rack farms. Collar me, and put me on probation. I've worked there before. It's not so bad. All the fresh tomatoes you can eat."

The more Mira thought about it, the more miserable she felt.

"But it won't come to that, Mira," Teddy said. "You've got to have more faith in people's goodwill."

They were down on the plain now, running straight as an arrow between fields of solar collectors toward the colony. Machines moved through the fields, removing dust from the faces of the collectors. It wouldn't be long now.

"I lied," Mira said. "My mother isn't sick."

Teddy looked at her. His blue eyes were wide and clear. His ears poked out sideways and his lips were pursed. He looked like a clown.

"That medical display. What about—"

"Don't be such an idiot, Teddy!"

He turned back to the road and gripped the wheel.

"You tricked me," he said quietly, and after a moment, staring straight ahead out the window, "You're not the first. Probably won't be the last."

Mira didn't say that they would probably think he had abducted her. It was the blackest crime the Society of Cousins could imagine; they would shove him into the stereotype of their worst nightmares, probably already had. She could save herself a lot of trouble by simply going along with that story.

Teddy was silent the rest of the way. The rimwall rose before them; at its base shone the lights of the south airlock. Another rover sped out to meet them; a couple of figures in surface suits who were riding on its back hopped off and skipped along beside Teddy's rover. Mira saw the constables' insignia on their shoulders. They pointed forcefully at the airlock entrance. Teddy nodded and waved at them.

Through the maze and into the open vehicle airlock they went. The other rover followed them in. More constables piled out. The constables stood impatiently on both sides of Teddy's rover while air was pumped into the lock. The constable on Mira's side was a woman, and the three on Teddy's were two women and a man. The minute pressure was equalized, they yanked the rover's doors open.

"Don't hurt him!" Mira yelled, but they had already seized Teddy by the collar and dragged him out onto the floor.

At the constabulary headquarters they questioned Mira and Teddy in different rooms. Mira told the truth, but they did not want to believe it.

Then eventually they seemed to believe it. Next came the scolding from Mira's mother. The constables reached her at Tranquility Spa, and after explaining the situation, turned Mira over to her. The screen seemed huge. Her mother was wearing a fancy low-cut blouse Mira had never seen before. Mira tried not to look her in the eyes. "How can I trust you?" her mother kept saying. "In a year and a half you're supposed to be an adult!" She and Richard were cutting short their vacation and would be home in another day.

Mira kept asking the constables what they were going to do with Teddy, but they wouldn't tell her. She insisted that they let her see him. Instead, they put a collar on Mira and took her home.

At least the constable who dropped her off let her go in alone. It was 0130 when she opened the door to the apartment, and almost tripped stepping in.

Marco had taken all of her horses off the shelf and set them out on the floor. There was a whole herd of them, bays and blacks and pintos and palominos, some prancing with foreleg raised and neck arched, others ears laid back in full gallop, others rearing with nostrils flared, others standing square on four legs, others with heads bent to crop the fabric floor. There were mares and foals, yearlings and ponies, stallions with little bumps between their hind legs to indicate they were boys. Some were twenty centimeters tall, others so tiny Mira could hide them in the palm of her hand.

Marco lay on the floor next to them, fully dressed, asleep with his head on his arm. Mira tiptoed through the field of horses and crouched down beside him. The sidewise shadows of the horses, cast by the nightlight, fell on his face. When she touched his shoulder he stirred. His eyelids fluttered and he blinked them open. It took him a moment to realize who she was.

"What are you doing here?" she asked. "You were supposed to stay with Grandmother Astrid."

He rubbed his eyes and sat up. A crease ran across his cheek from where he had been lying on the sleeve of his shirt. "It's boring there, so I came home. I can take care of myself!"

She didn't bother to disagree with him.

"The constables called looking for Mom," Marco said. "They said you would be sent home. What happened?"

"I'll tell you in the morning." She helped him get up and steered him, half asleep, toward his bedroom. She managed to get him into his bed, then sat down on the edge.

"Are you in trouble?" he asked.

"I'll just tell Mom it's your fault." She poked him in the side. "That usually works."

"Ha. Ha," he said, eyelids drooping. "Mom's onto that one."

He let out a big sigh and his eyes fell shut.

"Thanks for setting out the welcoming committee," Mira said.

"Knew you'd need to see some friendly faces," Marco whispered. His breathing became regular and he fell sleep.

Mira went back into the living room and began to gather up the horses and return them to her room. It wouldn't do for their mother to come home and find them all over the floor. As she did so she wondered, for the first time, how Marco spent the nights when everyone else was away. She had imagined it as a great freedom, one of the many privileges boys had over girls. Boys didn't get sent to retreats. When Marco wasn't being fawned over by some matron, he got to do whatever he wanted. He could hang out at the Men's House, stay up as late as he liked, meet with friends, and pull pranks all night.

But what if he just stayed home alone? That would get old fast. It would feel like nobody cared about you enough to pay attention.

Mira realized that being left alone wasn't always a privilege. Teddy was left alone. He was invisible. Mira didn't want Marco to end up invisible. Marco was her if she had been born a boy—their mother had him grown from one of Mira's own cells, with Mira's X chromosome switched to a Y the only difference between them.

When Mira had arranged the last of the horses on her shelves, she took Comet out of her pocket and set him in front. The little horse stared back at her, his long noble face intelligent and alert. She knew she would never really have a horse; horses didn't make any sense on the moon.

She went back out to the living room and sat in a chair, waiting for their mother to come home.

Sunlight or Rock

In Mayer colony, Erno lived in the Hotel Gijon, on Calle Viernes, in a two-by-three-meter room barely high enough for him to stand up in. The room contained a gel mattress, a false window, and a thousand bugs. He assumed that anything he said or did in the hotel was being recorded for later perusal, but in fact Erno could not imagine why anyone would care what any of the residents of Calle Viernes did.

Most likely the bugs were the remnants of some jackleg enterprise that had failed. Some would-be entrepreneur had seeded self-replicating monitors throughout the colony, hoping to sell the spy service, or the idea of the spy service, or protection against the spy service. The thing had fallen through, and now, unless you lived in the park and could afford scrubbers, you dealt with the bugs.

Erno sat up on the edge of the gel mat, cross-legged, trying to get himself moving. Too much wine last night. He stared out the window at an Earth landscape: sunrise over forested mountains, pink and blue sky with streaks of white cloud, river in the valley catching silver fire from the sun. In the distance an eagle circled above the cliffs. Erno took a deep breath of Mayer's slightly sour air and relaxed the muscles in his back and shoulders. The eagle froze dead in mid-glide, the foliage in the trees stopped moving—then the bird jumped back and repeated its swoop: a glitch in the ancient image generator.

Erno had been watching this stuttering eagle for six months now. After ten minutes he stretched to his feet, shook the bugs from his arms and legs, applied probiots to his groin and armpits, and drew on his stiff overalls. He drank the ounce of water left in the bulb by his bed and ate the leftover soycake from last night.

Outside his room he ran into Alois Reuther, who lived in the next room. Alois, about to scuttle through his door, raised his left arm in greeting. It looked completely normal. The last time Erno had seen him, Alois had sported a glittering metal hand with six digits and a special manipulator.

"New hand?" Erno asked.

"The newest," said Alois. He swiveled the hand 360 degrees and extended his index finger twenty centimeters. The fact that the hand looked like flesh rather than a machine was unsettling. "Watch," he said. Alois touched his finger to the dim light fixture in the ceiling and the light brightened.

"Nice," Erno said, completely repulsed. Alois had replaced much of his body with obsolete devices. His eyes were multifaceted lenses, his left arm was made of pink pseudo-flesh over a titanium armature, and servos in his legs clicked as he walked. The fingers of his flesh hand were stained yellow from the cigarettes that he smoked, imported from Clavius. His shabby blue suit, worn at the elbows, reeked of stale smoke, and every night Erno could hear him coughing through the thin wall that separated their rooms. Some of the other residents claimed that Alois had done hard time in Shackleton, others that he had a fortune stashed away in some secret account. Erno doubted it.

Alois shrank his finger and held his hand out for Erno to shake. Erno hesitated, then took it. The hand felt like warm flesh. Alois grinned fiercely and would not let go. "Look," he said.

When Erno looked down at their grasped hands, he saw that Alois's little finger bore a silver ring—the same ring that Erno wore on his own pinkie. Startled, he let go of Alois's hand, and the ring on Alois's finger gradually subsided into the flesh. Erno touched the ring on his own finger. It was the only thing he had from his mother. He always wore it turned around so that the turquoise stone sat toward his palm, making it look like a plain silver band—less chance for the inhabitants of Calle Viernes to notice he had anything of value.

"Perfect mimicry!" Alois said. As abruptly as he had engaged Erno, he turned and placed the new hand against his doorplate. The door flipped open and Alois hurried through it into his room.

Alois was only one of the eccentrics who lived in the hotel. On the other side of Erno lived Brian, an evolved dog who worked as a bonded messenger. One floor down the narrow stairs lived a couple of dwarfs who went by the names of Tessa and Therese, each only a meter tall. At first Erno thought their stature was a freak of nature, until the concierge told him they were an abandoned genetic mod that had been tried at Tycho, engineered at half-size to reduce the load on resources. But the mod never caught on, and Tessa and Therese were left to live in a world of giants. They earned their living selling pornographic vids that they produced somewhere in the e-swamp at the north end of the colony. Erno bought one and found it pretty hot. On disk, they had the ability to convey by expression and pose the desperate need to have a penis inserted somewhere, anywhere, into their bodies, immediately. Nothing strange about that: what was strange was to see that ability translated into money, something that he had heard about back home but never understood. Now, alone in a place where the sexual rules were all upside down, he understood it better. He was ashamed to admit how easily he had become a consumer.

The concierge was already at her desk when he hit the lobby. "Good morning, Mr. Pamson," she said. "Your rent is due."

"Tonight, Ana," Erno said. "I promise."

"I promise, too. I promise, if your door won't open for you tonight, I will not open it for you."

"I don't promise unless I mean it," Erno said.

"*Claro*. The deadly Mr. P."

He could not pay the rent. Anadem Benet had loaned him cash for two weeks now. Perhaps it was that he was an immigrant from the Society of Cousins, and she liked quizzing him about life in what she persisted in thinking was a dictatorship of women. The first time she had seen his penis, she'd asked him why it wasn't bigger. She had the idea that Erno had been born in a male harem, genetically engineered to give sexual pleasure. Erno's descriptions of everyday life among the Cousins only disappointed her. "Cousins are a gender-differentiated anarcho-social democracy," he insisted, "not a role-reversed sexual tyranny. The founders were women *and* men; first chair Nora Sobieski said—"

"So why were you exiled?"

"I—I made a mistake. Because of it, someone died."

"Ah." It was the only time he had ever impressed her. The deadly Mr. P. Maybe that was why she had let him ride so long. Anadem claimed she came from one of the wealthiest families on the moon, graced with prenatal mods that gave her lightning intellect and catlike balance. It was only through an unlikely series of investment reverses, and the malice of her great-aunt Amelia, Anadem allowed, that she had come to manage the Hotel Gijon. Erno found the story hard to reconcile with her lank hair and spotty skin, and as for preternatural balance, the only evidence Erno had seen of that was when she dodged out the back of the lobby whenever Felix Menas came down Calle Viernes looking for her.

Erno headed up the boulevard. The Mayer lava tube had been sealed with foamed basalt when it was pressurized seventy years earlier, and painted with white titanium dioxide. But where Erno lived the last paint upgrade had to have been thirty years before, and the alleys were draped in shadows. Calle Viernes, along with Calles Sabado and Domingo, was one of these short side streets. Hotel Gijon stood at the street's far end; one wall of the building was constructed of the face of the lava tube. Across Calle Viernes were another flophouse and a RIOP rental shop; next to it a loan shark and a gambling arcade, and on the corner the Café Royale.

As the boulevard wound its way through the heart of the lava tube, in places it broke into a flight of broad steps or ramps to negotiate rises or falls in the natural floor that the colony designers had deliberately retained. That, and the fact that the older buildings were decorated with red, blue, and yellow ceramic tiles, gave the place its old European look. The vistas were broken by the curve of the gray stucco buildings. Above, from the bright roof with its nest of catwalks, heliotropes fed sunlight down. From the roof of the hotel you could see a considerable way down the tube through hazy, high-CO_2 air until it twisted away, a ten-kilometer-long city stretched inside the hollow snakeskin that ancient lunar vulcanism had discarded several billion years ago.

The first place Erno had gone after he had been exiled from the Society of Cousins had been the scientific station at Tsander, but all they had there was a battery of radio and gamma-ray telescopes and a crew of Aspergered scientists. There was no work for an undocumented eighteen-year-old biotech apprentice. But he accessed the Lunar Labor Market and managed to snag a job with Dendronex Ltd. in Mayer, in the Lunar Carpathians.

Erno had heard little about Mayer among the Cousins. Founded by the EU in 2046, the colony been taken over by free marketers in the Lawyers' Coup of 2073. Here, Erno's lack of a citizenchip wasn't a problem; when the economy was humming, immigrants like him kept labor costs down. He busied himself as an assistant on a project for adding prion linkages to human growth hormone. It was mindless work, and he wondered why Dendronex was even interested in this, since HGH was a glut on the market and medically questionable anyway. Three months into his job he found out why when it was revealed that Dendronex was a shell corporation for an AI pyramid; in the ensuing market panic sixteen associated corporations failed, and Erno was on the street.

With the financial chaos, work became scarce. The rail gun was still in operation sending satellites to low-Earth orbit; the only other jobs there were in a factory producing cermet building struts, and in colony services. So every day Erno would go to the labor pool and sit in the waiting room with dozens of others hoping to be hired for day work. Since Erno had no membership in the colony corporation, he was paid in cash, one ducat a day. The labor pool took 20 percent off the top. He kept the remainder on his bracelet, bought protein bars and, when he could afford it, an apple or two, in the shop at the end of Calle Sabado.

Tony, the shop owner, pestered Erno about sex among the Cousins. Did Erno miss the sex with his sisters?

"I didn't have sex with my sisters," Erno told him.

"Why not? Were they ugly?"

"Cousins don't have sex with relatives."

"You can tell me the truth. I'm no bigot, like these others."

"Trust me, we don't. I mean, there's no actual law against it, but cultural imperatives don't need to be codified in law. The Society of Cousins isn't just about sex, it's a matter of—"

"Sure, Cuz. You need to buy something or get out. How about a lotto ticket?"

Tony earned more by selling lottery tickets than fruit or anti-senescents. The front of his shop was a big screen monitoring the latest winners. The residents of the Weekend would cycle through the remote celebrity cams: Balls Hakim, Sophonsiba Bridewell, Jun Yamada. Watch him move into his new luxury condo in the park, go shopping with her for clothes, see them have sex with famous people. Everyone talked about the winners with a mixture of envy and pride, as if they were relatives. Felix even claimed to be related to Gudrun Colt, who had won the jackpot three years ago—but if he was, why was he living in the Weekend?

From inside the shop Tony could watch the passersby stop and stare at the screen, and he would make vicious fun of them. Their bovine faces. Their fantasies. "Two kinds of tramps," he'd say, holding up one finger. "The unfettered, free spirit. Ultimate individual, self-reliant, not owned by anyone." He held up a second finger. "Then you've got the broken parasite feeding on the labors of good citizens, a beggar and prostitute, thief, and hustler. Social deviant who must be controlled, limited, quarantined. Freeze them all and forget the defrost."

Erno wondered what kind of tramp Tony considered Erno to be. He had a lot of time to think about it, because mostly he had no work. He was what they called "poor." All the people living in the Weekend were poor, even the shop owners that the other hotel residents spoke of with envy. Tony had stacks of cash, they told him, hidden away. Erno did not know what to believe.

Mostly, being poor was a matter of finding enough to eat and to pay the rent, and then sitting around with nothing to do and not much energy to do it. Poverty was boring. Even though Erno had spent most of his adolescence feeling ignored and underutilized, he had never felt this useless. He sat in the labor pool all morning and the Café Royale all afternoon.

This morning in the street outside the labor pool, a woman in shabby clothes peddled hot biscuits from a cart, and another, no older than Erno's little sister Celeste, sold jump blood in plastic bags. Inside, forty men and women sat on plastic chairs; some were eating biscuits they had bought outside, others played cards. The muñeco slouched in his cube off to the side with his feet up on his desk; if people tried to talk with him he just opened one lazy eye and cracked a joke. His white shirt and detachable collar were pristine, as if he expected to move up soon, but his demeanor belied that expectation. Down on the Miracle Kilometer, beyond the last pressure wall, the wealthy had their homes in the park. Erno had walked down there one time, ogling the large, clean banks of buildings, the conspicuous waste of water in the fountains, the lush hanging gardens. The muñeco would never live there. None of them would.

It reminded him a little of the apartments on the ring wall back at Fowler, but at home living in such a nice place was not a matter of having money. And here, even the rich had to breathe the same bad air, and they made people sit in a room waiting for work when they could just as easily register workers online and call them by remote.

Erno joined the crowd before the video wall watching the replay of last night's hockey game against Aristarchus. He sat next to Rudi, an old man he had worked with several times. "Any work today?"

"Not unless you're a dog." Rudi's cracked voice bore witness to too many years breathing agglutinate dust. "Fucking dogs. Who can compete with a dog?"

"Dogs are trustworthy, all right," Erno said. "But people are smarter. He glanced up at the screen. "How'd the Gunners do last night?"

Rudi snorted, which turned into a racking cough. He leaned forward and his face turned red. Erno slapped his back. When the cough at last petered out, Rudy drew a shuddering breath and continued as if nothing had happened, "They're getting paid to play that game? Professionals."

The video, subjective from the POV of Gunner's defenseman Hennessey Mbara, showed him cross-checking an Aristarchus forward into a high parabola out of the rink. The forward bounced off the restraining netting and landed on his feet, and deflected a chest-high pass from the center past the Gunner's goalie. The siren wailed. People in the labor pool shook their heads, smiled grim smiles. They stuffed another stick of mood gum and complained about the coach, the strategy, the star forward who was in a scoring slump. The goalie, according to the regulars, had lost all hand-eye coordination.

Erno was still musing over Rudi's comment. "Where does that word come from—'professional'? That makes it sound like, if you claim to be something, that makes you more than someone who just does that thing."

Rudi looked at him sideways. "They're freaks, they get paid big money, and they've got no balls anymore, and they're going to be dead before they're fifty."

"Yes, but what about the word? What does a professional profess?"

"Erno, please shut up."

Erno shut up. He had never gotten used to the way men here considered every conversation to be a competition.

The voice of the muñeco broke in. "I need six certified Remote Integrated Object Printer handlers for D'Agro Industries." The men and women in the room sat straighter in their chairs, the card games stopped. "Frazielo, Minh, Renker, Wolfe, Marovic, Tajik. Have your prods ready."

The laborers named all checked in at the window, ran their forearms through the scanner, and were let through the bubble where they would be hustled by cart out to their posting. They left a score of grumbling unemployed in their wake. Behind Erno, one of the card players threw in her hand, the cards sliding across the table and floating to the floor. "I've had enough for today," the woman said.

The room began to clear out—this late in the day there was little chance of any other work coming in. Erno stood, stretched his legs, touched Rudi on the shoulder, and left. The old man just sat there. Erno couldn't imagine a worse place to be at Rudi's age than the waiting room of the Mayer labor pool. Unless it was the debtor's freezer.

He wandered back toward the Weekend. When he got there, rather than continue on to the hotel, he slid into a seat on the patio of the Café Royale, a small patch of level concrete a couple of meters square, with yellowed fiberglass tables and tube chairs. The other buildings of Calle Viernes had grown up around it, leaving the café a little pit in the shadows. For ten centimes you could buy a tumbler of wine and sit and talk with the other unemployed. From the back came the smells of yeastcake and fried onions that made Erno's stomach growl. An onion sandwich cost a quarter.

Erno counted his change. He had exactly seventy-two centimes. He poked the coins around the palm of his hand, his finger gliding over the raised profile of Friedman on the two quarters, Smith on the two dimes, Jesus on the two pennies. He ordered a wine and watched the sparse traffic on the boulevard: pedestrians, electric carts, messenger dogs.

A trio of loiterers at the next table were arguing. "They make big money on Earth," insisted one of them, slender, with orange hair.

"Earth! You couldn't stand up for ten minutes on Earth," said the burly one with the shaved head.

"GenMod takes care of that," the third said, "Denser bones, better oxygenation."

These guys didn't have the money to buy new slippers, let alone therapy. As Erno listened to their aimless blather, Luis Ajodhia came by and sat at his table. Luis was tall, slender, and wore tight silver pants and a loose black shirt. Whenever he smiled, his wide mouth quirked higher at one corner than the other, and his eyes closed to a squint. When Luis had asked Erno for money after the first time they slept together, Erno didn't understand what he was talking about.

Today Luis leaned in toward him and whispered in Erno's ear. "I've got a business proposition."

"I'm not a bank, Luis."

"You only need forty ducats to get in on this."

Erno laughed. "I don't have forty ducats."

"Don't kid me. You came here with money, Cousins money."

"In that you are mistaken."

"You don't have forty? So how much do you have, sweet boy?" Luis tapped his long fingers on the scarred surface of the table.

The men in the emigration conversation were still going. "The Polity on Earth knows how to run a society."

"Yes, they run things. That's the problem. Laissez-faire for me."

"You go one step outside the standard here and the corporation will let you *faire* in the freezer."

"I'm not afraid of the freezer."

Besides his now sixty-two centimes, Erno had only the one ducat thirty on his bracelet, which he owed Anadem. "What's the proposition?"

Luis looked at him through those squinted eyes, as if assessing whether Erno was worth his confidence. "I know who's going to win tonight's hockey game."

"And how do you know this?"

"I spent last night at the Hotel Serentatis with the forward for the Aristocrats. He told me that the Aristocrats were going to throw the game."

"Why would he tell you that?"

"I have means of persuasion, dear boy. The odds are running 6–1 against the Gunners."

"And if the Gunners lose?"

"They won't lose. I know this, Erno."

"And now that you've told me, I know, too. What do I need you for?"

"You need me because I know the bookies, and can get the best odds."

As Erno and Luis haggled, Alois Reuther twitched by the café. He wore his blue suit and puffed nervously on a cigarette in his new left hand. The three men who had been arguing immediately got up. "Alois, old friend," said the shaven-headed man. "We've been waiting for you. You need to come with us."

Alois's lenses rotated as he focused in on the men. He attempted to push past them. "No, I don't."

"*Au contraire*," said the orange-haired man, putting his arm around Alois's shoulder and guiding him toward the alley behind the café. "Mr. Blanc worries about you."

"Your finances," said the first. "And your health."

"For instance, this hand," said the third, taking Alois's hand in his. "Has it been properly attached?"

With that they disappeared around the side of the building. In a minute came sounds of a beating. Erno got out of his seat. Luis did not move.

Nor did anyone else in the café. Erno circled around to the alley and saw the three men crouched over Alois's body in the shadows. "Hey!" Erno shouted. "Stop!"

The men looked up indifferently. "Where is it?" one of them asked the other, who was kicking around the trash in the alley.

"I don't know. It bounced over here, I thought. Why did you have to take it off?"

"Just find it."

A cloud of security midges was accumulating over their heads. Their tiny loudspeakers all spoke in unison, making an odd AI chorus: "In all disputes, entrepreneurs must relate to one another with complete transparency. Please wait here until the settlement agent arrives."

The bald man reached into his blouse pocket and tugged out a card. He held it up to the monitors. "I have accumulated a Social Deviance Credit," he announced.

"And your colleagues?"

The small man flashed his own card. But the orange-haired man did nothing. The bald man confronted him. "What? Don't tell me you're out of SDC."

"Okay, I won't tell you."

"Fuck!" said the small man.

"Fuck," said the big man. "I don't know why I married you. Let's go." They straightened and pushed past Erno into the street.

"Why are you—" Erno started.

"Mind your own business," the tall man said as he shouldered past.

Erno knelt over Alois. His shirt was torn, his leg was bent funny, and his hand had been torn off. A trickle of blood ran from his scalp, but he was breathing. Erno ran back to the café. Luis was talking to the manager. Erno returned with a wet towel and held it to the unconscious Alois's head. In fifteen minutes a bored settlement agent came by and loaded Alois onto an electric cart.

"Is he going to be all right?" Erno asked.

"Was he all right before this?" the agent said.

"Where will you take him?"

The agent ran his reader over Alois's good arm. "He's insured. I'll take him to the Magnificent Dividends HMO."

"What about the men who beat him?"

The agent calmly surveyed Alois's semiconscious body. "On the violence scale, this probably isn't outside of one standard deviation. You want to make a statement?"

"Uh—no."

"Good day, then." The agent climbed onto the cart and drove away, Alois's handless arm dangling off the side.

Luis emerged from the bystanders and pulled Erno back to the table. "So, are you done wasting time? This information is only valuable until game time."

"They just beat him up."

"You don't have anyone who'd like to beat you up?"

Not yet, Erno thought. But next week he could be Alois: if he paid all he had against his rent, he wouldn't have enough left to feed himself. He couldn't even sit in the café unless he bought something. Maybe he could put Ana off with one ducat on account, but any way he looked at it, in another week he would be destitute.

He could sell his possessions. He had the spex he had brought with him from home. He had his good suit, some other clothes. A few tabs of IQ boosters. "I can maybe raise some money."

"Go do it. I'll meet you back here at 1600. I'll have to lay off the bets at a couple of different bookies or somebody will figure out something's up. We need to get the money down by 1800. By midnight we'll be counting our winnings."

Erno left the café and went back to his room. He got the boosters from his drawer and stuffed them into an inner pocket. He put on his worn slippers, then folded his good ones up inside his suit, and tucked the suit under his jacket with the spex, hoping he could get them past Anadem. He left the hotel for the pawnshop.

The front of the shop was filled with racks of plasma shirts, boots, spex, jewelry, sex implants, toys; in the back were older and odder items: paper books, mutable sculptures, ugly lamps, antique drugs. A little boy sat on the floor playing with a wheel on a wire armature. Several other people were ahead of Erno, waiting for their moment with the woman behind the counter. Erno sat on a bench until his turn came. He went up to her and laid the suit and slippers down. Beside them he put the spex and the boosters.

With her index finger she pushed the spex back toward him across the counter. "Worthless."

She picked up the suit by its collar, shook it out. It had been one of Erno's prized possessions back at Fowler, dark synthetic silk, cut to look just like a dress suit of the mid twentieth century. She laid it back on the counter, ran her fingers along the lapel. She looked up at Erno. "Two ducats."

"Two ducats! You can't find a jacket like that anywhere in the colony."

"That, my friend, is not an argument in its favor."

Erno sighed. "All right." He pulled off his bracelet. "Take this, too. I've got one-thirty on it in cash." He hesitated, rotating his mother's ring on his finger. Finally he pulled it off and set it on the counter. "How about this?"

It looked so small, sitting alone there. The man behind Erno leaned over his shoulder to see. The silver setting of the ring shone in the soft light; the turquoise was rich blue.

The proprietor held the ring up to the light. "This is Earth turquoise?"

"Yes. My mother's family came from New Mexico. That's on Earth."

She gave him a withering look. "I know that." She put the ring back down. "I can give you twenty ducats."

Erno picked the ring up. "No thanks."

"Thirty. That's as much as I can offer."

"Forty," Erno said.

After a moment the woman nodded. Reluctantly, Erno handed her the ring. "Keep it in a safe place. I'll be back to get it later tonight."

"I won't be here. Come in the morning, when we open." The woman offered him a cash card, but he insisted on currency. She counted out four fabric ten-ducat bills, each with its video of the Heroic Founding Speculators on its face, and a few singles and change; Erno stuffed the money into his pocket and fled the shop, almost tripping over the boy on the way out.

Back at the café, Luis was waiting. "Have you got the money?"

Erno looked around the café to make sure no one was watching, and put the bills on the table. He took the coins from his pocket, reserving only a quarter. It came to forty-six ducats and ninety-eight centimes. "How much have you got?" he asked Luis.

"Twenty-three ducats."

For a moment Erno was annoyed; why was Luis coming to him for money when he couldn't even match what Erno contributed? But then he got over it. They both were taking a chance, and it didn't matter who took the bigger. At 6–1 he would clear 281 ducats. That would make all the difference in him getting out of the rut that was the weekend.

Luis scooped up the bills. "Right is right, then. I lay this off, and when we win I give you 225."

"What?" Erno said. "Should be more than that."

"Ten percent for information, and ten for risk," Luis said.

"What risk?"

"I got to lay this off at three different bookies, my son. I try to lay it off all at one and people gone to notice."

It was after 1600. "Then we better hurry."

"You wait here."

"Luis, I trust you, but I'm not crazy."

Luis protested, but gave in. They first went to a shop that Erno had always thought was a virtuality center. He watched through the doorway, and ten minutes later Luis came back smiling, with a tag. "Twenty-five down on the Gunners, at 6–1."

The next place was in the colony center, the business district with the efficient shopfronts and mentally augmented security. Luis left him at an arcade and went into a gold-fronted building of algorithmic design that dated back thirty years or more. Erno wandered around the plaza reading the quotations inlaid in the pavement. He stood for a while on "In the state of nature, Profit is the measure of Right," by someone named Hobbes. He was loitering on "I don't believe in a government that protects us from ourselves—Reagan," trying to avoid the gaze of the security midges, when Luis returned. This time he was not so cheerful. "I could only get 4–1. Bastards are too upscale to give odds."

The third bookie was a single person, a large man in a black jumpsuit standing on the street outside the warehouses near the railgun airlocks. Erno insisted on going up with Luis. The man smiled when he saw them. "Luis, my oldest and best friend. Who's your mark?"

"My name is Erno."

The man's smile grew very broad indeed. He had a video tooth. "What can I do for you?"

"Need to lay down some money on tonight's game," Luis said.

"It's late. They drop the puck in twenty minutes."

"You want our money or not?"

"I always want your money, Luis."

"So it is. We've got twenty ducats we want to put on the Gunners."

The man arched an eyebrow. "Entrepreneurs. I'll give you 2–1."

"Two to one?" Erno said.

"Been a lot of bets in the last hour laid on the Gunners," Black said. "Must be some access of team spirit, I think. Odds going down like a horny Cousin."

"Shit, team spirit. You can't—"

"2–1, Luis, declining as we speak. Maybe you want to bet a different game? I can offer 7–1 on the Shackleton game."

Luis pulled the bills out of his pocket. "No. We'll take it."

Erno was calculating what the reduced odds would cost them. He was going to say something, but Luis had already handed over the cash and received the tag.

"See you after the game," Luis said.

Black nodded, and smiled. "I'll be here, darling"—his tooth gleamed rose, then blue—"if it should prove necessary."

On their way back to the café, Erno asked Luis, "What was that about? 2–1?"

"The word must be out. Too many people must have bet the Gunners."

"You shouldn't have bet that last twenty."

"Relax. We still double our money. We're just lucky we got to the other bookies before the odds came down."

Erno bit his tongue. The whole thing smelled. He felt in his pocket for his last quarter. No rent. No job. His mother was dead and he'd pawned her ring.

They went back to the café and ordered two wines. Erno let Luis pay. By the time they got there the first period had started: they watched on Tony's front window across the street. The Gunners were skating with more energy than they had showed in a month. They spent as much time in the Aristocrats' end of the rink as in their own, a distinct novelty. They scored first, on a blue line slapshot. They kept the Aristos off balance with brutal fore checking. Erno sat on the edge of his seat. At the end of the first period, during a power play, the Gunner forward leapt over the crease, soaring over the defender who was trying to check him. The center slapped a shot into the air that the forward deflected with the blade of his stick over the goalie's right shoulder into the net. The arena exploded with cheers. Erno leapt out of his seat, flew three meters into the air; Luis caught him coming down, swung him around and hugged him. The sudden physical contact startled Erno; he realized he had not been touched by another human being since the last time he and Anadem had had sex.

"You see!" Luis shouted, kissing him.

What a strange place this was. Sex was rationed, money was rationed, sex was worth money and money was sexy. Erno thought about what he would do with his winnings. After getting back his ring he would go to the clinic and make sure Alois was all right. And then he would, one way or another—even if he had to pay for it—what did they call it?—"get laid."

Thirty seconds into the second period the Aristocrats scored. The second period was fought out at mid-ice, with few clear shots taken by either team. It began to worry Erno that the Aristocrats were playing as well as they were. They did not look like a team that was trying to lose. When he mentioned this, Luis replied that probably it was only a couple of players that were in the bag for the game.

"Why didn't you say that before!"

"What did you expect? It doesn't take a whole team to throw a game, Erno. A couple of key plays will do it."

In the third period the Aristocrats put on a furious rush. The puck ricocheted off the dome of netting; flying passes deflected by leaping front liners ended on the blade of a forward just hitting the crease, and only inspired goalkeeping by the Gunner netminder kept his team ahead. Five minutes in, the Aristocrats executed a three-carom shot off the dome that was slapped into the corner of the net by a lurking forward. A minute later they scored on a fluke deflection off the skate of a defenseman. Aristos up, 3-2.

Falling behind seemed to inspire the Gunners, and they fought back, putting several good shots on net, that the Aristocrats' goalie blocked. Erno could not sit down. He paced the café, hitting the concrete so hard with each step that he floated. When the clock hit ten minutes remaining he turned to Luis and said, "I can't stand this." He left and hurried down to the arena, hoping to get inside. But though the doors were open a uniformed chimera stood outside.

"Can I get in?" Erno asked.

"One ducat," the chimera said. His ears were pointed, his pale face smooth as a baby's, his ancient brown eyes impassive as agates. His uniform sported green lighted epaulets and a matching fluorescent belt. Attached to the belt was a stun baton.

"Please," Erno said. "There are only a few minutes left."

"You may enter if you have credit."

Erno could hear the crowd inside, shouting, occasionally cheering. He paced back and forth, staring at his feet. If he had any credit he could just walk through the door. But his bracelet was gone. He had given everything he owned to Luis Ajodhia. How could he have been so stupid?

Suddenly a huge roar burst from the arena doors. He ran over to the guard. "What is it? What happened?"

The chimera cupped a hand over his ear. "The Gunners tied the game. A wraparound goal."

"How much time is left?"

"Two minutes and fifty-two seconds."

"Please. Let me in."

"No."

Erno walked in circles. His scalp tingled and his ears rang. He closed his eyes and took a deep breath. *Please score*, he thought. *Please score*. He looked up at the roof of the lava tube. The air was hazy here, the light from the heliotropes dimmed down to indicate night. High up on the catwalks a couple of kids were screwing.

Erno kicked the pavement with his frayed slipper. Cheers came from the opened door. Erno could imagine the crowd, standing now, shouting, shaking their fists at the players. The last two minutes were taking an eternity. If they went to overtime, Erno did not think he could stand it.

Then came a huge gasp, an oceanic groan, punctuated by shouts and cries of anger, even despair.

A couple of minutes later the first of the people began to exit the arena, cursing, arguing, laughing bitterly, or completely silent. As she passed him, Erno heard one woman say to her surly companion, "Well, at least they played a good game."

Luis was not there when Erno got back to the café. Erno snuck back into his room and threw himself onto the gel mat. He lay on his back with his hands behind his head and stared at the ceiling. Three bugs were fixed motionless up there, microcams trained on him. No one, he reminded himself, cared enough to be watching. The ceiling was made of regolith adobe, so old that it probably had been constructed by people instead of RIOPs. Those swirls and grooves, laden with dirt, had been brushed into the surface by some long-dead hand. How many people had lain in this room and stared up at this ceiling? How many had been as broke as Erno? How many people had shouted rage and frustration at each other in this room, how many had made love here, how many children had been conceived, how many plans made and abandoned?

Well, he had to plan now. First thing he had to plan was how to get his things out of the hotel without Anadem seeing him. If he tried to carry a bag out, she would know at once that he was jumping. Which meant that he could take only what he could wear.

There wasn't much left anyway. He stripped and put on his two remaining shirts, and his jacket, and shorts beneath his trousers. He began sweating, and he felt like a fool, but in the mirror he didn't look too absurd. He stuffed his notebook into one pocket, his spex into another. He still had his quarter, his last money in the world.

Outside his room the light that Alois had made miraculously brighter by his touch that morning had burned out. One floor down he heard laughter coming from Tessa and Therese's room. When he hit the lobby he found Anadem sprawled on the chaise in her office.

"Your rent!" she called.

"Back in five minutes!" he said, saluting her as he walked out. He hurried down to the café hoping to find Luis. Night was falling: the heliotropes were masked. Music blared from the back—staccato drums and pipes, a song he remembered from home, the popstar Cloudsdaughter's *Sunlight or Rock*. The café was crowded, talk was loud. But when he asked around, Tony said Luis had not been there since the afternoon.

Suddenly the weight of the day, and of the last six months, came down on Erno so heavily that his knees buckled and he sat down on the pavement. He put his head in his hands. Through the buzz of conversations came Cloudsdaughter's sweet, mocking voice:

> *But it seems you were mistaken*
> *And the truth came as a shock*
> *About which one was stronger*
> *Sunlight or rock.*

He looked down the alley where Alois had been beaten. Anadem would not have him beaten, he reckoned. He'd just starve, be arrested, put into the freezers until some enterprise paid his way out as an indentured worker. Erno blinked his eyes quickly to keep back the tears.

Something moved in the shadows. In the alley, a dog was nosing around. Erno lifted his head, got to his feet, and went back to see. It was his neighbor Brian. "What are you doing here?" he asked it.

The dog raised its narrow white face. "Good evening, sir," it growled. "I smell something."

Something moved, scuttling beneath discarded papers. There were few small animals in this colony, not even birds—not in this misbegotten place, where they didn't even have a real ecology, just people. Brian tensed, ears laid back. "Stay!" Erno said, grabbing the collar of the dog's shirt. He reached forward, pushed aside the paper, and there, clenched into a fist, found Alois's artificial hand.

"Can I have it?" the dog whined piteously.

"No." Erno reached into his pocket, pulled out his quarter, and slipped it into Brian's breast pocket. "Good dog. Buy yourself a biscuit."

The dog looked uncertain, then raised its ears and walked away, nails clicking on the pavement.

Erno poked the hand with his finger. As soon as he touched it, it twitched away. In the dim light Erno could make out that the wrist was sticky with some fluid that might have been blood but was probably something more complex. This was not some cheap servo. It had independent power and rudimentary intelligence.

Erno cornered the hand, picked it up, and shoved it inside his shirt. It stopped moving, but it made a bulge that he hid by holding his arm against his side. It was warm. He could feel the fluid against his skin.

From Calle Viernes he went down to the Port Authority. The station was not busy at this hour, except for passengers waiting for the night train and aphasics preparing to bed down in dark corners. On the board were listed the biweekly cable car to Rima Sitsalis, another to Le Vernier, and the daily maglev to the southern colonies—Apollo 12, Hestodus, Tycho, Clavius, all the way down to Shackleton. A ticket to Shackleton cost sixty ducats. He didn't even have his quarter.

But he did have Alois's hand. A hand in which Alois had invested a great deal, maybe more than was immediately evident. The portal would read any standard credit chip.

Erno walked to the entrance to the maglev platform. He stood up straight, tried to act like he knew exactly where he was going, and had not the slightest worry in the world. A businessman passed through the portal ahead of him. Erno fell behind. He held his forearm against his side, pressing the hand inside his shirt against his belly. As they approached the portal, the fingers of the hand began to move. Erno did not flinch.

He passed through the portal. The hand, under his shirt, froze. He strode down the tube, and felt the air pressure change as he passed through the lock to the train waiting in the airless tunnel. He stepped into the maglev. The telltale at the door flashed green, and Erno was through.

He passed down the aisle of the car, checking out the compartments as he passed. Most of them were occupied by people who looked no more prosperous than Erno. He slid open the door of an empty compartment and took a seat by the window. Against his belly he felt the warmth of the artificial hand. Alois had stashed at least sixty ducats in there—how much more besides? He wondered what Alois was doing at that moment. He had probably been mustered out of the clinic as soon as they'd patched him up. Back at Hotel Gijon, could he even open the door to his room?

Ten minutes later, the doors closed, the umbilicus pulled away, and the train began to move. They passed out of the dark tunnel into the bright lunar day, and as the maglev swooped up into the Carpathians, the Earth, in its first quarter, swung into sight high above them. Erno still was not used to it; on the cable trip from Tsander he had been fascinated to see the planet rise above the horizon as they came from the farside to the near. That first sight of it in reality, only months ago, had seemed pregnant with meaning. He was moving into a new world. And it hung there still, turquoise and silver, shining with organic life, as it had hung for several billion years. It was strange to imagine a world with air and water on the outside, where you could walk out in shirtsleeves, even naked, where the sun shining down on you was not an enemy but a pleasure. But gravity there would press a lunar-bred boy like Erno to the ground and leave him gasping.

He leaned his head against the train's window, the light of the old Earth throwing shadows on his face, and fell asleep.

The Snake Girl

The winter of Ben Kwiatkowski's junior year was the coldest on record. The first blizzard hit on Halloween, and by Thanksgiving the snow was beaten flat on the slopes behind the women's dorm where students went sledding on trays stolen from the cafeteria. By early December the river, which curled around the campus like a question mark, was frozen. In the mornings, strung out, crossing the bridge over the railroad tracks on his way to thermodynamics, Ben would squint into a howling arctic wind that froze the tears in his eyelashes.

But when Ben met Linda it was still September, the skies were fair, and the upstate New York autumn still yielded sunny days when you could lie out on the quad and watch girls in short skirts throw Frisbees to dogs named Frodo. It was in this calm season that Linda first showed up in the dish room.

The dish room was in the dining hall of Stanton, the women's dorm, where most of the students from the outlying dorms ate every day. Ben had worked there since he was a freshman, and the dish crew had become his circle of friends. They tended to be scholarship kids like Ben who were trying to pick up some extra cash. The pay was minimum wage, but you could work your way up to thirty hours a week if you didn't mind smelling like grease most of the time. At least it kept gas in his car.

That Monday when Ben showed up for his first day of work, there was a new girl among the crew waiting for Mr. Hsu, the cafeteria manager.

"Quiet Man!" said Tony Spicelli. "How's the summer?"

"Not bad. How about you?"

"I got a job working in Lake Placid. I had a great time."

"Who's this?"

"This is Linda."

She was a skinny girl with large breasts. She wore her brown hair in a long braid that hung to the middle of her back, tied with a blue rubber band. Brown eyes, dark eyebrows, and very pale lips, a pretty face, and straight white teeth. There was a pimple on her chin.

"Nice boots," she said. She kicked him in the toe, leaving a scuff.

Ben was wearing the boots he had bought at a head shop in Yorkville, the hippie district of Toronto, at a considerable investment. Black, square toed, an inch of heel, halters around the ankle fastened with bright brass rings. He wore them all the time, part of his attempt at making himself into a hippie, a step up from physics nerd, which had been his identity the first two years of college. Hippies had at least a chance of success with girls.

Not that he knew how to talk to girls. "Thanks," was all he said to Linda, and then Mr. Hsu went on to describe to Linda the five jobs in the dish room: bussing tables, scraping plates, racking plates, glasses, and trays, pulling racks from the big Hobart machine, and sorting silverware. While Mr. Hsu talked Ben hung up his hat and jacket, rolled up his sleeves and put on an apron, and added a headband to hold back his hair.

Girls tended not to want to work the dish room, and Mr. Hsu would give them jobs in the serving line. Ben wondered whether Linda had asked to be on the crew, or whether Mr. Hsu had no other jobs available, or even whether he had something against her.

That first week Linda was put to work sorting silver, one of the cleaner jobs, though the tableware came out of the Hobart almost too hot to touch, and the job left you stuck in the corner at a stainless-steel table where you couldn't talk to anyone else. In the middle of her first shift Linda startled them by shouting, "Jesus H. Christ on a pogo stick! I hope this self-indulgent generation appreciates what I do for it!"

Ben's semester did not go well. His grades in physics skidded as the term wore on; he had carried a B+ average coming into the semester, but Advanced Classical Mechanics was busting his ass. He couldn't tell a Hamiltonian from l'Hôpital's rule. It took him an hour to read five pages of matrix algebra only to have it all evaporate the moment he closed the textbook. It probably didn't help that he was staying up late blowing dope four nights a week. He began to realize that he was not going to be any kind of scientist. Since that had been his goal since he was seven years old, whenever he thought about the future all he felt was panic. The only thing waiting for him after graduation was the draft.

Ben sat with his roommate Mitch Beckmann in Poli-Sci 310, The Age of Reform, the last of Ben's social science electives. Linda was also in the course, and one day she sat with them. Professor Goldberg was droning on about the Prohibition movement. Goldberg was one of those professors who had started to affect longer hair and sideburns. Ben leaned over to Linda. "Look," he said. "One of his sideburns is longer than the other."

Even though they were sitting in the middle of the large lecture hall, miles from the lectern, it was obvious that Goldberg's neatly trimmed left sideburn was at least an inch longer than his right. "How do you get them that far off?" Ben asked.

"I bet he's blind in one eye," Mitch said.

"Maybe he did it on purpose," Linda said. "Maybe it's a statement."

They went back and forth, speculating on the mystery of the sideburns until suddenly Ben realized that the room had fallen silent—Goldberg had stopped lecturing and was staring at them. "You want to tell us all what's so funny?" he asked.

Mitch leaned away as if he didn't know Ben and Linda. Linda slouched in her seat.

"Uh—no, professor," Ben started.

"Perhaps then you ought to pay better attention." Below the level of the seats, Linda kicked Ben's boot. "*Tell him!*" she whispered. "*It's a public service.*" Goldberg's blue eyes were locked on Ben.

"Yes, sir." Goldberg's sideburns had to be *more* than an inch out of whack. Ben couldn't help it: he burst out laughing. Linda exploded into giggles. Goldberg closed his book and said, "You two—please leave my class."

"Yes . . . sir . . ." Ben gasped helplessly, gathering up his backpack. The other students stared as he and Linda fled the lecture hall.

Out on the quad they fell against each other laughing. "Shit, shit, shit!" Ben said. "I am in a world of hurt. Poli Sci is the only class I'm doing well in."

"That's why he did his sideburns that way!" Linda crowed. "He's out to get you."

"The bastard!" Ben said. "I ought to egg his car."

They walked to the student union and drank coffee in the café. They talked about music and politics and feminism and Vietnam and what was the funniest movie they had ever seen. Ben voted for *The Crawling Eye.* Linda held out for some old movie called *The Awful Truth.* When Ben asked her what she intended to do after she graduated, Linda said, "I want to be a part of the world, not the enemy of it."

Linda came from money; her father was the mayor of Hartford, Connecticut. That explained why she had so many different pairs of bell-bottoms, and the embroidered Russian-collar shirts that cost twenty-five bucks each in any head shop. But if she didn't need the money, why did she work in the dish room, where the tropical heat was rivaled only by the reek of old vegetables? She could quote Shakespeare but she cussed like Ben's Uncle Stan, who was an ex-marine and a millwright.

On a Friday night in late October Ben and Mitch went over to Debbie Rosenbaum's room to smoke some dope. It was already turning cold, windy with freezing rain. Ben had a nickel bag in the pocket of his thick corduroy coat. While Cream's *Wheels of Fire* played on Debbie's stereo and Mitch fired up Debbie's hash pipe, Ben sat cross-legged on the knotted rug and started cleaning his dope. He didn't have a screen, so he creased a double thickness of newspaper down the middle, rested it on Debbie's history textbook, and rubbed the dry dope between his fingers, breaking the leaves and stems. The seeds and bits of stem fell into the crease of the paper, and rolled down it to another sheet of paper Ben had laid on the floor. Ben liked cleaning dope—it was a mindless task but made him feel like he was accomplishing something. After a few tokes on the pipe he was feeling very happy, when a knock came on Debbie's door.

"Shit!" Ben said, trying to slide the dope under Debbie's bed.

"Stay cool," Debbie said. "Who is it?" she called.

"It's Linda," came the voice from the hallway.

Debbie moved the rolled-up towel away from the crack beneath the door and opened it a sliver. "Come on in."

Ben did not know that Linda was tight with Debbie. Linda sat down opposite him on the floor. She was wearing bell-bottoms and a knit vest over a turtleneck. He retrieved his dope and continued cleaning it.

After a while, when *Wheels of Fire* quit and *Bringing It All Back Home* dropped onto the turntable, Linda started kicking Ben's boots. It shook the paper on his lap and a couple of seeds rolled off onto the floor and under her thigh. "Cut it out," he said.

"Cut what out?" Linda said. She kicked his boot, harder this time.

He looked up from the paper. Her brown eyes were studying him. "I'm gonna waste this dope."

"'Look out kid,'" she said. "'Don't matter what you did.'"

"Boy, am I thirsty," Debbie said.

"I have a bottle of wine in my room," said Linda.

"But this isn't your room, is it?" said Ben.

Linda shot him a look. "Come with me. We'll go get it."

"Yeah," said Mitch, leaning into Debbie. "You should go get the wine."

Ben set aside his dope again and slipped out with Linda into the hallway. Rather than wait for the elevator they cut through the fire doors and up the stairs three floors. Linda unlocked the door and led him in.

"Have a seat," she said while she opened her closet. The narrow room held a single unmade bed, a desk pushed into a corner, a bookshelf. A jar of pennies and a coffee mug full of pens bracketed her books—*The Era of Excess*, *A Separate Reality*, *An Economic Theory of Democracy*, *Siddhartha*, *The Way of Zen*, and *Alice's Adventures in Wonderland*. On top of her bookshelf stood a row of empty wine bottles. The desk chair was covered with dirty clothes, and Ben did not want to move the bra on top in order to sit there.

On the windowsill sat a large fish tank. Except it wasn't full of water, though it had an inch of sand and some rocks and a couple of dry sticks on the bottom. As Ben looked at it in a stoned daze, he was startled to see something move, uncoiling and sliding silently behind one of the rocks. The thing lifted a triangular head and looked at Ben.

"That's a snake," he said.

"Bingo." Linda pulled the bottle from the closet. "That's Lucifer."

The snake had to be at least three feet long, half an inch in diameter. It had a black face and rings of orange, black and copper. "What kind is it?"

"It's a he, not an it. He's a king snake."

"What do you feed it—him?"

"Mice."

"Mice? Where do you get them?"

"At the pet store on Hudson Street."

"I bet they come in packages, like hot dogs."

"Lucifer only eats live prey. He hasn't been fed for a week. Would you like to watch?"

Ben couldn't think of anything he wanted less. "Sure."

Linda went back into the closet and pulled out a cage with two white mice. She reached in and grabbed one of them, then tipped up the screen over the top of the snake's tank and dropped the mouse in. The mouse scrambled into the corner of the tank, face pressed into the angle, one little pink foot splayed on the glass.

At first the snake did nothing. Then, slowly, he began to slide from behind the rock. The mouse trembled and scrabbled against the glass. Leisurely, the snake slid toward it. Head turned sideways, Lucifer seemed indifferent to the mouse. He stopped, and Ben hoped that he wasn't hungry. Then, remarkably quick, the snake snapped his head toward the mouse and took it in his jaws, coiled his body around it, and crushed the life out of it. The mouse hardly struggled. Lucifer's mouth opened impossibly wide and swallowed the mouse, headfirst, in one huge gulp. For a second the mouse's tail remained trailing from the snake's mouth, but as peristalsis pushed the mouse down his gullet, the tail disappeared inside. Ben watched the bulge slide down the snake's body. Lucifer rested on the sand beneath the fluorescent light: beautiful, swollen, and bright.

"You want to hold him?" Linda asked.

"You're sure he won't eat me?"

She tilted her head sideways. "Not for another week or so."

Linda reached into the tank and lifted out Lucifer. It curled around her arm up to her elbow, the head peeking from between her thumb and forefinger. She held the snake out to Ben.

Awkwardly, Ben took it into his hands. Lucifer tried to slither away and almost fell.

"Catch him!" Linda said, holding out a hand.

Ben moved one hand after another in front of the snake whenever it slid forward to get away, as if it were a Slinky and he was trying to make it climb down the steps of his palms. "He's warm," Ben said in surprise.

"Lucifer's not crazy about being handled after he's eaten. Come sit on the bed."

They moved over to Linda's bed and sat. Lucifer stopped trying to get away and curled into a coil in the crook of Ben's knee. Linda lit a scented candle.

"He likes you," she said.

"Yeah, right."

Linda got a corkscrew from her desk; Ben was impressed with her dexterity at pulling the cork. She poured wine into two Dixie cups. They leaned back against the wall. Ben was acutely aware of Linda's breasts. She began tapping her shoe against the toe of his boot.

"Why do you keep doing that?" he asked.

"Doing what?"

"Kicking my boots."

"I've got to do something. You're not doing anything."

He felt his face get red. He reached out to touch her waist, and suddenly she was kissing him fiercely on the lips. Her breath tasted of wine. He worried about his own breath, he worried about Lucifer, he worried about his dope left back in Debbie's room, but pretty soon he wasn't worried about anything at all. He slid his hands up under her turtleneck, fumbled with the catch on her bra until, giggling, she pulled off her shirt and undid it herself. Ben thought he was going to faint. His dick was so hard in his jeans that it was painful. She unzipped them and they fumbled to pull off each other's pants.

"Wait," she said. Linda got up, found Lucifer under the pillow, and carried him to his tank. Ben pulled off his jeans. She returned with a foil-wrapped condom that she dropped on the bedside table. She kneeled down on the bed, straddling him, leaned over, and brushed her breasts against his face. His pulse raced in his ears.

Ben tried to act like he knew what he was doing, but it was his first time and it must have been obvious. Linda said nothing. He took in her extraordinary kiss, the touch of her warm skin, the scent of sweat and wine and incense. He felt dizzy, excited beyond words. When she guided him inside her he had never been so urgently alive. "Fuck," he gasped. "Fuck."

"That's the general idea," Linda said.

Outside the window he heard the wind howling in the leafless trees, and the click of frozen rain against the glass.

After she rescued him from his virginity, Ben saw Linda a lot. He couldn't believe how lucky he was. He couldn't believe how great sex was. He *loved* sex.

He remembered reading a story about a man who got a magical pocket watch that could stop time, so that whatever you were doing could last forever—but you could only use it once. The man kept waiting his entire life for the perfect moment, and never used the watch.

If Ben had owned that watch he would stop time tonight, while he was in bed with Linda. It didn't even have to be a big bed; the sprung single in Linda's dorm room would do. He wanted nothing more.

Ben went home for Thanksgiving, and it was misery. On Thanksgiving Day his Uncle Stan came over and he and Ben's father sat in front of the TV all afternoon, trading shots of Three Feathers while the Packers whipped Detroit. Ben sat at the kitchen table watching his mother and Aunt Stasia cook; his mother kept after him about getting a haircut before he took communion with her at mass on Sunday. At dinner hardly a word passed between his parents. His father treated his mother like an annoyance, as if the only reason she had been put on earth was to torment him. His mother returned the favor, though her hostility showed itself in much more subtle ways. They never touched each other. In his entire life, Ben could not remember seeing them touch each other. How had they managed to have a child?

Sunday afternoon he fled back to campus; Linda was back, too, and that night they went to a movie. He told her all about his visit home. She didn't say much. It was colder than Nixon's heart outside when they left the cinema, but Linda insisted they walk along the river road back to the dorm.

"Why?"

"Look at the stars! Let's get away from the lights. It's so clear!"

"It's clear because it's six degrees out."

She pointed at him, her mouth open in a round O of horror. "Serpent! Serpent!"

He had to laugh. "You're insane."

She scooped up a handful of snow and threw it at him. He ducked and it hit his shoulder, a dust of flakes sliding down his collar. By the time he turned back to her, she was running down the road. "Serpent!" she shouted.

He raced after her, his boots crunching on the snow. The river road was deserted; between the branches of the bare trees the lights of the houses on the other side gleamed on the frozen river. Snow, lifted by the wind, swirled across the ice.

Linda hopped down the riverbank and onto the ice.

"Wait!" Ben shouted. He picked his way between the trees down the brush-laced slope. There was a lot of trash at the river's edge, including a rusted, twisted bicycle frame.

"Come on!" She was already thirty feet out, headed for the other side.

Ben followed her, but before he had taken three steps his foot skidded out from under him and he did a desperate dance trying not to fall. Linda stood out in the middle, her hands on her hips, laughing. "Come on!"

He moved toward her, more slowly, and heard the ice moan beneath him. She waited until he was close. "Are you sure this is safe?" he said. "How thick is this?"

"How thick are you?"

Ben grabbed her around the waist and picked her up. She struggled, laughing; they fell. When she landed on top of him, his head snapped back and bounced on the ice. "Ouch."

"Are you all right?" she asked. Her breath fogged his glasses.

"What are we doing out here?"

"It's called fun. You should try it."

"I think I've heard about it."

She rolled over and pointed at the sky. "See the stars? There's Orion."

The back of his head hurt. "I know." He pointed. "Betelgeuse. Rigel. See those two?—that's Castor and Pollux. That bright one? That's Spica."

She leaned over and kissed him. He put his arms around her and held her tight. They were both so big, in their scarves and heavy coats, that they were like winter bears. He felt himself getting hard.

Linda got to her knees and stood. She reached down and grabbed his gloved hand. "Come on, Mr. Science. Get up."

He scrambled to his feet. The ice beneath them made a cracking sound. In the distance he could hear the traffic on Power Avenue.

"Don't worry. I've been out here a dozen times." She led him across the river to the city side. "We can get to Tony's Pizza from here."

They climbed the bank to the street and walked two blocks to Tony's. By the time they were there, Ben was frozen. They ordered calzones and drank two pitchers of beer. Linda drank more than he did, and he had to keep her from stumbling on the walk home. He made them go the long way around, by the bridge.

He knocked on Linda's door several times, but there was no answer. He went back to his dorm room and tried calling her, but still no answer. He tried every ten minutes until it was time for work, then hurried off to the dish room.

She was not there. Mr. Hsu said she had called in sick; either she had lied to Mr. Hsu or she was in her room so ill she couldn't answer the door. Ben worked through the dinner shift in increasing anxiety. As soon as work was over he threw his apron into the hamper and hurried back to her room. He knocked on the door repeatedly, to no answer. A couple of girls passing in the hall gave him odd stares; he glared back at them.

"Linda?" he called, his mouth up close to the door. Suddenly it opened, and Linda was there, inches away. "Are you all right?"

She was wearing sweatpants and a red T-shirt. Her hair was undone, hanging tangled around her shoulders. She rubbed her eyes. "I was asleep. What's going on?"

"I came by earlier, about five. Where were you?"

"I didn't hear you. I'm kind of strung out." She gave him a sleepy kiss. "What's the matter?"

He pushed her back into the room, took her in his arms. "I need you," he said.

She resisted a bit, but then relaxed. They fell onto the bed.

Ben decided that he wanted to make her feel as good as possible. Linda had taught him about oral sex, and, though he had been timid at first, it turned out that he liked going down on her. What he liked the best about it was how excited she got, how her hips trembled and heaved beneath him, how her nipples got hard and she gasped for breath. How she would laugh when she came.

It was only afterward that he realized he was halfway off the bed, his knees on the floor. The room was cold. He pulled himself up beside her and she drew the covers over him. "That was lovely," she said.

Lovely. A word he never used. It was the kind of word the daughter of the mayor of Hartford might use. "Why do you work in the dish room?" he asked. "Your parents are loaded."

"I want to be more than the daughter of loaded parents," she said. "Just like you want to be more than the son of a Catholic martyr."

"Too late," Ben said. "For both of us."

"You think so?" She lay on her back and folded her hands behind her head. "Do you believe in God?"

"'I believe in one holy catholic and apostolic church. I acknowledge one baptism for the remission of sins, and I look for the resurrection of the dead and the life of the world to come.'"

"Don't hold your breath."

"Did you know that prayer was written by a committee?" he said. "It was like a loyalty oath, hammered out in a negotiation in A.D. 380. They invented it so they could kill the people who wouldn't say it."

"How do you know that?"

"History 235: Early Christianity. That drove the stake through my Catholicism. So now I believe in the laws of thermodynamics, and that Alfred Bester is the best science fiction writer alive. What do you believe?"

"I believe when you're dead, you're dead, so don't waste any time. I believe Alfred Bester, whoever he is, isn't fit to wipe Shakespeare's ass. I believe I can do anything that I set my mind to, and nobody owns me."

He grabbed her around the hips, and kissed her belly. "Wrong. I do."

"You pig!" she laughed. They wrestled together and it became another bout of sex.

They lay in each other's arms for a long time after that. His hand rested where her hip narrowed to her waist; it gave him the oddest feeling of mild arousal and comfort just to touch her there. He was half asleep when Linda rolled away from him. "Come on, get up. It's time for you to go home."

He slipped on his glasses and looked up at her. She put on her T-shirt, pulled back her hair and tied it with a rubber band. Standing with her legs spread, wearing the red shirt and blue panties, she looked like Wonder Woman. She raised her eyebrows at him. Had he said something to make her mad? "That line about owning you?" he said. "That was just a joke."

"I know. Get going. I have to study."

"Study? It's eleven o'clock."

"I've got a paper for Anthro due Friday."

"I'll just lie here. I'll be quiet."

"No. Come on, go——or else I'll set Lucifer on you."

Reluctantly, he pulled on his clothes and left. She gave him a long, lingering kiss at the door. Ben went outside and walked back toward his dorm, but when he was halfway there he turned around. He circled to the back of Stanton, counted up five floors and six windows from the end of the wing. Her window was dark. If Linda was studying, she was doing it with the lights off. Or maybe he had counted windows wrong. But he thought he could make out Lucifer's tank sitting in the windowsill.

December saw eighteen consecutive days when the temperature did not rise above freezing. Though Ben wanted Linda to stay in town over Christmas, Linda insisted that she had to go home. "My parents will kill me," she said.

"I wouldn't like that," Ben said.

"But you could do me a huge favor——could you take care of Lucifer?"

Ben had never gotten used to the snake. He liked holding it well enough, but the thought of feeding it made him cringe, and he had never watched Linda do so after that first time. But he didn't want to look like a wimp, and he didn't want to lose Linda.

"All right," he said.

So they moved Lucifer into Ben's dorm room for the break, and she bought him three mice, enough to carry the king snake through the holidays. Something about the whole farewell bothered Ben. They made love in Linda's room, and in the morning he drove her to the train station. She thanked him profusely for taking care of Lucifer, and hugged him for at least thirty seconds before getting on the train, but as she turned from him and flew up the steps she seemed like a bird let out of its cage.

Mitch went home, but Ben stayed on the deserted campus most of the break, trying to catch up on his physics. There were only a handful of other men in the dorm. They watched NBA games and *Star Trek* on the TV in the lounge, and staged one snowball fight. Ben went home for four days over Christmas proper and the whole time his mother complained why didn't he stay longer. Back on campus by New Year's Eve, he and some guys got together to drink Southern Comfort and smoke weed, but Ben broke away before midnight and went down to the lounge to use the pay phone. He dropped in a buck and a half in change and dialed the Hartford number from the slip of paper in his wallet.

The phone rang a long time before anyone picked up. "Hello?" said a man's voice.

"Hello. May I speak with Linda Norton?"

"Who is this?" The man sounded a little drunk.

"This is Ben Kwiatkowski. I'm a friend of hers from college."

"Just a minute."

Much more than a minute went by. On the phone Ben heard music in the background, some Frank Sinatra record. He looked across the lounge. Outside the big plate-glass windows at the front of the dorm, snow swirled down out of the blackness to briefly catch the fan of light beneath the streetlights before hitting the ground.

The man's voice came back. "Linda can't speak with you now. She's not home."

"Can you tell her I called?"

"Who are you?"

"Her boyfriend Ben."

"Who?"

"Ben Kwiatkowski."

"All right."

"Are you her father?"

A burst of noise came from behind the voice on the phone. "Yes. Goddamn it. Happy New Year."

The phone clicked and the dial tone buzzed in Ben's ear. He looked at the clock above the dorm elevators. It was 12:01.

Instead of going back to the dope party, Ben went up to his room. He took Lucifer out of the tank, sat down on the bed, and held him. The snake liked the warmth of Ben's hands. It would try to slide up Ben's shirtsleeves and sometimes Ben even let him. At other times Lucifer would dangle from his hands, head down, like a piece of rope.

"Are you hungry, Lucifer? How about a mouse to bring in the New Year?"

Ben put the snake into its tank and got one of the mice out of the cardboard box in his closet. He clutched it in his hand, a little ball of fur, useless claws pricking his palm. As soon as Lucifer saw it his head perked up. Ben dangled the terrified mouse over the tank by its tail, then dropped it inside.

Ben was at the station at the end of Christmas break to meet Linda. She was standing on the platform with her red suitcase and matching overnight case, wearing her peacoat, a red and green tartan scarf, and a red stocking cap. A dark green skirt and green kneesocks. Very New England prep school. There was a line between her brows.

She granted Ben a tepid kiss and they loaded her bag into the trunk of his '63 Plymouth. On the way back to campus she said, very simply, "I don't want to sleep with you anymore."

It seemed that she had done some thinking over Christmas. It seemed that things had gone too fast. It seemed that he was taking things much more seriously than she had intended them. It was fun, and she liked him, and everything, but he was too intense. She was only nineteen, he was only twenty. What did he expect to happen?

"I expect to get married," he said. The bright sun glared on the snowy streets. He felt like he was from another planet. Linda didn't say anything, and when they stopped at the next red light he turned to her.

She was looking at him, and for the first time ever he saw what he might call anxiety in her eyes. If it had ever been there before, he had not noticed it.

"That's sort of the problem," Linda said softly. "I mean, how many girlfriends have you had?"

"What difference does that make?"

"Well, it ought to make some kind of difference. What do you know about me?"

"I know I love you."

The driver of the car behind him leaned on his horn. "The light's changed," Linda said.

Ben pulled away from the signal. His mind was in complete confusion. They said nothing to each other until they pulled into the parking circle in front of Stanton. The place was busy with students returning from break for the rump session and finals. He turned off the car's engine and the blower on the fan stopped, leaving them in silence. "How can you say this to me?" he asked.

"I know you love me, Ben," Linda said. "But why do you love *me*?"

"What are you talking about? You don't make any sense."

"Please don't get mad."

"Don't get mad! What am I supposed to do? You wouldn't even talk to me on the phone!"

"I'm sorry. That was my father."

"You could have called."

A snowball splatted against the windshield. Ben looked out and saw Mitch wave from the sidewalk, then hurl another at the car. Linda opened the door and got out.

Ben walked around to open the trunk while Linda said hi to Mitch. Ben put her suitcases on the sidewalk. Another car was idling behind him, exhaust smoking the chill air. The driver rolled down his window and asked Ben to move.

"We need to talk," Ben told Linda. Linda looked uncertain and, while Mitch watched, leaned up to Ben's shoulder and whispered in his ear, "I don't think there's much to say." She turned and picked up her bags.

Ben got into the Plymouth and drove to the student lot. He sat in the parked car and hit his forehead on the steering wheel until it began to throb with pain.

The rump session was two weeks of classes and a week of finals, followed by a five-day break and the start of the second semester. Linda wouldn't talk with him. She quit the dish room. Pretty soon the others knew what was going on. Some of them talked behind his back, and others acted like it was no big deal. Mitch told Ben he was crazy to get hung up on a girl who used a snakeskin as a bookmark. He ought to just study hard and forget about her.

At least Ben still had Lucifer, and if Linda wanted her snake back she was going to have to come to him. He would make her give him a better explanation, a real one. What she had told him meant that she didn't really love him, had never loved him. When they had sex together that was all it was—sex. He tried to get his mind around that. He didn't talk to anyone. He wrote Linda a long letter, tore it up, wrote another, and sent it. He got no reply.

He didn't sleep. He would lie in bed and think of Linda, imagine making love to her, masturbate desperately, and end up just as sleepless as he started, only filled with self-loathing.

He saw her in Poli Sci, but he did not sit with her. She was always with Susan Meredith. Ben sat two rows behind her and to her left. He watched the back of her head and wondered what she had told Susan about him. Professor Goldberg's sideburns were still out of balance. Ben wondered if Goldberg noticed that he and Linda no longer sat together.

That weekend the campus cinema had a Marx Brothers double feature, *Monkey Business* and *Duck Soup*. Ben went in order to cheer himself up. In *Monkey Business* Groucho put the moves on a sexy blond woman who was falling out of her dress. "I want to dance, I want to sing, I want to ha-cha-cha!" They danced a loopy tango that was aborted when the woman's husband entered the room and Groucho fled into the closet. Ben laughed until tears came to his eyes. Fuck her, Groucho! Fuck them both!

At the break between films Ben got up to go to the men's room, and when he walked up the aisle he saw Linda sitting in the theater with some other guy. Ben immediately fell into a funk. He came back from the men's room and sat through the second movie, but did not remember a single thing about it, so full was his mind of shame and humiliation and desire.

He went so far as to try studying like Mitch suggested. In order to get out of the dorm and away from the dope smokers, after work in the dish room he would go to the library stacks. He found a carrel hidden in a corner on the eighth floor. Beside the carrel the thick masonry wall was pierced by a narrow window, like the loopholes in medieval castles through which defenders shot arrows. Through it he could spy a slice of one of the paths on the quad, the glitter of a streetlamp on the snow, where occasionally a lone student would pass, bell-bottoms flapping, head hunched against the cold and breath steaming the air.

The light in the stacks was dim. After reading pages of thermodynamics he would raise his head and look down the aisle of bookshelves under a row of dying lightbulbs in wire cages. By eleven at night the stacks were silent. Ben would think about Linda and imagine he was the only person left in the world, like some character in a science fiction book. One time, as he pored over a page of classical mechanics, a powerful feeling came over him that he had slipped out of reality. He became convinced that, if he raised his head and looked down the aisle, he would see a vision of the Virgin Mary floating beneath the sixty-watt lights. His breath trembled in his chest as he tried to decide whether to look. The equations lay stark black on the white page before him. Do it, he told himself. Lift your head. There's nothing there. But if there were something, if he did see the Virgin Mary, crushing a snake beneath her heel, then he would know that he was insane. No matter how bad he felt, he didn't want to be insane. He was supposed to be a scientist; he didn't believe in visions or in the Virgin Mary.

He kept his head bowed over his textbook, and eventually the moment passed.

Finals were a disaster. The worst was Advanced Classical Mechanics. Ben carried a C+ average into the exam. Students were allowed to bring a single crib sheet of equations into the test. Ben worked over his sheet meticulously; he was nervous but as prepared as he had been all semester.

The moment the test papers were handed out, he panicked. There were ten questions. Ben could not make himself understand a single one. Everything he had learned was caught in some barbed-wire tangle in his brain, neurons firing randomly. He wrote down equations, did hectic calculations, but it was all vapor. He might as well have been on acid. When the professor announced the end of the three hours, Ben couldn't believe it. It had seemed like no more than twenty minutes. What had he been doing for all that time?

After handing in his paper he put on his coat and scarf and stumbled out of the physics building. The sky was leaden, but the setting sun shot in from below the clouds, giving ten minutes of weird sunshine before it turned dark. The wet sidewalks glared with polarized light and heaps of dirty snow dripped into the gutters. Ben threw his mechanics textbook into a trash can and went to see Linda.

He went right up to her door and pounded on it. One of the girls on the corridor peeked out at the noise, and then ducked back into her room. "Linda! Linda, open up!" he shouted. No one answered. Maybe she wasn't there. Or maybe she was afraid. "Please," he said, quieter now, leaning in to the door, one hand on either side, speaking to the battered oak. "I have to talk to you. Something's wrong."

No response. He closed his eyes.

He was about to give up and go when he heard the latch click and the door swung slightly open: he opened his eyes to see Linda's face in the gap. Her brow was furrowed. "What's the matter?"

He swallowed hard. "Please. Let me come in."

Instead, she came out into the hall. "We can talk here."

He wanted so much to hold her. She stood with her arms crossed over her chest and would not look him in the eye. When he spoke he was surprised at the resentment in his own voice. "When are you going to come and get your snake?"

"Is he all right?" There was more concern in her voice than he had heard from her since she had gotten on the train to Connecticut before Christmas.

"Him? What about me! Why don't you care whether *I'm* all right?"

"I do care, Ben."

"Well, I'm not all right. I'm fucked up. You fucked me up."

"*I* fucked you up?" She laughed. "You were fucked up long before I met you."

"You dumped me."

"If you keep this up I won't be the last, Ben. Get a grip."

"Get a grip? I'll give you a grip." He grabbed her arm.

She pulled away. "Let go of me!"

This wasn't what he wanted. This wasn't what he wanted at all. He let go, and turned from her. Other girls had come out of their rooms to stare. The resident advisor was hurrying down the corridor toward them.

Ben looked at Linda, made a fist, and with all of his strength slammed it into the door beside her head. Pain shot up his arm. Then he fell to his knees and cradled his hand in his palm.

In the student health center, they bandaged his knuckles, put a brace on his wrist, and made him talk to a shrink, Dr. Thompson. Ben didn't want to talk to anyone. Dr. Thompson asked him a lot of questions about his appetite and his sleeping habits and whether he smoked dope. He prescribed a drug called Triavil and kept Ben in the clinic overnight. In the morning Campus Security wrote up a report and sent him back to his dorm. His anger had dissipated the instant he had hit his hand. He felt stupid, embarrassed. How was he ever going to face anyone again? What a clown.

Somehow he managed to make it through the rest of his finals. The five days between the semesters was a big all-campus party, but Ben stayed in his room and read science fiction novels. If he let himself get caught up in the story, time would pass, and he would not have to think about anything. Second semester started. He saw Dr. Thompson once a week and talked about his parents and the fact that he didn't know what he was going to do. The Triavil didn't seem to do anything but make him thirsty. He was not supposed to drink alcohol while taking it, but when he finally let Mitch take him out for pizza, they split a pitcher of beer. It didn't seem to do any harm.

He'd flunked the classical mechanics final but out of pity the prof gave him a D for the course. In the spring semester he enrolled in the second half of thermodynamics and an astronomy class, but for a free elective he decided to go off the reservation and sign up for Milton. He studied hard and managed to start well enough in the science classes, and to his amazement actually enjoyed the Milton class, though his wrist brace made note taking hard. In the dish room he was stuck in the corner sorting tableware. Between classes and work, he made it through the days.

He avoided talking to Dr. Thompson about her. He didn't say anything about the times he imagined her dead, or the more frequent times he imagined himself dying and her called to his bedside. Stupid fantasies of resentment and revenge. How he hated her. But then, when Thompson asked him what he wanted to do after he graduated, without thinking Ben said, "I want to be a part of the world, not the enemy of it."

He saw Linda in the dining hall, or in the student post office or on the quad. Mitch told him that Linda told Debbie that she missed Lucifer, but she never came to see Ben about it. Was the snake his now? Did he want it? He hardly had the extra cash to spend on mice, but on the other hand he had gotten used to having the snake around. He read up on king snakes. Lucifer, Ben discovered, was a false coral snake, camouflaged with the red, gold and black bands in order to look venomous, but actually harmless to humans. Red on yellow, kill a fellow; red on black, friend to Jack. Ben cleaned the tank regularly, set out a fresh bowl of water daily, and visited the pet store on Hudson Street to buy mice. Ben would take Lucifer out of his tank and hold him, let him spiral around his forearm and taste the air with his tongue. "Close the serpent sly, insinuating, wove with Gordian twine his braided train"—Ben chanted—"and of his fatal guilt gave proof unheeded. Serpent! Serpent!"

Mitch looked across the room and said, "What was that?"

"Milton meets *Alice in Wonderland*." Ben was almost ready to ask Mitch to help him out. He couldn't face Linda himself, but Mitch could contact her for him. Mitch could tell her Ben was ready to give Lucifer back. Mitch could even bring the snake back to her dorm room, and Ben would not have to see her at all.

Except Ben wasn't sure that was the right thing to do. Maybe he should see her in person, talk to her like an adult, and show her that he could behave himself without putting any expectations on her. Maybe, even, he could ask her what she thought had been going on between them, since he so obviously could not figure it out himself. But whenever he got to this stage in the scenario, his emotions would rise up and leave him in anger and confusion. So he let it slide.

One Monday evening in early March when Ben showed up at the dish room, two campus cops were waiting for him. They pulled him aside, took him into Mr. Hsu's office in the kitchen. The cafeteria staff all watched through the plate-glass window.

"You're Ben Kwiatkowski?"

"Yes."

"When did you last see Linda Norton?"

"Maybe a week ago, in the dining hall." She had been sitting with some tall guy with curly hair. He'd had to turn around and go back to the dish room, and couldn't think of anything but her for the next hour. "I haven't spoken with her in almost two months."

He looked at the cops, who looked back levelly at him.

"You must know about that," Ben said. "You've got the report. What's going on?"

"She's been missing since Saturday night."

Linda had gone out with Susan and two other girls to a club in a run-down neighborhood. They drank some beer. About midnight Linda begged off and said she was going back to campus. No one noticed she was missing until Monday when she did not show up for classes and her friends realized they hadn't seen her in the dorm or dining halls all Sunday.

After the campus cops came the city police. They made Ben come down to the station and questioned him at length. They accused him of abduction, rape, murder. They asked him where he'd hidden her body. His parents hired a lawyer. For a week or two the newspapers were full of it. But there was nothing to connect him with Linda's disappearance, and eventually they let him go back to his classes and attempt to reconstruct his life. Other students treated him like he had a disease. Ben was scared witless: he stopped smoking and threw away his stash. Linda's father hired a private detective to investigate him. Her parents drove up from Hartford and emptied her room.

Ben contemplated dropping out, but if he did he'd lose his draft deferment and then what would he do? So instead he stuck it out, worked in the dish room, studied spherical astronomy and black body radiation, read *Areopagitica* and *Samson Agonistes*.

Whenever his concentration failed he thought about Linda. Late at night he imagined himself lying next to her in her dorm bed. He remembered how she looked while she slept, her hair spread across her face, her eyelashes trembling with some dream. He thought about how he had wished her dead.

He wanted to imagine that she had run off to some better place, booked a bargain flight to France under another name and was working in some *pension*. But he knew better. As time passed the likelihood increased that she was dead. He could not imagine her committing suicide; no, somebody had assaulted her as she walked home from the club. He wondered what she had been thinking as she approached the river.

Then he remembered her fearlessness on the river ice, and realized that perhaps nobody had alerted the police about that. She could easily have fallen through. He imagined how her last moments would be, in the freezing water, struggling and failing. What a horrible way to die. He should call the police and tell them. He owed her that much.

But if he did, it would only renew their suspicions. They had to know already.

In late March, when the winter finally broke and the ice cleared, Linda's body was found tangled among some dead tree limbs on a bridge abutment in the heart of the city, a mile downriver from the campus.

Paradise Lost, Ben found out, was not about the discovery of sex, but about the discovery of shame, selfishness, exploitation, and guilt. Adam and Eve had lots of sex before the Fall; it was in fact their chief delight. But afterward, after they had eaten the forbidden fruit and gained the knowledge of good and evil, it was not the same. Not that sex became evil, but it was drawn into the world of good and evil and could not ever again be separated from it.

Ben got an "A" in Milton, the only one he received that semester.

He kept Lucifer with him all through graduate school. His new friends called him "the snake guy."

It's All True

On the desk in the marina office a black oscillating fan rattled gusts of hot air across the sports page. It was a perfect artifact of the place and time. The fan raised a few strands of the harbormaster's hair every time its gaze passed over him. He studied my papers, folded the damp sheets, and handed them back to me.

"Okay. Mr. Vidor's yacht is at the end of the second row." He pointed out the open window down the crowded pier. "The big black one."

"Is the rest of the crew aboard?"

"Beats me," he said, sipping from a glass of iced tea. He set the perspiring glass down on a ring of moisture that ran through the headline: "Cards Shade Dodgers in 12; Cut Lead to 5-1/2." On the floor beside the desk lay the front page: "New Sea-Air Battle Rages in Solomons. Japanese Counterattack on Guadalcanal."

I stepped out onto the dock, shouldered my bag, and headed toward the yacht. The sun beat down on the crown of my head, and my shirt collar was damp with sweat. I pulled the bandana from my pocket and wiped my brow. For midweek the place was pretty busy, a number of Hollywood types down for the day or a start on a long weekend. Across the waterway tankers were drawn up beside a refinery.

The *Cynara* was a 96-foot-long two-masted schooner with a crew of four and compartments for ten. The big yacht was an act of vanity, but King Vidor was one of the most successful directors in Hollywood and, though notorious for his parsimony, still capable of indulging himself. A blond kid who ought to have been drafted by now was polishing the brasswork; he looked up as I stepped aboard. I ducked through the open hatchway into a varnished oak companionway, then up to the pilothouse. The captain was there, bent over the chart table.

"Mr. Onslow?"

The man looked up. Mid-fifties, salt-and-pepper hair. "Who are you?" he asked.

"David Furrow," I said. I handed him the papers. "Mr. Welles sent me down to help out on this cruise."

"How come I never heard of you?"

"He was supposed to call you. Maybe he asked Mr. Vidor to contact you?"

"Nobody has said a word about it."

"You should call Mr. Welles, then."

Onslow looked at me, looked at the papers again. There was a forged letter from Welles, identifying me as an able-bodied seaman with three years' experience. Onslow clearly didn't want to call Welles and risk a tirade. "Did he say what he expected you to do?"

"Help with the meals, mostly."

"Stow your gear in the crew's compartment aft," he said. "Then come on back."

I found an empty bunk and put my bag with the portable unit in the locker beneath it. There was no lock, but I would have to take the chance.

Onslow introduced me to the cook, Manolo, who set me to work bringing aboard the produce, poultry, and a case of wine the caterer had sent. When I told him that Welles wanted me to serve, he seemed relieved. About mid-afternoon Charles Koerner, the acting head of production at RKO, arrived with his wife and daughter. They expected to be met by more than just the crew, and Koerner grumbled as he sat at the mahogany table on the afterdeck. Manolo gave me a white jacket and sent me up with drinks. The wife was quiet, fanning herself with a palm fan, and the daughter, an ungainly girl of twelve or thirteen, all elbows and knees, explored the schooner.

An hour later a maroon Packard pulled up to the dock and Welles got out, accompanied by a slender dark woman whom I recognized from photos as his assistant, Shifra Haran. Welles bounded up onto the deck. "Charles!" he boomed, and engulfed the uncomfortable Koerner in a bear hug. "So good to see you!" He towered over the studio head. Koerner introduced Welles to his wife Mary.

Welles wore a lightweight suit; his dark hair was long and he sported a mustache he had grown in Brazil in some misguided attempt at machismo. He was over six feet tall, soft in the belly but with little sign of the monstrous obesity that would haunt his future. A huge head, round cheeks, beautifully molded lips, and almond-shaped Mongol eyes.

"And who's this?" Welles asked, turning to the daughter. His attention was like a searchlight, and the girl squirmed in the center of it.

"Our daughter Barbara."

"Barbara," Welles said with a grin, "do you always carry your house key in your ear?" From the girl's left ear he plucked a shiny brass key and held it in front of her face. His fingers were extraordinarily long, his hands graceful.

The girl smiled slyly. "That's not my key," she said.

"Perhaps it's not a key at all." Welles passed his left hand over his right, and the key became a silver dollar. "Would you like this?"

"Yes."

He passed his hand over the coin again, and it vanished. "Look in your pocket."

She shoved her hand into the pocket of her rolled blue jeans and pulled out the dollar. Her eyes flashed with delight.

"Just remember," Welles said, "money isn't everything."

And as quickly as he had given the girl his attention, he turned back to Koerner. He had the manner of a prince among commoners, dispensing his favors like gold yet expecting to be deferred to at any and every moment. Haran hovered around him like a hummingbird. She carried a portfolio, ready to hand him whatever he needed—a pencil, a cigar, a match, a cup of tea, a copy of his RKO contract. Herman Mankiewicz had said about him, "There but for the grace of God—goes God."

"Shifra!" he bellowed, though she was right next to him. "Get those things out of the car."

Haran asked me to help her. I followed her to the pier and from the trunk took an octagonal multi-reel film canister and a bulky portable film projector. The label on the canister had *The Magnificent Ambersons* scrawled in black grease pencil. Haran watched me warily until I stowed the print and projector safely in the salon, then hurried back on deck to look after Welles.

I spent some time helping Manolo in the galley until Onslow called down to me: it was time to cast off. Onslow started the diesel engine. The blond kid and another crewmember cast off the lines, and Onslow backed the *Cynara* out of the slip. Once the yacht had left the waterway and entered San Pedro Bay, we raised the main, fore, and staysails. The canvas caught the wind, Onslow turned off the engine, and, in the declining sun, we set sail for Catalina.

On my way back to the galley I asked the passengers if I could freshen their drinks. Welles had taken off his jacket and was sprawled in one of the deck chairs, regaling the Koerners with stories of voudun rituals he had witnessed in Brazil. At my interruption he gave me a black look, but Koerner took the break as an opportunity to ask for another scotch. I asked Barbara if she wanted a lemonade. Welles's hooded eyes flashed his impatience, and I hurried back belowdecks.

It was twilight when I served supper: the western horizon blazed orange and red, and the awning above the afterdeck table snapped in the breeze. I uncorked several bottles of wine. I eavesdropped through the avocado salad, the coq au vin, the strawberry shortcake. The only tough moment came when Onslow stepped out on deck to say good-night. "I hope your dinner went well." He leaned over and put a hand on Welles's shoulder, nodding toward me. "You know, we don't usually take on extra crew at the last minute."

"Would anyone like brandy?" I interjected.

Welles, intent on Koerner, waved a hand at Onslow. "He's done a good job. Very helpful." Onslow retired, and afterward I brought brandy and glasses on a silver tray.

Welles put to Koerner the need to complete the *It's All True* project he had gone to Rio to film. RKO had seen the rushes of hordes of leaping black people at Carnival, gone into shock, and abandoned it. "Three segments," Welles said. "'The Jangladeros,' 'My Friend Bonito,' and the story of the samba. If you develop the rest of the footage I sent back, I can have it done by Thanksgiving; for a small additional investment, the studio will have something to show for the money they've spent, Nelson Rockefeller will have succeeded in the Good Neighbor effort, and I can go on and make the kind of movies RKO brought me out here to make."

Koerner avoided Welles's eyes, drawing lines on the white tablecloth with a dessert fork. "Orson, with all due respect, I don't think the studio is interested anymore in the kind of movies you were brought out here to make. *Kane* took a beating, and *Ambersons* doesn't look like it's going to do any better—worse, probably."

Welles's smile was a little too quick. "The version of *Ambersons* that's in the theaters now bears only passing resemblance to what I shot."

"I've never seen either version. But I saw the report on the preview in Pomona. The audience was bored to tears by your tragedy. 'People want to laugh,' they said. The comment cards were brutal."

"I saw the cards, Charles. Half the audience thought it was the best movie they had ever seen. The ones who didn't like it spelled 'laugh' l-a-f-f. Are you going to let the movies you release be determined by people who can't spell 'laugh'?"

"We can't make money on half-full theaters."

I went back and forth, clearing the table, as they continued to spar. Haran was busy doing something in the salon. After I helped him clean up, Manolo headed for his bunk, and except for the pilot and me, the crew had turned in. I perched on the taffrail in the dark, smoking a twentieth-century cigarette and eavesdropping. So far Koerner had proved himself to be an amusingly perfect ancestor of the studio executives I was familiar with. The type had not changed in a hundred years. Barbara, bored, stretched out on a bench with her head in Mary Koerner's lap; Mary stroked Barbara's hair and whispered, "In the morning, when we get to Catalina, you can go swimming off the yacht."

"Mother!" the girl exclaimed. "Don't you know? These waters are infested with sharks!"

Mother and daughter squabbled about whether "infested" was proper language for a well-bred young woman to use. They fell silent without reaching a decision. It was full night now, and the moon had risen. Running lights glowed at the top of the masts and at the bowsprit and stern. Aside from the snap of the flag above and the rush of the sea against the hull, there was only the sound of Welles's seductive voice.

"Charles, listen—I've got the original cut of the movie with me—the print they sent down to Rio before the preview. Shifra!" he called out. "Have you got that projector ready?" Welles finished his brandy. "At least have a look at it. You'll see that it's a work of merit."

Barbara perked up. "Please, father! Can we see it?"

Koerner ignored his daughter. "It's not about the merit, Orson. It's about money."

"Money! How can you know what is going to make money if you never take a chance?" His voice was getting a little too loud. Mrs. Koerner looked worried. "What industry in America doesn't spend some money on experiments? Otherwise the future surprises you, and you're out of business!"

Haran poked her head out of the doorway. "I have the projector set up, Orson."

"Orson, I really don't want—" Koerner said.

"Come, Charles, you owe me the favor of at least seeing what I made. I promise you that's all I'll ask."

They retired to the salon. I crept up alongside the cabin and peeked in one of the windows. At one end on a teak drop table Haran had set up the projector, at the other a screen. The film canister lay open on the bench seat, and the first reel was mounted on the projector.

"I'm tired," Mary Koerner said. "If you'll excuse me, I think I'll turn in."

"Mother, I want to see the movie," Barbara said.

"I think you should go to bed, Barbara," said Koerner.

"No, let her see it," Welles said. "It may be a little dark, but there's nothing objectionable."

"I don't want her to see any dark movies," Koerner said.

Welles clenched his fists. When he spoke it was in a lower tone. "Life is dark."

"That's just the point, Orson," said Koerner, oblivious of the thin ice he was treading. "There's a war on. People don't want to be depressed." As an afterthought, he muttered, "If they ever do."

"What did you say?"

Koerner, taking a seat, had his back to Welles. He straightened and turned. "What?"

Welles stepped past Haran and, with jerky movements, started to remove the reel from the projector. "Forget it, Shifra. Why waste it on a philistine?"

Barbara broke the charged silence. "What's a philistine?"

Welles turned to her. "A philistine, my dear girl, is a slightly better-dressed relative of the moron. And you have the bad fortune to have a complete and utter philistine for a father."

"I've had just about enough—" Koerner sputtered.

"YOU'VE had enough?" Welles bellowed. "I am SICK to DEATH of you paltry lot of money-grubbing cheats and liars! When have any of you kept your word to me? When? Traitors!" He lurched forward and pitched the projector off the table. Koerner's wife and daughter flinched at the crash and ducked down the companionway. Haran, who had clearly seen such displays before, did nothing to restrain her boss.

Koerner's face was red. "That's it," he said. "Whatever possessed me to put my family in the way of a madman like you, I am sure I don't know. If I have anything to say about it, you will never work in Hollywood again."

"You bastard! I don't need your permission. I'll work—"

Koerner poked a finger into Welles's heaving chest. "Do you know what they're saying in every clubroom in the city? They're saying, 'All's well that ends Welles.'" He turned to the cowering secretary. "Miss Haran— good night."

With that he followed his wife and daughter to their room.

Welles stood motionless. I retreated from the window and went up to the pilothouse. "What was that about?" the man on duty asked.

"Mr. Welles just hit an iceberg. Don't worry. We're not sinking."

In German, "Rosebud" is "Rosenknospe."

My mother fancied herself an artist. She was involved in *Les Cent Lieux*, the network of public salons sponsored by Brussels, and so I grew up in a shabby gallery in Schwabing where she exhibited her tired virtualities. I remember one of them was a sculpture of a vagina, in the heart of which a holographic projector presented images that switched whenever a new person happened by. One was of a man's mouth, a mustache above his lip, whispering the word "rosebud."

I could tell that this was some archival image, and that the man speaking wasn't German, but I didn't know who he was. It wasn't until I left Munich for NYU film school that I saw *Citizen Kane*.

I was going to be the artist my mother never was, in no way wedded to old Europe or the godforsaken twentieth century. I was fast and smart and persuasive. I could spin a vision of Art and Commerce to potential backers until they fainted with desire to give me money. By the time I was twenty-six I had made two independent films, *The Fortress of Solitude* and *Words of Christ in Red. Words* even won the best original screenplay award in the 2037 Trieste Film Festival. I was a minor name—but I never made a dime. Outside of a coterie, nobody ever saw my movies.

I told myself that it was because the audience were fools, and after all, the world was a mess, what chance did art have in a world in flames, and the only people who made money were the ones who purveyed pretty distractions. Then time travel came in and whatever else it helped, it was a disaster for films; making commercial movies came to be about who could get Elizabeth Taylor or John Wayne to sign up. I got tired of cruising around below the radar. When I was thirty I took a good hard look in the mirror and found the job with Metro as a talent scout.

That sounds plausible, doesn't it? But there's another version of my career. Consider this story: I used to be a good tennis player. But my backhand was weak, and no matter how much I worked on it, it never got to be first-rate. In a key moment in every match my opponent would drive the ball to my backhand side, and that damn tape at the top of the net would rise up to snare my return. I could only go so far: I couldn't pull genius out of thin air. And so the films and disks and the Trieste trophy sat in the back of my closet.

I was transferring the contents of that closet into boxes when the call came from DAA. I had a headache like someone driving spikes into my brain, and Moira the landlord hectored me from the doorway. The only personal possessions I had that were worth auctioning online had already been auctioned, and I was six months in arrears.

My spex, on the bedside table, started beeping. The signal on the temple was flashing.

"I thought your service was cancelled," Moira said.

"It is."

I fumbled for the spex, sat spraddle-legged on the floor, and slipped them on. My stomach lurched. The wall of my apartment faded into a vision of Gwenda, my PDA. I had Gwenda programmed to look like Louise Brooks. "You've got a call from Vannicom, Ltd.," she said. "Rosethrush Vannice wants to speak with you."

I pulled off the spex. "Moira, dear, give me five minutes alone, would you?"

She smirked. "Whoever she is better owe you money." But she went away.

I pawed through the refuse on the bedside table until I found an unused hypo and shot it into my arm. My heart slammed in my chest and my eyes snapped fully open. I put the spex back on. "Okay," I said.

Gwenda faded and Vannice's beautiful face took her place. "Det? Are you there?"

"I'm here. How did you get me?"

"I had to pay your phone bill for you. How about giving me a look at you?"

The bedroom was a testimony to my imminent eviction, and I didn't want her to see what I looked like. "No can do—I'm using spex. How can I help you?"

"I want to throw some work your way."

After I had helped Sturges desert the studio, Vannice had told me that I would never work for her again. Her speech might be peppered with lines from Nicholas Ray or Quentin Tarantino, but her movie lust was a simulation over a ruthless commercial mind, and I had cost the company money. For the last six months it looked like I wouldn't work for anyone. "I'm pretty busy, Rosethrush."

"Too busy to pay your phone bill?"

I gave up. "What do you need?"

"I want you to end this Welles runaround," she said.

I might be on the outs, but the story of the wild goose chase for Orson Welles was all around town. Four times talent scouts had been sent back to recruit versions of Welles, and four times they had failed. "No," said Welles at the age of forty-two, despite being barred from the lot at Universal after *Touch of Evil*. They tried him in 1972, when he was fifty-seven, after Pauline Kael trashed his reputation; "No," he said. Metro even sent Darla Rashnamurti to seduce him in 1938, when he was the twenty-three-year-old wunderkind. Darla and that version of Welles had a pretty torrid affair, but she came back with nothing more than a sex video that drew a lot of hits on the net and some clippings for her book of memories. I knew all this, and Rosethrush knew I knew it, and it didn't make a damn bit of difference. I needed the work.

"Can you send me some e-cash?" I asked.

"How much?"

I considered Moira. "Ah—how about ten thousand for now?"

"You'll have it in an hour. By which time you'll be in my office. Right?"

"I'll be there."

A week later, shaved and briefed and buffed to a high luster, I stood in the center of the time-travel stage at DAA. I set down the kit bag that held my 1942 clothes and the portable time-travel unit, and nodded to Norm Page up in the control booth. Vannice stood outside the burnished rail of the stage. "No screw-ups this time, right, Det?"

"When have I ever let you down?"

"I could give a list . . ."

"Ten seconds," said Norm from the booth.

Vannice pointed her finger at me like a gun, dropped her thumb as if shooting it, and spoke out of the corner of her mouth, doing a passable imitation of a man's voice.

"Rosebud—dead or alive," she said, and the world disappeared.

The thing that separates me from the run-of-the-mill scout is that I can both plan and improvise. Planning comes first. You must know your mark. You are asking him to abandon his life, and no one is going to do that lightly. You need to approach him at his lowest ebb. But you also want to take him at a time when his talents are undiminished.

This situation had fallen together rather nicely. I went down to the afterdeck and smoked another cigarette. Tobacco, one of the lost luxuries of the twentieth century. Through a slight nicotine buzz I listened to Welles shouting at Haran in the salon, and to the sounds of the demolition of what was left of the projector. I heard her tell him to go to hell. The moon was high now, and the surface of the sea was rippled in long, low swells that slapped gently against the hull as we bore south. Behind us, the lights of San Pedro reflected off our subsiding wake.

A few minutes later Welles came up onto the deck lugging the film canister, which he hefted onto the table. He sat down and stared at it. He picked up the brandy bottle and poured a glass, gulped it down, then poured himself another. If he was aware of my presence, he gave no sign.

After a while I said, quietly, "That might have gone better."

Welles lifted his big head. His face was shadowed; for a moment he looked like Harry Lime in *The Third Man.* "I have nothing to say to you."

"But I have something to say to you, Orson." I moved to the table.

"Go away. I'm not about to be lectured by one of Vidor's lackeys."

"I don't work for Mr. Vidor. I don't work for anyone you know. I'm here to talk to you."

He put down his glass. "Do I know you?"

"My name is Detlev Gruber."

He snorted. "If I were you, I'd change my name."

"I do—frequently."

For the first time since he'd come aboard the yacht, he really looked at me. "So speak your piece and leave me alone."

"First, let me show you something."

I took my bandana from my pocket and spread it flat on the table between us. I tugged the corners that turned it rigid, then thumbed the controls to switch it on. The blue and white pattern of the fabric disappeared, and the screen lit.

Welles was watching now. "What is this?"

"A demonstration." I hit play, the screen went black, and words appeared:

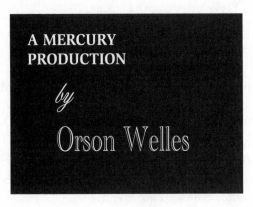

And then the title:

Ominous music rose. Fade in, night, on a chain-link fence with a metal sign that reads "No Trespassing."

"What the hell . . . ?" Welles said.

I paused the image.

Welles picked up the flatscreen. He shook it, rigid as a piece of pasteboard, turned it over and examined its back. "This is amazing. Where did you get it?"

"It's a common artifact—in the year 2048."

Welles laid the screen down. With the light of "No Trespassing" shining up into his face, he looked like no more than a boy. He was twenty-seven years old.

"Go on," he said. "I like a tall tale."

"I got it because I come from the future. I've come here just to see you, because I want you to come back with me."

Welles looked at me. Then he laughed his deep, booming laugh. He pulled a cigar out of his jacket pocket and lit it. "What does . . . the future . . . want with me?" he said between puffs.

"I represent an entertainment company. We want you to do one thing: make movies. We have technology that you don't have and resources you can't imagine. This screen is only the most trivial example. You think that optical printing is a neat trick? We can create whole landscapes out of nothing, turn three extras into an army, do for a fraction of the cost what it takes millions to do here, and do it better. The movie technology of the future is the best toy train set a boy ever had.

"More to the point, Orson, is this: you can fool these people around you, but you can't fool me. I know every mistake you've made since you came to Hollywood. I know every person you've alienated. Koerner's hostility is only the tip of the iceberg."

"I won't argue with you about that. But I have possibilities yet. I'm certainly not ready to fly off with you like Buck Rogers. Give me a couple of years—come back in 1950, and we'll see."

"You forget, what's the future for you is history to me. I know your entire life, Orson. I know what will happen to you from this moment on, until you die of a heart attack, completely alone, in a shabby house in Los Angeles in 1985. It's not a pretty life."

The notion of Welles's death hung in the air for a moment like the cigar smoke. He held the cigar sideways between his thumb and fingers, examining it. "'An ill-favored thing, sir, but mine own,'" he said, as if addressing the cigar—and then his eyes, cold sober, met mine.

"You can joke," I said, "but you will never make another movie as unfettered as you were for *Kane*. The butchery RKO performed on *Ambersons* is only the beginning. No studio will let you direct again until 1946, and that's just a potboiler completely under the thumb of the system. When you try for something more ambitious in *The Lady from Shanghai*, the film gets taken from you and an hour chopped out of it. Hollywood exiles you; you escape to Europe. You spend the last forty years of your life begging for cash, acting small parts in increasingly terrible films as you struggle to make movies on your own. Your entire career? Eleven films—and that includes *Kane* and *Ambersons*."

"Sounds like I'm a flop. Why do you want me?"

"Because, despite fools nipping at your ankles and a complete lack of support, a couple of those films are brilliant. Think what you could do if you had the support of a major studio!"

"Don't you care that if I come with you, I'll never make these works of genius you tell me about?"

"On the contrary, I can show them to you right now. What I'm doing is plucking you from an alternate version of our history. In our world you will have gone on to live exactly the life I've been telling you about. So we will still have all of those movies, but you won't have to struggle to make them. Instead, you can make the dozens of other projects that you never could find backing for in this history. Before you shot Kane, you wanted to do *Heart of Darkness*. In 2048, still nobody has made a decent film of that book. It's as if the world has been waiting for you.

"In 2048 you will be celebrated instead of mocked. If you stay here, you will spend the rest of your life as an exile. If you must be an exile, be one in a place and time that will enable you to do the work that you love."

Welles moved a coffee cup, tapped ash into the saucer, and rested his cigar on the edge. "I have friends. I have family. What about them?"

"You have no family: your parents are dead, your brother estranged; you're divorced from your wife and, frankly, not interested in your daughter. Most of your friends have abandoned you."

"Joe Cotten hasn't."

"You want Joseph Cotten? Look." I called up the clip on the flatscreen, then slid it back in front of Welles. The screen showed a café patio. Street noises, pedestrians with UV hats, futuristic cars passing by. A man and a woman sat at table under a palm tree. The camera closed in on the couple: Joseph Cotten, wearing white trousers and an open-necked shirt, and his wife, Lenore. "Hello, Orson," they said, grinning. Cotten spoke directly into the camera. "Orson, Detlev tells me he's going to show you this clip. Listen to what the man is saying—he's telling the truth. It's much nicer here than you can imagine. In fact, my biggest regret about coming to the future is that you're not here. I miss you."

I stopped the image. "Another scout brought him to the future four years ago," I said.

Welles took another sip of brandy and set his glass down on Cotten's nose. "If Joe had stood by me, the studio wouldn't have been able to reshoot the ending of *Ambersons*."

I could see why my predecessors had all failed. For every argument I gave, Welles had a counterargument. It wasn't about reason; he was too smart, and the reasons he offered for declining were not reasonable. He needed convincing on some visceral level. I had a brutal way to get there, and would have to use it.

I moved the brandy glass off the screen. "We're not quite done with the movies yet," I said. "You have trouble controlling your weight? Well, let me show you some pictures."

First, an image of Welles from *The Stranger*, slender enough that you could even see his Adam's apple. "Here you are in 1946. You still look something like yourself. Now here's *Touch of Evil*, ten years later." A bloated hulk, unshaven and sweating. The photos cycled, a dismal progression of sagging jaws, puffy cheeks, a face turned from boyishly handsome to suet, a body from imposing size to an obese nightmare. I had film clips of him waddling across a room, of his jowls quivering as he orated in some bad mid-sixties European epic. Numerous clips of him seated on talk-show sets, belly swelling past his knees, a cigar clutched between the fingers of his right hand, full beard failing to disguise his multiple chins.

"By the end of your life you weigh somewhere between three hundred and four hundred pounds. No one knows for sure. Here's a photo of an actress named Angie Dickinson trying to sit on your lap. But you have no lap. See how she has to hold her arm around your neck to keep from sliding off. You can't breathe, you can't move, your back is in agony, your kidneys are failing. In the 1980s you get stuck in an automobile, which must be taken apart for you to be able to get out. You spend the last years of your life doing commercials for cheap wine that you are unable to drink because of your abysmal health."

Welles stared at the images. "Turn it off," he whispered.

He sat silently for a moment. His brow furrowed, his dark eyes became pits of self-loathing. But some slant of his eyebrows indicated that he took some satisfaction in this humiliation, as if what I had shown him was only the fulfillment of a prophecy spoken over his cradle.

"You've gone to a lot of trouble, I can see," he said quietly.

I felt I was close now. I leaned forward. "This doesn't have to happen. Our medical science will see that you never become that gross parody of yourself. We'll keep you young and handsome for the rest of your life."

Welles stirred himself. "I'm dazzled by your generosity. What's in it for you?"

"Very good. I don't deny it—we're no charitable organization. You don't realize the esteem in which your works are held in the future. A hundred years from now, *Citizen Kane* is considered the greatest movie ever made. The publicity alone of your return is worth millions. People want to see your work."

"You sound exactly like George Schaefer persuading me to come out to Hollywood after *The War of the Worlds*. I'm a genius, unlimited support, people love my work. And the knives were sharpened for me before I even stepped off the plane. Three years later Schaefer is out on the street, I'm a pariah, and his replacement won't even watch my movie with me. So, have studio executives in the future become saints?"

"Of course not, Orson. But the future has the perspective of time. RKO's cuts to *Ambersons* did nothing to protect their investment. Your instincts were better than theirs, not just artistically, but even from the point of view of making money."

"Tell it to Charles Koerner."

"I don't have to. It's considered the greatest tragedy of cinema history. In 2048, nobody's ever seen your movie. This print"—I touched the film canister—"is the only existing copy of your version. When it goes missing, and the negatives of the excised footage are destroyed, all that's left is the botched studio version."

"This is the only print?"

"The only print."

Welles ran his long-fingered hand through his hair. He heaved himself to his feet, went to the rail of the schooner, grabbed a shroud to steady himself, and looked up at the night sky. It was a dramatic gesture, as he undoubtedly knew. Without looking back at me, he said, "And your time machine? Where do you keep that?"

"I have a portable unit in my bag. We can't use it on the ship, but as soon as we are back on land—"

"—we're off to 2048!" Welles laughed. "It seems I dramatized the wrong H.G. Wells novel." He turned back to me. "Or maybe not, Mr. . . . ?"

"Gruber."

"Mr. Gruber. I'm afraid that you'll have to return to the future without me."

Rosethrush had spent a lot of money sending me here. She wasn't going to let me try another moment universe if this attempt failed. "Why? Everything I've told you is the simple truth."

"Which gives me a big advantage in facing the next forty years, doesn't it?"

"Don't be a fool. Your situation here is no better tomorrow than it was yesterday." One of the rules is never to get involved, but I was into it now, and I cared about whether he listened to me or not. I could say it was because of my bank balance. I gestured toward the cabins, where Koerner and his family slept. "Worse, after tonight. You're throwing away your only chance to change your fate. Do you want to mortgage your talent to people like Charles Koerner? Sell yourself for the approval of people who will never understand you?"

Welles seemed amused. "You seem a little exercised about this—Detlev, is it? Detlev, why should this mean so much to you?" He was speculating as much as asking me. "This is just your job, right? You don't really know me. But you seem to care a lot more than any job would warrant.

"What that suggests to me is that you must really like my movies—I'm flattered, of course—or you are particularly engaged with the problem of the director in the world of business. Yet you must work in the world of business every day.

"So let me make a counter-proposition: You don't take me back to the future; you stay here with me. I question whether any artist can succeed outside of his own time. I was born in 1915. How am I even going to understand 2048, let alone make art that it wants to see?

"On the other hand, you seem quite familiar with today. You say you know all the pitfalls I'm going to face. And I'll bet you know your twentieth-century history pretty well. Think of the advantage that gives you here! A few savvy investments and you'll be rich! You want to make movies—we'll do it together! You can be my partner! With your knowledge of the future we can finance our own studio!"

"I'm a talent scout, not a financier."

"A talent scout—we'll use that, too. You must know who the great actors and actresses of the next thirty years are going to be—we'll approach them before anyone else does. Sign them to exclusive contracts. In ten years we'll dominate the business!"

He paced the deck to the table, put a brandy glass in front of me, and filled it. "You know, if you hadn't told me, I would never have thought you were anything other than a servant. You're something of an actor yourself, aren't you? A manipulator of appearances. Iago pouring words into my ear? Good, we can definitely use that, too. But don't tell me, Detlev, there aren't aspects of the future you wouldn't like to escape from. Here's your chance. We can both kiss the Charles Koerners of the world good-bye, or better yet, succeed in their world and rub their faces in it!"

This was a new one. I had been resisted before, I had been told to get lost, I had faced panic and disbelief. But never had a target tried to seduce me.

The thing was, what Welles was saying made a lot of sense. Maybe if I could bring him back I would come out okay, but that didn't look like it was going to happen. Everything I had told him about himself— his lack of family connections, his troubles with the industry, his bleak prospects—applied to me in 2048. And since I had burned this moment universe by coming here, there was no way anyone from the future was going to come to retrieve me, even if they wanted to. I could make movies with Orson Welles—and eventually, I could make them without him.

I stared at the *Ambersons* film canister on the table in front of me and got hold of myself. I knew his biography. Welles hadn't just been abandoned by others. When necessary, he had seduced and abandoned even his most trusted friends. It was always love on his terms.

"Thank you for the offer," I said. "But I must go back. Are you coming with me?"

Welles sat down in the chair beside me. He smiled. "I guess you'll have to tell your studio head, or whoever sent you, that I was more difficult than he imagined."

"You'll live to regret this."

"We shall see."

"I already know. I showed you."

Welles's face darkened. When he spoke his voice was distant. "Yes, that was pleasant. But now, it seems our business is finished."

This was not going to play well when I got back to DAA. I had one chance to salvage my reputation. "Then, if you don't mind, I'll take this." I reached across the table to get the print of *Ambersons.*

Welles surged forward from his chair, startlingly quick, and snatched the canister before I could. He stood, holding it in his arms, swaying on the unsteady deck. "No."

"Come now, Orson. Why object to our having your film? In the hundred years after that botched preview in Pomona, no one has ever seen your masterpiece. It's the Holy Grail of lost films. What possible purpose could be served by keeping it from the world?"

"Because it's mine."

"But it's no less yours if you give it to us. Didn't you make it to be admired, to touch people's hearts? Think about—"

"I'll tell you what to think," Welles said. "Think about this."

He seized the canister by its wire handles, twirled on his feet as he swung it round him like a hammer thrower, and hurled it out into the air over the side of the boat. He stumbled as he let it go, catching himself on the rail. The canister arced up into the moonlight, tumbling, and fell to the ocean with only the slightest splash, disappearing instantly.

I was working at my video editor when Moira came into the apartment. She didn't bother to knock; she never did. I drained the last of my gin, paused the image of Anne Baxter that stood on my screen, and swiveled my chair around toward her.

"Jesus, Det, are you ever going to unpack?" Moira surveyed the stacks of boxes that still cluttered my living room.

I headed to the kitchen to refill my glass. "That depends—are you going to throw me out again?"

"You know I didn't want to," she said. "It was Vijay. He's always looking over my shoulder." She followed me into the kitchen. "Is that twentieth-century gin? Let me have some." She examined a withered lime that had been sitting on the windowsill above the sink since before my trip to 1942, then put it back down. "Besides, you're all paid up for now."

For now. But Rosethrush had not put me back on salary. She was furious when I returned without Welles, though she seemed to enjoy humiliating me so much that I wondered if that alone was worth what it had cost her. She rode me for my failure at the same time she dismissed it as no more than might be expected. Her comments combined condescension and contempt: not only was I a loser, but I served as a stand-in for the loser Welles.

According to Rosethrush, Welles's turning me down showed a fatal lack of nerve. "He's a coward," she told me. "If he came with you, he'd have to be the genius he pretended to be, with no excuses. His genius was all sleight of hand."

I didn't mention Welles's offer to me. Not arguing with her was the price I paid for avoiding another blackballing.

On the editor, I was working on a restoration of *The Magnificent Ambersons*. By throwing the only existing print overboard, Welles had made my job a lot harder—but not impossible. The negatives of the discarded footage in the RKO archives hadn't been destroyed until December, 1942, so I'd had time to steal them before I came back. Of course Rosethrush didn't want *Ambersons*; she wanted Welles. Hollywood was always about the bottom line, and despite my sales job to Welles, few beyond a bunch of critics and obsessives cared about a hundred-year-old black-and-white movie. But I was banking on the possibility that a restoration would still generate enough publicity to restart my career.

Or maybe I had other reasons. I had not edited a film since the end of my directorial ambitions, twelve years before, and working on this made me realize how much I had missed the simple pleasure of shaping a piece of art with my hands. The restored *Ambersons* was brilliant, harrowing, and sad. It told the story of the long, slow decline of a great mercantile family, destroyed by progress and bad luck and willful blindness—and by the automobile. It was the first great film to address the depredations of technological progress on personal relations in society; but it was also a human tragedy and a thwarted love story. And it centered on the life of George Minafer, a spoiled rich boy who destroyed himself while bringing misery to everyone around him.

Moira gave up and took the lime off the windowsill. "Where's a knife? You got any tonic?"

I liked Moira; the very fact that she cared nothing about movies made her refreshingly attractive. But I had work to do. I went back to the editor while she poked around the kitchen. I hit play. On the screen Anne Baxter, as Lucy Morgan, was telling her father, played by Joseph Cotten, the legend of a mythical young Indian chief, Vendonah. Vendonah meant "Rides-Down-Everything."

"Vendonah was unspeakable," Lucy said as they walked through the garden. "He was so proud he wore iron shoes and walked over people's faces. So at last the tribe decided that it wasn't a good enough excuse for him that he was young and inexperienced. He'd have to go. So they took him down to the river, put him in a canoe, and pushed him out from the shore. The current carried him on down to the ocean. And he never got back."

I had watched this scene before, but for the first time the words sent a shiver down my spine. I hit pause. I remembered the self-loathing in Welles's eyes when I had shown him the images of himself in decline. Now I saw that he had made a movie about himself—in fact, he'd made two of them. Both Kane and George Minafer were versions of Welles. Spoiled, abusive, accusing, beautiful boys, aching for their comeuppance. Which they had gotten, all three of them, almost as if they had sought it out, directing the world and the people around them to achieve that aesthetic result. No wonder Welles abused others, pushing until they said "no"—because at some level he felt he deserved to be said "no" to. Maybe he turned down my "yes" because he needed that "no." The poor bastard.

I stared at the screen. It wasn't all sleight of hand—or if it was sleight of hand, it was brilliant sleight of hand. Welles had pulled a masterpiece out of the air the way he had pulled the key out of Barbara Koerner's ear. And to keep it, he had thrown the last print of that masterpiece into the ocean.

Within a week I would have it back, complete, ready to give to the world, both a fulfillment of Welles's immense talent and the final betrayal of his will, sixty-three years after his death. And I would be a player again.

If I ever let anyone else see the film. If I didn't? What, then, would I do to fill my days?

Behind me, I heard Moira come back out of the kitchen, and the tinkle of ice in her glass. She was going to say something, something irrelevant, and I would have to tell her to get lost. But nothing came. Finally I turned on her, just as she spoke. "What's this?" she asked.

She was playing idly with an open box of junk. In her hands she held a trophy, a jagged lucite spike on a black base.

"That?" I said. "That's—that's the best original screenplay award from the 2037 Trieste Film Festival."

She turned it over and put it back into the box. She looked up at me and smiled.

"Anyway, Det, the reason I'm here is to ask if you want to go swimming. It's been record low UV all this week."

"Swimming."

"You know. Water? The beach? Naked women? Come with me, sweetheart, and I promise you won't get burned."

"The burn doesn't worry me," I said. "But these waters are infested with sharks."

"Really? Where'd you hear that?"

I turned off the editor and got out of my chair. "Never mind," I said. "Give me a minute and I'll find my suit."

The Last American

The Life of Andrew Steele
Recreated by Fiona 13

Reviewed by The OldGuy

> "I don't blame my father for beating me. I don't blame
> him for tearing the book I was reading from my hands,
> and I don't blame him for locking me in the basement.
> When I was a child, I did blame him. I was angry, and I
> hated my father. But as I grew older I came to understand
> that he did what was right for me, and now I look upon
> him with respect and love, the respect and love he always
> deserved, but that I was unable to give him because I was
> too young and self centered."
>
> —Andrew Steele, 2077
> Conversation with Hagiographer

During the thirty-three years Andrew Steele occupied the Oval Office
of what was then called the White House, in what was then called the
United States of America (not to be confused with the current United
State of Americans), on the corner of his desk he kept an antiquated
device of the early twenty-first century called a taser. Typically used by
law-enforcement officers, it functioned by shooting out a thin wire that,
once in contact with its target, delivered an electric shock of up to 300,000
volts. The victim was immediately incapacitated by muscle spasms and
intense pain. This crude weapon was used for crowd control or to subdue
suspects of crimes.

When Ambassador for the New Humanity Mona Vaidyanathan first

visited Steele, she asked what the queer black object was. Steele told her
that it had been the most frequent means of communication between his
father and himself. "When I was ten years old," he told her, "within a
single month my father used that on me sixteen times."

"That's horrible," she said.

"Not for a person with a moral imagination," Steele replied.

In this new biography of Steele, Fiona 13, the Grand Lady of
Reproductions, presents the crowning achievement of her long career
recreating lives for the Cognosphere. Andrew Steele, when he died in
2100, had come to exemplify the twenty-first century, and his people, in a
way that goes beyond the metaphorical. Drawing on every resource of the
posthuman biographer, from heuristic modeling to reconstructive DNA
sampling to forensic dreaming, Ms. 13 has produced this labor of, if not
love, then obsession, and I, for one, am grateful for it.

Fiona presents her new work in a hybrid form. Comparatively little
of this biography is subjectively rendered. Instead, harking back to a
bygone era, Fiona breaks up the narrative with long passages of *text*—
strings of printed code that must be read with the eyes. Of course this
adds the burden of learning the code to anyone seeking to experience
her recreation, but an accelerated prefrontal intervention is packaged
with the biography. Fiona maintains that *text*, since it forces an artificial
linearity on experience, stimulates portions of the left brain that seldom
function in conventional experiential biographies. The result is that the
person undergoing the life of Andrew Steele both lives through significant
moments in Steele's subjectivity and is drawn out of the stream of sensory
and emotional reaction to contemplate the significance of that experience
from the point of view of a wise commentator.

I trust I do not have to explain the charms of this form to those
of you reading this review, but I recommend the experience to all
cognizant entities who still maintain elements of curiosity in their affect
repertoire.

CHILD

Appropriately for a man who was to so personify the twenty-first
century, Dwight Andrew Steele was born on January 1, 2001. His mother,

Rosamund Sanchez Steele, originally from Mexico, was a lab technician at the forestry school at North Carolina State University; his father, Herbert Matthew Steele, was a land developer and on the board of the Planter's Bank and Trust. Both of Steele's parents were devout Baptists and attended one of the new "big box" churches that had sprung up in the late twentieth century in response to growing millennialist beliefs in the United States and elsewhere.

The young Steele was "home-schooled." This meant that Steele's mother devoted a portion of every day to teaching her son herself. The public school system was distrusted by large numbers of religious believers, who considered education by the state to be a form of indoctrination in moral error. Home-schoolers operated from the premise that the less contact their children had with the larger world, the better.

Unfortunately, in the case of Andrew this did not prevent him from meeting other children. Andrew was a small, serious boy, sensitive, and an easy target for bullies. This led to his first murder. Fiona 13 realizes this event for us through extrapolative genetic mapping.

>*We are in the playground, on a bright May morning. We are running across the crowded asphalt toward a climbing structure of wood and metal, when suddenly we are falling! A nine-year-old boy named Jason Terry has tripped us and, when we regain our feet, he tries to pull our pants down. We feel the sting of our elbows where they scraped the pavement; feel surprise and dismay, fear, anger. As Terry leans forward to grab the waistband of our trousers, we suddenly bring our knee up into Terry's face. Terry falls back, sits down awkwardly. The other children gathered laugh. The sound of the laughter in our ears only enrages us more—are they laughing at us? The look of dismay turns to rage on Terry's face. He is going to beat us up, now, he is a deadly threat. We step forward, and before Terry can stand, kick him full in the face. Terry's head snaps back and strikes the asphalt, and he is still.*
>
>*The children gasp. A trickle of blood flows from beneath Terry's ear. From across the playground comes the monitor's voice: "Andrew? Andrew Steele?"*

I have never experienced a more vivid moment in biography. There it all is: the complete assumption by Steele that he is the victim. The fear and rage. The horror, quickly repressed. The later remorse, swamped by desperate justifications.

It was only through his father's political connections and acquiescence in private counseling (that the Steeles did not believe in, taking psychology as a particularly pernicious form of modern mumbo jumbo) that Andrew was kept out of the legal system. He withdrew into the family, his father's discipline and his mother's teaching.

More trouble was to follow. Keeping it secret from his family, Herbert Steele had invested heavily in real estate in the late oughts; he had leveraged properties he purchased to borrow money to invest in several hedge funds, hoping to put the family into a position of such fundamental wealth that they would be beyond the reach of economic vagaries.

When the Friends of the American League set off the Atlanta nuclear blast in 2012, pushing the first domino of the Global Economic Meltdown, Steele senior's financial house of cards collapsed. The U.S. government, having spent itself into bankruptcy and dependence on Asian debt support through ill-advised imperial schemes and paranoid reactions to global terrorist threats, had no resources to deal with the collapse of private finances. Herbert Steele struggled to deal with the reversal, fell into a depression, and died when he crashed a borrowed private plane into a golf course in Southern Pines.

Andrew was twelve years old. His mother, finding part-time work as a data-entry clerk, made barely enough money to keep them alive. Andrew was forced into the public schools. He did surprisingly well there. Andrew always seemed mature for his years, deferential to his elders, responsible, trustworthy, and able to see others' viewpoints. He was slightly aloof from his classmates, and seemed more at home in the presence of adults.

Unknown to his overstressed mother, Andrew was living a secret life. On the Internet, under a half dozen false IP addresses, he maintained political websites. Through them he became one of the world's most influential "bloggers."

A blog was a personal web log, a site on the worldwide computer system where individuals, either anonymously or in their own names, commented on current affairs or their own lives. Some of these weblogs had become prominent, and their organizers and authors politically important.

Andrew had a fiction writer's gift for inventing consistent personalities, investing them with brilliant argument and sharp observation. On the "Political Theater" weblog, as Sacré True, he argued for the impeachment of President Harrison; on "Reason Season," as Tom Pain, he demonstrated why Harrison's impeachment would prove disastrous. Fiona sees this phase of Steele's life as his education in manipulating others' sensibilities. His emotion-laden arguments were astonishingly successful at twisting his interlocutors into rhetorical knots. To unravel and respond to one of Steele's arguments rationally would take four times his space, and carry none of his propagandistic force. Steele's argument against the designated-hitter rule even found its way into the platform of the resurgent Republican Party.

INTERROGATOR

"You don't know why I acted, but I know why. I acted because it is necessary for me to act, because that's what, whether you like it or not, you require me to do. And I don't mind doing it because it's what I have to do. It's what I was born to do. I've never been appreciated for it but that's okay too because, frankly, no one is ever appreciated for what they do.

"But before you presume to judge me realize that you are responsible. I am simply your instrument. I took on the burden of your desires when I didn't want to—I would just as gladly have had that cup pass me by—but I did it, and I have never complained. And I have never felt less than proud of what I have done. I did what was necessary, for the benefit of others. If it had been up to me I would never have touched a single human being, but I am not complaining

"I do however ask you, humbly, if you have any scrap of decency left, if you have any integrity whatsoever, not to judge me. You do not have that right.

"Ask Carlo Sanchez, ask Alfonso Garadiana, ask Sayid Ramachandran, ask Billy Chen. Ask them what was the right thing to do. And then, when you've got the answer from their bleeding corpses, then, and only then, come to me."

—Andrew Steele, 2020
Statement before Board of Inquiry

Contemporary readers must remember the vast demographic and other circumstantial differences that make the early twenty-first century an alien land to us. When Steele was sixteen years old, the population of the world was an astonishing 6.8 billion, fully half of whom were under the age of twenty-five, the overwhelming majority of those young and striving individuals living in poverty, but with access, through the technologies that had spread widely over the previous twenty years, to unprecedented unregulated information. Few of them could be said to have been adequately acculturated. The history of the next forty years, including Steele's part in that history, was shaped by this fact.

In 2017 Steele was conscripted into the U.S. army pursuing the Oil War on two continents. Because he was fluent in Spanish, he served as an interrogator with the 71st infantry division stationed in Venezuela. His history as an interrogator included the debriefing of the rightfully elected president of that nation in 2019. Fiona puts us there:

> We are standing in the back of a small room with concrete walls, banks of fluorescent lights above, an HVAC vent and exposed ducts hanging from the ceiling. The room is cold. We have been standing for a long time and our back is stiff. We have seen many of these sessions, and all we can think about right now is getting out of here, getting a beer, and getting some sleep.
>
> In the center of the room Lieutenant Haslop and a civilian contractor are interrogating a small brown man with jet-black shoulder-length hair. Haslop is very tall and stoop shouldered, probably from a lifetime of ducking responsibility. The men call him "Slop" behind his back.
>
> The prisoner's name is Alfonso Garadiana. His wrists are tied

together behind him, and the same rope stretches down to his ankles, also tied together. The rope is too short, so that the only way he can stand is with his knees flexed painfully. But every time he sways, as if to fall, the contractor signals Haslop, who pokes him with an electric prod. Flecks of blood spot Garadiana's once brilliant white shirt. A cut over his eyebrow is crusted with dried blood, and the eye below it is half-closed.

The contractor, Mr. Gray, is neat and shaved and in control. "So," he says in Spanish, "where are the Jacaranda virus stores?"

Garadiana does not answer. It's unclear whether he has even understood.

Gray nods to Haslop again.

Haslop blinks his eyes, swallows. He slumps into a chair, rests his brow in one hand. "I can't do this anymore," he mutters, only apparently to himself. He wouldn't say it aloud if he didn't want us to hear it, even if he doesn't know that himself. We are sick to death of his weakness.

We step forward and take the prod from his hand. "Let me take care of this, sir." We swing the back of our hand against Garadiana's face, exactly the same motion we once used to hit a backhand in high school tennis. The man's head snaps back, and he falls to the floor. We move in with the prod.

Upon the failure of the Oil War and the defeat of the government that pursued it, a reaction took place, including war-crimes investigations that led to Steele's imprisonment from 2020 to 2025. Fiona gives us a glimpse of Steele's sensorium in his third year in maximum-security prison:

We're hungry. Above us the air rattles from the ventilator. On the table before us in our jail cell is a notebook. We are writing our testament. It's a distillation of everything we know to be absolutely true about the human race and its future. There are things we know in our DNA that cannot be understood by strict rationality, though reason is a powerful tool and can help us to communicate these truths to those who do not, because of incapacity or lack of experience, grasp them instinctively.

The blogs back when we were fourteen were just practice. Here, thanks to the isolation, we are able to go deep, to find the roots of human truth and put them down in words.

We examine the last sentence we have written: "It is the hero's fate to be misunderstood."

A guard comes by and raps the bars of our cell. "Still working on the great opus, Andy?"

We ignore him, close the manuscript, move from the table, and begin to do push-ups in the narrow space beside the cot.

The guard raps again on the bars. "How about an answer, killer?" His voice is testy.

We concentrate on doing the push-up correctly. Eleven. Twelve. Thirteen. Fourteen . . .

When we get out of here, all this work will make a difference.

This was indeed the case, Fiona shows us, but not in the way that Steele intended. As a work of philosophy his testament was rejected by all publishers. He struggled to make a living in the Long Emergency that was the result of the oil decline and the global warming–spawned environmental disasters that hit with full force in the 2020s. These changes were asymmetric, but though some regions felt them more than others, none were unaffected. The flipping of the Atlantic current turned 2022 into the first Year Without a Summer in Europe. Torrential rains in North Africa, the desertification of the North American Great Plains, mass wildlife migrations, drastic drops in grains production, die-offs of marine life, and decimated global fish stocks were among only the most obvious problems with which worldwide civilization struggled. And Andrew Steele was out of prison, without a connection in the world.

ARTIST

"The great artist is a rapist. It is his job to plant a seed, an idea or an emotion, in the viewer's mind. He uses every tool available to enforce his will. The audience doesn't know what it wants, but he knows what it wants, and needs, and he gives it to them.

"To the degree I am capable of it, I strive to be a great artist."

—Andrew Steele, 2037
"Man of Steele"
Interview on *VarietyNet*

At this moment of distress, Steele saw an opportunity, and turned his political testament into a best-selling novel, *What's Wrong with Heroes?* A film deal followed immediately. Steele insisted on being allowed to write the screenplay, and against its better judgment, the studio relented. Upon its release, *What's Wrong with Heroes?* became the highest-grossing film in the history of cinema. In the character of Roark McMaster, Steele created a virile philosopher king who spoke to the desperate hopes of millions. With the money he made, Steele conquered the entertainment world. A series of blockbuster films, television series, and virtual adventures followed. This photo link shows him on the set of *The Betrayal*, his historical epic of the late twentieth century. The series, conflating the Vietnam with two Iraq wars, presents the fiascos of the early twenty-first as the result of Machiavellian subversives and their bad-faith followers taking advantage of the innocence of the American populace, undermining what was once a strong and pure-minded nation.

Fiona gives us a key scene from the series:

INT. AMERICAN AIRLINES FLIGHT 11

Two of the hijackers, wearing green camo, are gathered around a large man seated in the otherwise empty first-class cabin of the 757. The big man, unshaven, wears a shabby Detroit Tigers baseball cap.

WALEED
(frantic)
What shall we do now?

MOORE
Keep the passengers back in coach. Is

Mohammad on course? How long?

                    ABDULAZIZ
            (calling back from cockpit)
            Allah willing—three minutes.

Moore glances out the plane window.

MOORE'S P.O.V.—through window, an aerial view of
Manhattan on a beautiful clear day.

CLOSE ON MOORE

Smirks.

                    MOORE
            Time to go.

Moore hefts his bulk from the first-class seat, moves
toward the on-board baggage closet near the front of
the plane.

                    ABDULAZIZ
            What are you doing?

From out of a hanging suit bag, Moore pulls a parachute,
and straps it on.

                    WALEED
            Is this part of the plan?

Moore jerks up the lever on the plane's exterior door
and yanks on it. It does not budge.

                    MOORE
            Don't just stand there, Waleed! Help me!

Waleed moves to help Moore, and reluctantly, Abdulaziz joins them.

> ATTA
> (from cockpit)
> There it is! Allah akbar!

Moore and the other two hijackers break the seal and the door flies open. A blast of wind sucks Abdulaziz and Waleed forward; they fall back onto the plane's deck. Moore braces himself against the edge of the door with his hands.

> MOORE
> In the name of the Democratic Party, the compassionate, the merciful—so long, boys!

Moore leaps out of the plane.

The Betrayal was the highest rated series ever to run on American television, and cemented Steele's position as the most bankable mass-appeal Hollywood producer since Spielberg. At the age of thirty-eight, Steele married the actress Esme Napoli, leading lady in three of his most popular films.

RELIGIOUS LEADER

The next section of Fiona's biography begins with this heartrending experience from Steele's middle years:

> *We are in a sumptuous hotel suite with a blonde, not wearing much of anything. We are chasing her around the bed.*
> *"You can't catch me!"*
> *We snag her around the waist, and pull her onto the bed. "I've already caught you. You belong to me." We hold up her ring finger, with its platinum band. "You see?"*

"I'm full of nanomachines," she says breathlessly. "If you catch me you'll catch them."

The Scarlet Plague has broken out in Los Angeles, after raging for a month in Brazil. We have fled the city with Esme and are holed up in this remote hotel in Mexico.

"When are we going to have these children?" we ask her. "We need children. Six at least."

"You're going to have to work harder than this to deserve six children," Esme says. "The world is a mess. Do we want to bring children into it?"

"The world has always been a mess. We need to bring children into it because it's a mess." We kiss her perfect cheek.

But a minute later, as we make love, we spot the growing rash along the inside of Esme's thigh.

The death of Steele's wife came near the beginning of the plague decade, followed by the Sudden War and the Collapse. Fiona cites the best estimates of historiographers that, between 2040 and 2062 the human population of the Earth went from 8.2 to somewhat less than two billion. The toll was slightly higher in the less developed nations; on the other hand, resistance to the plagues was higher among humans of the tropical regions. This situation in the middle years of the century transformed the Long Emergency of 2020 to 2040—a condition in which civilization, although stressed, might still be said to function, and with which Steele and his generation had coped, into the Die-Off, in which the only aspect of civilization that, even in the least affected regions, might be said to function was a desperate triage.

One of the results of the Long Emergency had been to spark widespread religious fervor. Social and political disruptions had left millions searching for certitudes. Longevity breakthroughs, new medicine, genetic engineering, cyborging, and AI pushed in one direction, while widespread climactic change, fights against deteriorating civil and environmental conditions, and economic disruptions pushed in another. The young warred against the old, the rich against the poor. Reactionary religious movements raged on four continents. Interpreting the chaos of the twenty-first century in terms of eschatology was a winning business.

Terrorism in the attempt to bring on utopia or the end of the world was a common reality. Steele, despite his grief, rapidly grasped that art, even popular art, had no role in this world. So he turned, readily, to religion.

"Human evolution is a process of moral evolution. The thing that makes us different from animals is our understanding of the ethical implications of every action that we perform: those that we must perform, those that we choose. Some actions are matters of contingency, and some are matters of free will.

"Evolution means we will eventually come to fill the universe. To have our seed spread far and wide. That is what we are here for. To engender those children, to bear them, to raise them properly, to have them extend their—and our—thought, creativity, joy, understanding, to every particle of the visible universe."

—Andrew Steele, 2052
Sermon in the Cascades

Steele's Church of Humanity grew rapidly in the 2040s; while the population died and cities burned, its membership more than doubled every year, reaching several millions by 2050. Steele's credo of the Hero transferred easily to religious terms; his brilliantly orchestrated ceremonies sparked ecstatic responses; he fed the poor and comforted the afflicted, and using every rhetorical device at his command, persuaded his followers that the current troubles were the birth of a new utopian age, that every loss had its compensation, that sacrifice was noble, that reward was coming, that from their loins would spring a new and better race, destined to conquer the stars. Love was the answer.

His creed crossed every ethnic, racial, sexual, gender-preference, class, and age barrier. Everyone was human, and all equal.

The Church of Humanity was undeniably successful in helping millions of people, not just in the United States but across the bleeding globe, deal with the horrors of the Die-Off. It helped them to rally in the face of unimaginable psychological and material losses. But it was not the only foundation for the recovery. By the time some semblance of order was restored to world affairs in the 2060s, genetically modified humans, the superbrights, were attempting to figure a way out of the numerous dead ends of capitalism, antiquated belief systems, and a dysfunctional system of nation-states. This was a period of unexampled experimentation, and the blossoming of many technologies that had been only potentialities prior to the collapse, among them the uploading of human identities, neurological breakthroughs on the origins of altruism and violence, grafted information capacities, and free quantum energy. Most of these developments presented challenges to religion. Steele came to see such changes as a threat to fundamental humanity. So began his monstrous political career.

POLITICIAN

> "The greatest joy in life is putting yourself in the circumstance of another person. To see the world through his eyes, to feel the air on her skin, to breathe in deeply the spirit of their souls. To have his joy and trouble be equally real to you. To know that others are fully and completely human, just as you are. To get outside of your own subjectivity, and to see the world from a completely different and equally valid perspective, to come fully to understand them. When that point of understanding is reached, there is no other word for the feeling that you have than love. Just as much as you love yourself, as you love your children, you love this other.
>
> "And at that point, you must exterminate them. That is the definition of hard."
>
> —Andrew Steele, 2071
> *What I Believe*

Steele was swept into office as President of the reconstituted United States in the election of 2064, with his Humanity Party in complete control of the Congress. In his first hundred days, Steele signed a raft of legislation comprising his Humanity Initiative. Included were The Repopulation Act, which forced all women of childbearing age to have no fewer than four children; a bold space-colonization program; restrictions on genetic alterations and technological body modifications; the wiping clean of all uploaded personalities from private and public databases; the Turing Limit on AI; the Neurological Protection Act of 2065; and the establishment of a legal "standard human being."

In Steele's first term, "nonstandard" humans were allowed to maintain their civil rights, but were identified by injected markers, their movements and employment restricted by the newly established Humanity Agency. Through diplomatic efforts and the international efforts of the Church of Humanity, similar policies were adapted, with notable areas of resistance, throughout much of the world.

In Steele's second term, the HA was given police powers and the nonstandard gradually stripped of civil and property rights. By his third term, those who had not managed to escape the country lost all legal rights and were confined to posthuman reservations, popularly known as "Freak Towns." The establishment of the Protectorate over all of North and South America stiffened resistance elsewhere, and resulted in the uneasy Global Standoff. Eventually, inevitably, came the First and Second Human Wars.

Fiona includes a never-before-experienced moment from the twenty-third year of Steele's presidency.

> *We are in a command bunker, a large, splendidly appointed room, one whole wall of which is a breathtaking view of the Grand Tetons. We sit at a table with our closest advisors, listening to General Jinjur describe their latest defeat by the New Humans. There are tears in her eyes as she recounts the loss of the Fifth Army in the assault on Madrid.*
>
> *We do not speak. Our cat, Socrates, sits on our lap, and we scratch him behind his ears. He purrs.*
>
> *"How many dead?" Chief of Command Taggart asks.*
>
> *"Very few, sir," reports Jinjur. "But over ninety percent converted. It's their new amygdalic bomb. It's destroys our troops' will to fight. The soldiers just lay down their arms and go off looking for something to eat. You try organizing an autistic army."*
>
> *"At least they're good at math," says Secretary Bloom.*
>
> *"How can these posthumans persist?" Dexter asks. "We've exterminated millions. How many of them are left?"*

"We can't know, sir. They keep making more."

"But they don't even fight," says Taggart. "They must be on the point of extinction."

"It has never been about fighting, sir."

"It's this damned subversion," says Taggart. "We have traitors among us. They seed genetic changes among the people. They turn our own against us. How can we combat that?"

General Jinjur gathers herself. She is quite a striking woman, the flower of the humanity we have fought to preserve for so many years. "If I may be permitted to say so, we are fighting ourselves. We are trying to conquer our own human élan. Do you want to live longer? Anyone who wants to live longer will eventually become posthuman. Do you want to understand the universe? Anyone who wants to understand the universe will eventually become posthuman. Do you want peace of mind? Anyone who wants peace of mind will eventually become posthuman."

Something in her tone catches us, and we are finally moved to speak. "You are one of them, aren't you?"

"Yes," she says.

The contemporary citizen need not be troubled with, and Fiona does not provide, any detailed recounting of the war's progress, or how it ended in the Peace that Passeth All Understanding of 2096. The treatment of the remaining humans, the choices offered them, the removal of those few persisting to Mars, and their continued existence there under quarantine, are all material for another work.

Similarly, the circumstances surrounding Steele's death—the cross, the taser, the Shetland pony—so much a subject of debate, speculation and conspiracy theory, surely do not need rehearsing here. We know what happened to him. He destroyed himself.

AWAITING FURTHER INSTRUCTIONS

"The highest impulse of which a human being is capable
is to sacrifice himself in the service of the community
of which he is a part, even when that community does

not recognize him, and heaps opprobrium upon him for that sacrifice. In fact, such scorn is more often than not to be expected. The true savior of his fellows is not deterred by the prospect of rejection, though carrying the burden of his unappreciated gift is a trial that he can never, but for a few moments, escape. It is the hero's fate to be misunderstood."

What's Wrong with Heroes? (unpublished version)

Fiona 13 ends her biography with a simple accounting of the number of beings, human and posthuman, who died as a result of Steele's life. She speculates that many of these same beings might not have lived had he not lived as well, and comes to no formal conclusion, utilitarian or otherwise, as to the moral consequences of the life of Dwight Andrew Steele.

Certainly few tears are shed for Andrew Steele, and few for the ultimate decline of the human race. I marvel at that remnant of humans who, using technologies that he abhorred, have incorporated into their minds a slice of Steele's personality in the attempt to make themselves into the image of the man they see as their savior. Indeed, I must confess to more than a passing interest in their poignant delusions, their comic, mystifying pastimes, their habitual conflicts, their simple loves and hates, their inability to control themselves, their sudden and tragic enthusiasms.

Bootlegged Steele personalities circulate in the Cognosphere, and it may be that those of you who, like me, on occasion edit their capacities in order to spend recreational time being human, will avail themselves of this no doubt unique and terrifying experience.

Downtown

So at the end of the week I shut down my left brain, got charged, and told anyone who would listen that I was going Downtown.

"And who is it that's supposed to care?" the Group Average said.

"Certainly not you," I said, pulling on my weekend skin. GA and I used to be featured, and they still held it against me.

"What you gonna do down there?" the Duck asked. The Duck was puny and naïve.

"Tell me something I *ain't* gonna do," I shot back.

Well, that seemed to intrigue the Duck. "Can I come, too?"

"It's a free domain," I said. "Long as you got your own charge."

We left the Group by the lockers and walked out of there. The sun was dying and on the horizon the murder trees were stirred by the offshore breeze. We walked up to the transit stop, plugged in, bought a couple of passages, and stood on the platform in the sultry evening waiting for the slip. Far down the slipway glowed the lights of the city.

"Will there be boys and girls there?" the Duck asked.

"You bet your feathers," I replied. "Ducks, too."

When the slip drew up we settled in and before we knew it we were stepping out into the colorful Calle Rosinante. Boys! Girls! Snakes! Metatron the Archangel, Available for 23 Amps! Ducks!

Hot jazz filled my right brain, singing Go! Go!, along with the Four Noble Truths:

> Life sucks.
> It sucks because you're stuck on things.
> This can be remedied.
> Fake left, fake right, go up the middle.

Just like Downtown to kill your buzz while pushing it. Stuck on things? I wasn't going to be stuck on anything tonight longer than it took me to drink it or smoke it or poke it. Remedy me no remedies.

First, food. We got some food. A CosmicBoy accosted us in front of the cheesetaurant. "You're outliers, right? For a very reasonable price, I can provide an interstellar experience."

"How much?" the Duck asked.

Before Cosmic could answer I put the bigger of my two hands—my pushing hand—on his chest. I pushed. "We aren't interested, Chaz. My friend may look like a Duck, but he wasn't fledged yesterday."

Cosmic sauntered off. "Why did you chase him away?" the Duck asked.

My right brain informed me that I regretted saying the Duck could come. Thanks, right brain. "Look, Duck, let's split up. I'll meet you back here at daybreak and a half."

His display feathers drooped, but he didn't protest.

So I had me a night and a day and a night. Various transactions were made, physical and psychological. Fluids were transferred. Charges were discharged. Frankly, I don't remember most of it.

What I do remember is waking in an alley between a tavern and a frothel. The Duck was leaning over me. He had lost most of his feathers; his downy cheeks made him look like a girl. Holy calamity—he *was* a girl.

"Duck?" I said groggily.

"The one and only," she replied. She levered herself under my arm and helped me to stand. My weekend skin was ruined. My right brain whirled. "Come on, Schmee," she said. "Time to slip home."

"I can't slip," I croaked. "I'm completely discharged."

"I'll take care of it."

We limped through the street. Downtown was just as bright and attractive as it had been when we arrived, in a completely meretricious sort of way. Meretricious. That was my left brain coming back.

We stood on the platform waiting for the slip. Ahead: another week in the reality mines. "Life sucks," I muttered.

"This can be remedied," the Duck said. To my utter and complete surprise, she kissed me on the cheek.

She is really quite attractive, for a duck.

Powerless

It's always struck me that the expression of George Washington on the dollar bill is that of a man unhappy with my behavior but unwilling to tell me what I am doing wrong. This explains my sad income history, and the marriage to Della who owns a barbershop. Every time I went there to get a haircut, I was impressed by the size of Della's tits, and she was always talking about how she hadn't seen her husband Toby in three or five months since he was stationed in San Diego or Diego Garcia or Garcia Lorca or one of those places. She never said she didn't love him, but you didn't have to be Stephen Hawking to figure out that any woman who's got two kids under the age of five and the only time she sees her husband is when he stops by to knock her up, is ready for a change. So Gary O'Halloran—that would be me—made his move.

That was a good marriage for a while. Della earned enough to support us, and I worked on perfecting the Foucault engine that was going to make us rich. I would have done it, too, if her brats hadn't been coming into the workshop every thirty-seven minutes to ask me to make them a PB&J or bind up their wounds. Though Della could still arrange my body in any way she saw fit, I began to understand Toby and the service he did for his country a little better.

At MIT I majored in physics but I didn't graduate because of the death of my father and growing fondness for cannabis and a number of other matters that I am less able to define clearly and to tell the truth about it I have some trouble remembering them. Romantic conundrums. By the time I was a second-semester junior I understood thermodynamics better than I understood women, and women better than I understood myself. Thermodynamics is about the behavior of particles, viewed statistically; that is, you can't tell what one particle is going to do, but if you get a couple of trillion of them together, you can pretty much predict exactly what they will do as a group. Women, though you can say some things about them as a group, will still surprise you. As for me, I always surprise myself, and I pay for it.

When Della threw me out I took my engine and moved into a studio apartment in a big brick 1940s-era building in a slightly dicey part of town. The apartment was completely empty except for a box of twelve brand-new Titleist golf balls I found on the floor of the closet. The engine I set up beside the old claw-footed bathtub in the bathroom.

The problem with an engine powered by the rotation of the Earth is that you cannot turn it off. If you built enough of them, they would gradually steal all of the Earth's angular momentum and the day would lengthen until the sun stood still in the sky, and then eventually start going backward. Of course that would probably take thirty or forty billion years, so I would say that the environmental drawbacks of the Foucault engine are relatively minor.

But if I am ever to become rich and powerful, this is my ticket.

Past the gate, behind the houses, is an alley. A trickle of water runs down the middle of the broken concrete spotted with oil, trashcans along the board fences, chicken wire, gravel parking spots. Behind one of the houses two men are working on a 1965 Ford Galaxie, a car that strikes you as absurdly large, maybe a block long. The driver's door is open and a girl sits in the front seat, smoking a cigarette.

The men have the hood up and are bent over the engine compartment. The distributor cap is off. One of them is using a set of feeler gauges to reset the points. A transistor radio on the fender plays "Help Me Rhonda" by the Beach Boys. It's a bright, cool day, blue sky and a breeze from the lake.

The girl, maybe eighteen, wears black pedal pushers and a yellow blouse. Her hair is pulled back into a ponytail. The men both wear white T-shirts and blue jeans with engineer boots. One of them has a denim jacket over his T-shirt. The other has a pack of cigarettes rolled up in the short sleeve over his biceps; without taking his eyes from the engine he unwraps the pack from his sleeve and pulls out a cigarette.

The guy in the denim is fitting a timing light to the lead spark plug. He takes a piece of chalk and marks the flywheel to make the timing mark show better in the dim interior. The cigarette guy calls out, "Start the engine." The girl turns the ignition, there is a click, but the starter motor does not catch. She tries again. Nothing.

"Okay, quit it!" the jacketed man says in annoyance.

The two young men stand back. One of them spits on the ground. "Shit!" he says. "We need a new starter."

These are the kind of guys who made you nervous all the time you were growing up, what they called "delinquents." Their cerebrum is okay for car repairs, but something inside them is broken. Now that you are older you can see how they are trying to fill out their shirts and make themselves into something. They aren't even aware that they are doing this. But it makes them no less dangerous—perhaps even more so.

Or maybe they aren't dangerous at all. Just boys.

"Have you checked the solenoid?" you ask.

All three heads turn your way. They see you. Neurons fire. "What are you talking about, Melvin?"

"My name is not Melvin," you say. You walk up close. "That's a big car."

"Three-fifty horses."

"All of them useless if your solenoid is burnt out."

The girl snickers. The guy with the cigarettes in his sleeve turns on her. "What?" he says.

"All those horses and a bad solenoid," she says.

The guy in the denim jacket laughs. T-shirt guy stares at you. He peers as if he has trouble recognizing your face. Are you an object? An animal? He can't make you out.

Something is off. You squint up at the sky. Cirrus clouds, high wispy commas in deep, deep blue. You don't belong here, too old, trying to prove something, baiting a couple of bullies.

The kid in the white shirt puts his greasy hand on your chest and shoves. You stumble, trip, land on your butt. The boy who shoved you laughs, the other boy laughs. The girl looks at you and smiles.

Archaeological discoveries of traumatic injuries in primitive hominid skulls strongly suggest that our species has a long history of violence [12]. Despite repeated attempts throughout history, including the imposition of criminal sanctions, we have yet to dispel our violent nature. Consequently, criminal violence remains a common feature of most societies. As policy-makers seek deeper understanding of deviant behavior, many contemporary neuroscientists assume that the essential ingredients of the human condition, including free will, empathy, and morality, are the calculable consequences of an immense assembly of neurons firing. Studies have concentrated on the behavioral effects of damage to regions of the brain associated with anti-social behavior, including the pre-frontal cortex [PFC], hippocampus, amygdala, corpus callosum, and hypothalamic–pituitary–adrenal axis [13]. Early damage to the orbitofrontal cortex in particular appears to result in poor acquisition of moral and social rules [14].

A couple of months after I moved out, Della showed up on my doorstep. I had just got back from the auto-parts warehouse where I was working. She was sitting on the front stoop when I came back to the apartment. She wore a green top and blue jeans. She looked good.

"To what do I owe the pleasure?" I asked.

"I haven't seen a dime from you so far, Gary. I've got kids to feed."

"Cut more hair."

"Come on, Gary."

"Look, they aren't my kids, dear. They don't even like me."

"They still have to eat, and you are my ex."

"I'm not your ex yet. And I never was their dad. When was the last time Toby sent you a check?"

"Toby's in Hawaii. I can't reach him."

I wished I were in Hawaii. "Della, I need every cent I got to put into the engine. You know that it's all I care about. When I get it working right, I'll be glad to give you all the money you want. You can dress the kids in hundred-dollar bills."

Ben Franklin's expression was more approving of me than George's. Probably because I had less experience with Ben.

"I don't deserve to be treated like this, Gary." Della crossed her arms and looked at the sidewalk. "Did that guy come round to see you?"

"Guy? What guy?"

"Tall guy, dark suit. Looked like an FBI man. He said he had some money for you. Why do you think I came here? I wouldn't expect money from you otherwise."

Halbo ducked under the massive wooden table that dominated the dining hall of Lord Karlovy's castle. The footsteps from the hall came closer. "Dimli!" Halbo hissed, "They're coming!"

The dwarf dropped the goblet, which clanged on the flagstones, and scuttled to join Halbo beneath the table.

The sound of the Dark Lord's boots stopped when he entered the room. "Did I hear a little mouse?" his voice rumbled. They saw his hand, and the black ermine sleeve, reach down to retrieve the golden goblet. "Did some little mouse knock over the Chalice of Dreams?" The steps came closer, and they heard Karlovy place the goblet on the table directly above their heads. "Or perhaps it was not mice, but *rats*."

Halbo's sweaty hand clutched the elven dagger—the same dagger that Advil son of Elavil had given him lo those many months ago, long before they had ever thought that they would dare to enter the Burned Lands—which rested still in the sheath at his belt. What was it Advil had said on that misty morning? *An edged weapon may serve you well on some day when that edged tongue of yours fails.*

"No, Halbo!" Dimli hissed. "Use the jewel!"

Yes, he could use the Jewel of Reduction—it gave him a power that even Lord Karlovy could not resist. But Halbo's job was to destroy the jewel, not use it. If once he took that world-shaping power into his hands, he would never see the lovely face of Marika again. Or, if he did see it, he would not care. Having experienced that ur-Power, he would laugh in scorn that anyone might ever hope to move him through affection.

"These rats are undoubtedly in my cupboard," Lord Karlovy said. He moved away from them across the floor. Then stopped. "Or, mayhap they are under my *table*."

Jean Bernard Léon Foucault (1819–1868) invented the Foucault pendulum, which demonstrates the rotation of the Earth. The other Foucault, Michel (1926–1984), didn't care about pendulums, but he was way into prisons and what they revealed about structures of social control. He also liked sex. Psychiatry, psychology, sociology, and criminology, this other

Foucault asserted, define standards against which people are measured: the sane man, the law-abiding citizen, and the faithful wife are all "normal" people. But an idea of the "normal" also implies the existence of the abnormal: the madman, the criminal, the prostitute. Deviance is possible only where norms exist. For Foucault, norms are concepts constantly used to evaluate and control us, and to exclude those who cannot or will not conform. The submission of our bodies to abstract systems of behavior is the payment we make to norms that define what we owe society.

"I'm here to collect. Your landlord, Darby, owes me, and you owe him, so he said to come to you directly and leave out the middleman. Normally I would not do Darby's collecting for him, but I run a salvage business, and he tells me you've got a pile of scrap metal in your bathroom."

"I don't have any scrap metal."

"That's not what Darby says. Why don't you take me up to your bathroom and show me?"

"I don't think so. I don't even know you."

The man in the black suit turned from me to look across the street. The neighbor's dog, an extraordinarily timid animal that would not leave the boundaries of his yard, was watching us steadily, standing motionless, feet planted with its head slightly lowered in a pantomime of menace. The man in the black suit calmly stared back at the dog. The dog broke eye contact and trotted along the sidewalk to sniff at the roots of a hydrangea bush at the street corner.

"I must know you at least a little," the man said. "I know you've got a pile of junk in your bathroom."

"Go away."

"You owe Darby. I'll give you two hundred dollars for that junk."

"No deal."

"Six hundred."

"Please go away."

The man in black flipped his cigarette onto the sidewalk and ground it out with his highly polished black shoe. He looked up into the cloudless blue sky. "It's a hot day, isn't it?" he said. "I don't know why I wear this black suit."

"Because it's supposed to intimidate people like me," I said. "But it's not working, is it. Tell whoever it is you work for that you're not getting you hands on my engine."

Three Ecuadorian Indians are installing the new irrigation pump. As they wrestle the engine toward the ditch, their curses in Quechua fog the thin air of the high valley. In the distance towers Mt. Cotopaxi, a plume of white smoke drifting from its volcanic summit.

"This better work," declares Hakan.

"The agent said it would," says Tintaya.

"It will work," says Pamakana, the youngest of them. "I saw it work in Quito."

"Does it truly use no fuel?" asks Tintaya.

"No fuel," says Pamakana.

"You believe anything a Spanish tells you."

Pamakana does not reply. They work the engine across two planks and onto the concrete pallet they constructed for it. Tintaya bolts it to the base while Pamakana and Hakan connect the flexible pipe that will draw water from the reservoir. Within an hour they are ready to test it out.

"Well," says Hakan. "Let's see this magic."

Without ceremony, Pamakana opens the panel over the gauges and flips the switch. Slowly at first, and then increasing in pitch, the pump begins to whir. The pipe stiffens, and suddenly, water shoots from the opposite side into the spillway that leads to the network of irrigation ditches. Tintaya lets out a whoop. He seizes Pamakana's arms, forcing him into a crazy dance. Even Hakan grins.

They run down to the village and a number of men, women and children follow them out to see it. They stand in a small group. "This is good," one of the old men says. "God bless that great and selfless benefactor, Gary O'Halloran."

"He has transformed the world," says an old woman.

"If he were here right now," says Kusi, one of the local girls, "I would have sex with him."

"How does it work?" asks the old man. "There is no gasoline."

"It uses the Earth itself for power," Pamakana says quietly. "As long as the sun rises and sets, it will run."

They stand silent for a moment, contemplating the tumbling waters, and the future.

Hakan wipes his brow. "This noon hour is lasting forever."

I was getting nowhere on the engine. Working in the parts store left me without two functioning brain cells to rub together. On the bus to and from work I would watch the other passengers. A woman with a hyperactive little boy fussed with her kid's hair, tugged his shirt straight. She was very patient. My Dad would belt me on the ear whenever I gave him any trouble.

Maybe Della's kids did deserve better than me for a father. Any kid should be taken care of.

When I got home from AutoWorld I couldn't bring myself to work. Instead I lay about the apartment and read. A heat wave had gripped the city and the building's air conditioning was on the fritz. At night I would soak a T-shirt in cold water, put it on, and let a room fan blow across my body all night to cool me off. In the morning when I woke the shirt would be bone dry.

One Saturday night Lewis from the third floor said let's get out of this sweatbox. He took me out for a beer and a roast beef sandwich at Karlovy's on the corner of 29th and Main. As we were sitting there sipping the last of our pilsners and I was complaining about how I missed Della, Lewis suggested that we check out one of the porn shops on Main on the way back to the apartment. I admitted I had never been into a porn shop.

That was all the encouragement Lewis needed. "Brother, you need to get educated. Here's what we'll do. Between here and 39th there must be a half-dozen peep shows and stroke-book stores. You and I will walk down those ten blocks, and we will stop in every one."

When I resisted, he said, "What you got better to do? Lie around reading more bad fantasy books?"

It was about 8:30 when we set out, and the street was getting busy. A hot night, smell of car exhaust and food from the greasy-spoon restaurants along the way. Guys in cars cruised the street looking to pick up hookers. The first store, Eddie's Books & Movies, had a front room lit by overhead fluorescents, several wooden racks of magazines, posters of women in provocative poses on the walls, and a glass counter at the back behind which a bald guy sat on a stool and smoked a cigarette, dispensing tokens for the movies in the cubicles in back. The place smelled of Lysol and cigarettes. A couple of men shuffled between the books and magazines, avoiding eye contact. Beneath a big red glass ashtray filled with cigarette butts, the display case held a rack of dildoes of prodigious size, wild color, and extravagant conformation, with knobs, spikes, grooves, ridges. One was double-ended. Another case held a display of whips and studded leather straps and ball-gags.

Lewis and I bought some tokens and slipped behind the curtained doorway into the back.

I entered one of the cubicles. It was about the size of an old-fashioned telephone booth and smelled of bleach and cum. A shelf seat faced a video screen on the opposite wall, next to which was a slot for the token. Gingerly, I sat. I deposited a token: Two women sitting in bras and panties on a sofa in a shabby apartment were surprised by the miraculous appearance beneath their coffee table of a naked man with an erection. But they were not so surprised that they failed to perform certain exercises that he prescribed.

I watched two other videos. Only one of them was very arousing: the women in the other films had spotty skin and gravity-defying robo-boobs, but this woman was stunningly beautiful. She had dark hair and a wide mouth; she looked exactly like one of the women in the poster-size photos of hairstyles that hung on the wall of Della's shop, and a little like the wife of a professor I'd had in college.

I left the booth. The men I ran into in the narrow aisle between the cubicles kept their heads down, but as I passed one of the niches, just before the door closed, I could have sworn that inside was the man in the black suit.

We hit three other shops in the odyssey; by ten-thirty I'd had enough. When we came to the Dunkin Donuts on the corner of 37th, I suggested we get a coffee.

There were three police cruisers in the lot beside the donut shop, and inside a flock of cops sat at the counter. In the corner a TV hanging from the ceiling was tuned to CNN with the sound turned down.

Two of the cops, one in his mid-forties with a gut pushing his blue shirt over his belt, and a fair-haired one in his twenties, were arguing about what made some people criminals. Lewis and I bought coffee and some crullers and sat at a table.

"What do you think?" Lewis asked me.

"I think those places are gross."

Lewis raised his eyebrows and leaned forward. "Right. And you never whack off, neither."

"That's between me and the Pope."

"What amazes me is the size on those guys in those videos. *Madon'!*"

"They have their jockey shorts made special," I said. What I was really wondering about was the woman with the dark hair in the video. What had she done to end up making porn? Was it the money? Did she like someone sticking a camera (among other things) up her crotch? Did some women get a feeling of power from their sex; did they revel in all the lonely losers who, years later, would get hard seeing them on various screens? Or were they forced into it, desperate just to make a buck, by pimps who arranged their bodies for the camera like a buffet in a cheap restaurant?

We finished our coffee and hiked back to the apartment. Lewis chattered; I was quiet.

When I got to the second floor, I found the door to my apartment ajar. Warily, I pushed the door wide. The light was on in the back. Heart pounding, I edged my way into my bedroom and got a clear look through the bathroom door. The shower curtain was pulled back from the tub. The engine sat on the floor just as I had left it, incomplete, useless, and unharmed.

The television is tuned to CNN, no sound, caption crawl along bottom. The President and some Arab prince in traditional bisht, ghutra, and igal are sitting in armchairs for a photo op in the Oval Office. Cut to them walking to dual podiums in the Rose Garden. Lots of photo flashes. ". . . New Mideast Power Sharing Agreement . . ." the news crawl along the bottom announces. ". . . weapons sales to Twilight Emirates guarantee the peace, President says . . ."

The senior seminar in the history of science meets for the last class of the semester at the home of professor Albrecht. The class contains four students, Arnold, Bill, Gene, and you. It is the first week of December and snow has been falling for two weeks. You caught a ride with Gene in his battered old Plymouth to Albrecht's house, which you hunted down following the directions he gave you on a mimeographed sheet of paper at the last class.

You walk up the shoveled path to the front door. It's an old house in an urban neighborhood, well kept. The house is painted a deep red with a white rail on the covered porch. You knock on the front door and Professor Albrecht greets you, rather more friendly than you are used to. You step into the foyer, he takes your coats and scarves and asks you to remove your shoes and leave them on a rubber mat in the entryway. He has a box of heavy gray wool socks, which he invites you to pull on over your own socks as the two of you move into the rest of the house. It is an odd feeling entering a history class wearing your professor's socks.

Arnold and Bill are already there, sitting in the living room on a sofa in front of a small coffee table. The room is overheated and stuffed with antique furniture. You sit down. Professor Albrecht settles into a wingback armchair and takes up that night's subject, the work of Michael Faraday.

Professor Albrecht is an awkward man in his mid-thirties, dark hair cut shorter than your own. His degree is from Stony Brook and he has been teaching at MIT for five years, specializing in the history of science. He is not popular. The only reason you are there is that you need a history class to further your rather desultory undergraduate career. The truth is, Professor Albrecht is a very poor teacher, witness the fact that there are only four of you left in the class, down from seven at the start of the semester. Had you realized it, the fact that the department even ran a class with only seven students enrolled is a sign that the scheduling officer took pity on Albrecht, or they had nothing else to do with his time. In a year he will be denied tenure.

Albrecht is a timid man, which does not earn him your respect. He seems to know his subject well enough, and at times when he lectures about Newton and the development of the calculus, or of Boyle and the ideal gas law, an enthusiasm will come to his voice that bespeaks some spirit that is not immediately discernible in his tall, awkward person. He has three jackets that he wears in rotation, and three ties in the same combination with those jackets, wool slacks, desert boots, oversized Clark Kent glasses pathetically out of style.

To top it all off, Professor Albrecht stutters. He will begin a sentence well enough, setting sail from the harbor of his subject, but soon enough become tangled in a Sargasso of syntax and stop dead. All of the class will know what word he next wants to say, usually something like "tensor" or "empiricism." He will freeze, his lips slightly parted, trying to form the syllables. You lean forward in your chairs, tempted strongly to supply the word, but don't, because he has put himself into that sentence himself and he can very well find his way out. It is your first realization that someone in authority over you might be vulnerable. You never thought there could be any reason to feel sorry for one of your professors. Whatever time you and Gene spend speaking of Professor Albrecht outside of class is dedicated to mockery. But that is not how you feel when you think of him.

Tonight, Albrecht goes on about Faraday and his discovery of the magnetic field around a current-carrying conductor, electromagnetic induction, diamagnetism, and electrolysis. He laid the foundation of modern electrodynamics. Albrecht praises Faraday's brilliant practical applications of these principles in the first electric motors. As he warms to his topic Albrecht's voice rises in pitch. Soon, he says, this invention transformed the world.

Albrecht speaks of Faraday's character. His father was a blacksmith and so he could never be a gentleman. So Faraday served as both scientific assistant and valet to Sir Humphrey Davy. Faraday was a devout Christian, and saw no conflict between the pursuit of nature's secrets and the tenets of his faith. Throughout his entire career, his increasing success and fame, he remained a humble man; he rejected a knighthood and twice turned down the Presidency of the Royal Society because he felt he did not deserve them. He refused to participate in the preparation of chemical weapons in the Crimean War.

"He rejected all"—Albrecht gets caught here, and the moment stretches—"all p-p-"—You close your eyes. Albrecht is foundering—"all p-pomp and power!" Albrecht gasps.

He has actually used the word "pomp" in a sentence. You have never heard a person use that word.

Albrecht makes the point that Faraday was not, like Newton or Maxwell, a genius. He did not grasp any mathematics beyond algebra. Instead, Faraday was the best experimentalist in the history of physics, a keen observer of nature and an ingenious deviser of ways, gently, to tease out her truths, to penetrate her secrets.

As you sit there and Professor Albrecht drones on—he occasionally pauses and looks at you with his pleading brown eyes—you find yourself, in your bulky sweater, getting sleepy. The solenoid, you think, Faraday invented the solenoid, right? Outside the frosted windows behind Albrecht, it is beginning to snow, big flakes swirling out of the darkness into the porch light. What can any of this possibly mean? There are family photographs on the mantel, old people wearing nineteenth century clothes, men in four-button suits, cravats clenching their necks, with hair that stands up in a Teutonic brush, reminding you of Bismarck and the Hohenzollerns. What are you doing here?

Just then Albrecht looks up, eyes focused on something behind you. You turn. A young woman has come into the room carrying a tray.

"I thought the boys might like some hot cider," she says.

"Gentlemen, this is my wife, Irene."

You are stunned. Irene is perhaps the most beautiful woman you have ever seen. Thick, lustrous brown hair, very dark eyes, a straight nose—it might even have been called sharp—but in the constellation of her face it indicates only intelligence. Her figure is stunning. The dress she wears is not designed to accentuate it, but there is no denying that she has the body of a Victoria's Secret model.

How can Albrecht possibly deserve her?

It has long been known that ablation of the monkey temporal lobe, including the amygdala, results in blunted emotional responses [26] (Figure 5C). In humans, brain-imaging and lesion studies have suggested a role for the amygdala in a theory of mind, aggression [27], and the ability to register fear and sadness in faces [28]. According to the violence inhibition model, both sad and fearful facial cues act as important inhibitors when we contemplate violence towards others. In support of this model, recent investigations have shown that individuals with a history of aggressive behavior have poorer recognition of facial expressions [29], which might be due to amygdala dysfunction [30]. Others have recently demonstrated how the low expression of X-linked monoamine oxidase A (MAOA)— which is an important enzyme in the catabolism of monoamines, most notably serotonin (5-HT), and which has been associated with an increased propensity towards reactive violence in abused children [31]—is correlated to volume changes and hyperactivity in the amygdala [32].

The four cops at the counter are talking about criminal behavior.

"Did you see that report on TV? Some guy says perps do bad things because of brain damage."

"If a perp wasn't damaged before you arrested him, Stoney, he is by the time you get him to the station."

"Social deviants resisting arrest," Stoney says.

"I don't believe that science crap," says the youngest.

"They say it's all because of their prefrontal complex."

"Psychiatrists. It's just a way to keep bad people from getting what they deserve."

The oldest cop there shifts his considerable bulk on his stool. "Listen, kid. I been doing this for twenty-four years. Nobody ever gets what's coming to him, except maybe by accident. Most of the victims don't deserve what they get. Most of the perps don't get what they deserve. Justice is a fairy tale."

"How can you say that? I couldn't be a cop if you're right."

"I'm right."

"It's a cop's job to make sure people get what they deserve. Otherwise, why be a cop?"

The fourth one, silent until now, speaks up. "Stoney does it so he can bust someone's prefrontal complex every week and get away with it."

"That's right, Mr. Social Worker. The state gives me that power. I use it."

"Forget about the word 'deserves,'" the old cop said. "Nobody deserves anything."

I awoke from fervid dreams and perfervid nightmares. As I slid out of bed I knocked volume six of *The Burned Lands* heptology from my bedside table, and a brown roach scurried for the baseboard. In the bathroom I splashed cold water in my face. There was grease under my fingernails and the pouches under my eyes could hold my passport and several hundred in travelers' checks.

Behind me in the mirror's reflection I saw the engine, sitting up beside the old bathtub like a scrapwork sculpture from the MOMA. There was an idea—a career change. But no, I didn't have the temperament or haircut for a career in the arts.

I had wired the golf balls I had found to the vertical shaft. If I ever got it to work, centrifugal force would make them rise up and spin like a circus ride. But now they just hung limply. Story of my life.

Then, looking at the engine in the mirror, with everything reversed, I realized that I had constructed it backward. It was a matter of the hemispheres. In the north, the Coriolis effect means cyclonic winds and whirlpools always move counterclockwise; in the southern hemisphere clockwise.

I turned from the sink, got down on my hands and knees, and set to work. About ten the phone started ringing, and when the machine picked up I heard it was my boss from AutoWorld asking me why I hadn't come in yet. I let the machine take it. He called again an hour later, and in the afternoon a third time to tell me I was fired. I didn't care.

I worked through the day, stopping only to grab a sandwich and some yogurt when my stomach started growling too much. I had to run out and hunt down some machine parts in the late afternoon, and then again in the morning.

I caught a few hours' sleep each night for three days. While I worked I hummed songs to myself. I felt light-headed, but that was all right. My head had been too heavy for too long.

His conception of power lies at the center of Michel Foucault's work. Essentially, questions of power arise in any relationship between people where one affects another's actions. Power does not reside only in force or violence, which affect the body physically. It involves making a free subject do something that he would not otherwise have done: power therefore involves restricting or altering someone's will. Power is present in all human relationships, and penetrates throughout society.

The state does not have a monopoly over power, because power relations are deeply unstable and changeable. Having said that, patterns of domination do exist in society. The employer and employee. The police officer and the citizen. The parent and child. The husband and wife. The lover and the beloved.

The relationship between power and knowledge, Foucault tells us, is also an important one. A major source of power comes from claims of knowledge. To claim that a statement is true is to make a claim to power because, according to Foucault, truth can only be produced by power. Criminology, for example, can make claims that exclude the delinquent by creating theories of human behavior that place the delinquent outside of "established norms." From this derives a system of power relations in which the delinquent is dominated.

The other Foucault—the pendulum one—who fortunately died long before the later Foucault was born, and was therefore blissfully ignorant of his theories, did not believe that truth was a matter of power relationships. Truth, for him, stood outside the constructions of human minds. Foucault's pendulum did not work because he had established a theoretical system that accounted for it, and that excluded systems in which it did not work. It worked because the Earth rotated, and would rotate whether or not human theoretical structures defined such rotation as "normal."

Outside the cave, the storm raged. Lightning split the skies, followed seconds later by the long rolling tumble of thunder. Halbo felt Dimli's fevered brow. The dwarf was burning up. Halbo ran to the mouth of the cave where the cold rain pelted down, soaked Dimli's bloody shirt, and brought it back to moisten his dying friend's cracked lips. Dimli struggled to speak. "Halbo, leave me," he gasped. "You must—"

"Rest, good friend. I know what I must do."

Not for the first time, Halbo vowed to survive this ordeal, and to change the world. In the new world, all would be well, and no faithful soul like Dimli would ever die. Through his tears he could see this new world, bright and clear enough almost to grasp. It only required that Halbo and those like him act boldly against the evil that oppressed them, and vanquish it forever.

"Nothing," Faraday said, "is too wonderful to be true."

Della called on the third day. When I heard her begin to speak into the answer machine, I lurched out of the bathroom to catch the phone. "Hello! Della!"

"Where are you, Gary? You said—"

"I've got it, Della! I really think this is it. It's an angular momentum thing. You have to confer a mechanical advantage—"

"Spare me, Gary. You told me you were going to take the boys today—"

"The boys! What day is it?"

"It's Saturday." Della's voice was very patient.

"I'm sorry, Del. I can't help you. I'm on the two-yard line here! If I don't punch it in I'm afraid it will all evaporate. You'll understand, right?"

The silence stretched a moment. The phone line clicked with static. "I understand," Della said quietly.

"I'll make it up to you. Promise!" I hung up and went back to work.

About seven in the evening of the fourth day I flipped the switch. The engine began to hum. The humming rose in pitch. The shaft began to spin. Centrifugal force lifted the golf balls to the ends of the wires. They spun so fast they became a blur. It worked.

I jumped up and down. My knees were so tight from crouching that I could hardly move, but I didn't care. I stumbled into the kitchen and pulled the bottle of rum from the cupboard, sloshed a couple of inches into a tumbler. I ran back to the bathroom. The engine was still humming, the golf balls buzzing in a white blur as they revolved. "To the future!" I called, raising my glass. "To unlimited power!" I slugged down the rum. "To the transformation of the world!"

This was going to change everything. Me, Gary O'Halloran, mankind's benefactor! I would be rich. I would live in a big house. I would sleep with whoever I wanted to sleep with.

Della, I thought. I dashed into the other room to call her, but when I picked up the phone, there was no dial tone. I clicked the plunger repeatedly, but still nothing. Had I forgotten to pay the bill? But then when I hung up the handset, it immediately rang. I picked up the receiver, "Della?"

No voice responded. I listened. Was there the sound of breathing?

I set the receiver down gently in the cradle.

I ran back into the bathroom. The engine purred. The spiraling golf balls set up a little breeze. It felt good.

I went back to the kitchen and refilled my glass. Threw in some more ice cubes, a splash of Coke. The next step was to figure out how to license the thing. I didn't fool myself that I could manufacture the Foucault engine by myself. I needed a patent lawyer, and an agent, and pretty soon after that an accountant, and a business manager. The world was complicated.

I sat on the sofa sipping rum. I had been working so hard on perfecting the engine that I had hardly spent a minute thinking about what would happen when I did so. At some level I guess I thought I might never succeed. It was as if I had been trying to batter down a door, kicking it, shoving on it, leaning into it, and now suddenly it was yanked open from the other side, and I sprawled on the floor unbalanced. On the other side of that door I'd imagined a vague fantasy land, a magic place of freedom and happiness. Now, the door was open and I stood on the verge. Could I step through? What was really on the other side?

I got pretty drunk, and the lack of sleep over the past days hit me hard. Eventually I shuffled into the bedroom and passed out on my bed.

In the morning I woke with a throbbing headache and a mouth dryer than death. Sun slanting through the curtains hurt my eyes. The apartment was still. For some reason that bothered me.

I dragged myself from the bed and into the bathroom, and remembered why it should not have been still. The Foucault engine was in pieces—bits of it, levers and cogs and shafts and springs, wires and gauges, in the bathtub, on the floor, in the sink, in the corner of the room way behind the toilet. I stepped on a golf ball and almost fell over.

I filled the toothbrush glass with tap water and drank it down. I repeated that three times. My temples throbbed. I sat on the toilet seat and assessed the wreckage.

It could, I suppose, have torn itself apart as it ran. But how could it have done that without waking me?

Unless someone tore it apart, carefully, dismantled it piece by piece and scattered them about the bathroom in order to make me think it had fallen apart. Weeks in advance they'd drugged my rum, planted a micro-camera in my bathroom, watched me until I got the engine perfected.

What about the phantom phone call? I made my way into the other room and picked up the handset. The dial tone was steady. I slumped on the sofa.

Who was I kidding? Maybe the engine had never worked. Maybe I had smashed it myself. I wasn't Thomas Edison, I was Gary O'Halloran. I hadn't slept properly in days.

I got up. I moved the pieces out of the tub, filled it with hot water, and climbed in. I took a very long bath. My headache subsided.

Afterward, I wrapped a towel around me and shuffled into the bedroom. I felt a little better. The window was open and a light breeze wafted the curtains toward me. I heard someone singing outside. I sat on the edge of the bed and looked out.

A young woman was setting out her recycling by the curb. I had never noticed her in the neighborhood before. She had a red Radio Flyer wagon carrying a bin full of newspapers, another of bottles. She sang softly to herself. Her very dark hair was pulled back into a ponytail. Though she was not acting sexual in any way, as she bent over to lift one of the bins out of the wagon, I looked down her blouse. Somehow she must have sensed me watching; she turned her face upward and caught me. Her face, heart shaped, was very beautiful. Her dark eyes locked with mine. She smiled.

Pride and Prometheus

Had both her mother and her sister Kitty not insisted upon it, Miss Mary Bennet, whose interest in Nature did not extend to the Nature of Society, would not have attended the ball in Grosvenor Square. This was Kitty's season. Mrs. Bennet had despaired of Mary long ago, but still bore hopes for her younger sister, and so had set her determined mind on putting Kitty in the way of Robert Sidney of Detling Manor, who possessed a fortune of six thousand pounds a year, and was likely to be at that evening's festivities. Being obliged by her unmarried state to live with her parents, and the whims of Mrs. Bennet being what they were, although there was no earthly reason for Mary to be there, there was no good excuse for her absence.

So it was that Mary found herself in the ballroom of the great house, trussed up in a silk dress with her hair piled high, bedecked with her sister's jewels. She was neither a beauty, like her older and happily married sister Jane, nor witty, like her older and happily married sister Elizabeth, nor flirtatious, like her younger and less happily married sister Lydia. Awkward and nearsighted, she had never cut an attractive figure, and as she had aged she had come to see herself as others saw her. Every time Mrs. Bennet told her to stand up straight, she felt despair. Mary had seen how Jane and Elizabeth had made good lives for themselves by finding appropriate mates. But there was no air of grace or mystery about Mary, and no man ever looked upon her with admiration.

Kitty's card was full, and she had already contrived to dance once with the distinguished Mr. Sidney, whom Mary could not imagine being more tedious. Hectically glowing, Kitty was certain that this was the season she would get a husband. Mary, in contrast, sat with her mother and her Aunt Gardiner, whose good sense was Mary's only respite from her mother's silliness. After the third minuet Kitty came flying over.

"Catch your breath, Kitty!" Mrs. Bennet said. "Must you rush about like this? Who is that young man you danced with? Remember, we are here to smile on Mr. Sidney, not on some stranger. Did I see him arrive with the Lord Mayor?"

"How can I tell you what you saw, Mother?"

"Don't be impertinent."

"Yes. He is an acquaintance of the Mayor. He's from Switzerland! Mr. Clerval, on holiday."

The tall, fair-haired Clerval stood with a darker, brooding young man, both impeccably dressed in dove gray breeches, black jackets, and waistcoats, with white tie and gloves.

"Switzerland! I would not have you marry any Dutchman—though 'tis said their merchants are uncommonly wealthy. And who is that gentleman with whom he speaks?"

"I don't know, Mother—but I can find out."

Mrs. Bennet's curiosity was soon to be relieved, as the two men crossed the drawing room to the sisters and their chaperones.

"Henry Clerval, madame," the fair-haired man said. "And this is my good friend Mr. Victor Frankenstein."

Mr. Frankenstein bowed but said nothing. He had the darkest eyes that Mary had ever encountered, and an air of being there only on obligation. Whether this was because he was as uncomfortable in these social situations as she, Mary could not tell, but his diffident air intrigued her. She fancied his reserve might bespeak sadness rather than pride. His manners were faultless, as was his command of English, though he spoke with a slight French accent. When he asked Mary to dance she suspected he did so only at the urging of Mr. Clerval; on the floor, once the orchestra of pianoforte, violin, and cello struck up the quadrille, he moved with some grace but no trace of a smile.

At the end of the dance, Frankenstein asked whether Mary would like some refreshment, and they crossed from the crowded ballroom to the sitting room, where he procured for her a cup of negus. Mary felt obliged to make some conversation before she should retreat to the safety of her wallflower's chair.

"What brings you to England, Mr. Frankenstein?"

"I come to meet with certain natural philosophers here in London, and in Oxford—students of magnetism."

"Oh! Then have you met Professor Langdon, of the Royal Society?"

Frankenstein looked at her as if seeing her for the first time. "How is it that you are acquainted with Professor Langdon?"

"I am not personally acquainted with him, but I am, in my small way, an enthusiast of the sciences. You are a natural philosopher?"

"I confess that I can no longer countenance the subject. But yes, I did study with Mr. Krempe and Mr. Waldman in Ingolstadt."

"You no longer countenance the subject, yet you seek out Professor Langdon."

A shadow swept over Mr. Frankenstein's handsome face. "It is unsupportable to me, yet pursue it I must."

"A paradox."

"A paradox that I am unable to explain, Miss Bennet."

All this said in a voice heavy with despair. Mary watched his sober black eyes, and replied, "'The heart has its reasons of which reason knows nothing.'"

For the second time that evening he gave her a look that suggested an understanding. Frankenstein sipped from his cup, then spoke: "Avoid any pastime, Miss Bennet, that takes you out of the normal course of human contact. If the study to which you apply yourself has a tendency to weaken your affections, and to destroy your taste for simple pleasures, then that study is certainly unlawful."

The purport of this extraordinary speech Mary was unable to fathom. "Surely there is no harm in seeking knowledge."

Mr. Frankenstein smiled. "Henry has been urging me to go out into London society; had I known that I might meet such a thoughtful person as yourself I would have taken him up on it long 'ere now."

He took her hand. "But I spy your aunt at the door," he said. "No doubt she has been dispatched to protect you. If you will, please let me return you to your mother. I must thank you for the dance, and even more for your conversation, Miss Bennet. In the midst of a foreign land, you have brought me a moment of sympathy."

And again Mary sat beside her mother and aunt as she had half an hour before. She was nonplussed. It was not seemly for a stranger to speak so much from the heart to a woman he had never previously met, yet she could not find it in herself to condemn him. Rather, she felt her own failure in not keeping him longer.

A cold March rain was falling when, after midnight, they left the ball. They waited under the portico while the coachman brought round the carriage. Kitty began coughing. As they stood there in the chill night, Mary noticed a hooded man, of enormous size, standing in the shadows at the corner of the lane. Full in the downpour, unmoving, he watched the town house and its partiers without coming closer or going away, as if this observation were all his intention in life. Mary shivered.

In the carriage back to Aunt Gardiner's home near Belgravia, Mrs. Bennet insisted that Kitty take the lap robe against the chill. "Stop coughing, Kitty. Have a care for my poor nerves." She added, "They should never have put the supper at the end of that long hallway. The young ladies, flushed from the dance, had to walk all that cold way."

Kitty drew a ragged breath and leaned over to Mary. "I have never seen you so taken with a man, Mary. What did that Swiss gentleman say to you?"

"We spoke of natural philosophy."

"Did he say nothing of the reasons he came to England?" Aunt Gardiner asked.

"That was his reason."

"I should say not!" said Kitty. "He came to forget his grief! His little brother William was murdered, not six months ago, by the family maid!"

"How terrible!" said Aunt Gardiner.

Mrs. Bennet asked in open astonishment, "Could this be true?"

"I have it from Lucy Copeland, the Lord Mayor's daughter," Kitty replied. "Who heard it from Mr. Clerval himself. And there is more! He is engaged to be married—to his cousin. Yet he has abandoned her, left her in Switzerland and come here instead."

"Did he say anything to you about these matters?" Mrs. Bennet asked Mary.

Kitty interrupted. "Mother, he's not going to tell the family secrets to strangers, let alone reveal his betrothal at a dance."

Mary wondered at these revelations. Perhaps they explained Mr.

Frankenstein's odd manner. But could they explain his interest in her? "A man should be what he seems," she said.

Kitty snorted, and it became a cough.

"Mark me, girls," said Mrs. Bennet, "that engagement is a match that he does not want. I wonder what fortune he would bring to a marriage?"

In the days that followed, Kitty's cough became a full-blown catarrh, and it was decided against her protest that, the city air being unhealthy, they should cut short their season and return to Meryton. Mr. Sidney was undoubtedly unaware of his narrow escape. Mary could not honestly say that she regretted leaving, though the memory of her half hour with Mr. Frankenstein gave her as much regret at losing the chance of further commerce with him as she had ever felt from her acquaintance with a man.

Within a week Kitty was feeling better, and repining bitterly their remove from London. In truth, she was only two years younger than Mary and had made none of the mental accommodations to approaching spinsterhood that her older sister had attempted. Mr. Bennet retreated to his study, emerging only at mealtimes to cast sardonic comments about Mrs. Bennet and Kitty's marital campaigns. Perhaps, Mrs. Bennet said, they might invite Mr. Sidney to visit Longbourn when Parliament adjourned. Mary escaped these discussions by practicing the pianoforte and, as the advancing spring brought warm weather, taking walks in the countryside, where she would stop beneath an oak and read, indulging her passion for Goethe and German philosophy. When she tried to engage her father in speculation, he warned her, "I am afraid, my dear, that your understanding is too dependent on books and not enough on experience of the world. Beware, Mary. Too much learning makes a woman monstrous."

What experience of the world had they ever allowed her? Rebuffed, Mary wrote to Elizabeth about the abrupt end of Kitty's latest assault on marriage, and her subsequent ill temper, and Elizabeth wrote back inviting her two younger sisters to come visit Pemberley.

Mary was overjoyed to have the opportunity to escape her mother and see something more of Derbyshire, and Kitty seemed equally willing. Mrs. Bennet was not persuaded when Elizabeth suggested that nearby Matlock and its baths might be good for Kitty's health (no man would marry a sickly girl), but she was persuaded by Kitty's observation that, though it could in no way rival London, Matlock did attract a finer society than sleepy Meryton, and thus offered opportunities for meeting eligible young men of property. So in the second week of May, Mr. and Mrs. Bennet tearfully loaded their last unmarried daughters into a coach for the long drive to Derbyshire. Mrs. Bennet's tears were shed because their absence would deprive Kitty and Mary of her attentions, Mr. Bennet's for the fact that their absence would assure him of Mrs. Bennet's.

The two girls were as ever delighted by the grace and luxury of Pemberley, Mr. Darcy's ancestral estate. Darcy was kindness itself, and the servants attentive, if, at the instruction of Elizabeth, less indulgent of Kitty's whims and more careful of her health than the thoroughly cowed servants at home. Lizzy saw that Kitty got enough sleep, and the three sisters took long walks in the grounds of the estate. Kitty's health improved, and Mary's spirits rose. Mary enjoyed the company of Lizzy and Darcy's eight-year-old son William, who was attempting to teach her and Darcy's younger sister Georgiana to fish. Georgiana pined after her betrothed, Captain Broadbent, who was away on crown business in the Caribbean, but after they had been there a week, Jane and her husband Mr. Bingley came for an extended visit from their own estate thirty miles away, and so four of the five Bennet sisters were reunited. They spent many cordial afternoons and evenings. Both Mary and Georgiana were accomplished at the pianoforte, though Mary had come to realize that her sisters tolerated more than enjoyed her playing. The reunion of Lizzy and Jane meant even more time devoted to Kitty's improvement, with specific attention to her marital prospects, and left Mary feeling invisible. Still, on occasion she would join them and drive into Lambton or Matlock to shop and socialize, and every week during the summer a ball was held in the assembly room of the Old Bath Hotel, with its beeswax-polished floor and splendid chandeliers.

On one such excursion to Matlock, Georgiana stopped at the milliners while Kitty pursued some business at the butcher's shop—Mary wondered at her sudden interest in Pemberley's domestic affairs—and Mary took William to the museum and circulating library, which contained celebrated cabinets of natural history. William had told her of certain antiquities unearthed in the excavation for a new hotel and recently added to the collection.

The streets, hotels, and inns of Matlock bustled with travelers there to take the waters. Newly wedded couples leaned on one another's arms, whispering secrets that no doubt concerned the alpine scenery. A crew of workmen was breaking up the cobblestone street in front of the hall, swinging pickaxes in the bright sun. Inside she and Will retreated to the cool quiet of the public exhibition room.

Among the visitors to the museum Mary spied a slender, well-dressed man at one of the display cases, examining the artifacts contained there. As she drew near, Mary recognized him. "Mr. Frankenstein!"

The tall European looked up, startled. "Ah—Miss Bennet?"

She was pleased that he remembered. "Yes. How good to see you."

"And this young man is?"

"My nephew, William."

At the mention of this name, Frankenstein's expression darkened. He closed his eyes. "Are you not well?" Mary asked.

He looked at her again. "Forgive me. These antiquities call to mind sad associations. Give me a moment."

"Certainly," she said. William ran off to see the hall's steam clock. Mary turned and examined the contents of the neighboring cabinet.

Beneath the glass was a collection of bones that had been unearthed in the local lead mines. The card lettered beside them read: *Bones, resembling those of a fish, made of limestone.*

Eventually Frankenstein came to stand beside her. "How is it that you are come to Matlock?" he inquired.

"My sister Elizabeth is married to Mr. Fitzwilliam Darcy, of Pemberley. Kitty and I are here on a visit. Have you come to take the waters?"

"Clerval and I are on our way to Scotland, where he will stay with friends, while I pursue—certain investigations. We rest here a week. The topography of the valley reminds me of my home in Switzerland."

"I have heard it said so," she replied. Frankenstein seemed to have regained his composure, but Mary wondered still at what had awakened his grief. "You have an interest in these relics?" she asked, indicating the cabinets.

"Some, perhaps. I find it remarkable to see a young lady take an interest in such arcana." Mary detected no trace of mockery in his voice.

"Indeed, I do," she said, indulging her enthusiasm. "Professor Erasmus Darwin has written of the source of these bones:

> "Organic life beneath the shoreless waves
> Was born and nurs'd in ocean's pearly caves;
> First forms minute, unseen by spheric glass,
> Move on the mud, or pierce the watery mass;
> These, as successive generations bloom,
> New powers acquire and larger limbs assume;
> Whence countless groups of vegetation spring,
> And breathing realms of fin and feet and wing.

"People say this offers proof of the Great Flood. Do you think, Mr. Frankenstein, that Matlock could once have been under the sea? They say these are creatures that have not existed since the time of Noah."

"Far older than the Flood, I'll warrant. I do not think that these bones were originally made of stone. Some process has transformed them. Anatomically, they are more like those of a lizard than a fish."

"You have studied anatomy?"

Mr. Frankenstein tapped his fingers upon the glass of the case. "Three years gone by it was one of my passions. I no longer pursue such matters."

"And yet, sir, you met with men of science in London."

"Ah—yes, I did. I am surprised that you remember a brief conversation, more than two months ago."

"I have a good memory."

"As evidenced by your quoting Professor Darwin. I might expect a woman such as yourself to take more interest in art than science."

"Oh, you may rest assured that I have read my share of novels. And even more, in my youth, of sermons. Elizabeth is wont to tease me for a great moralizer. 'Evil is easy,' I tell her, 'and has infinite forms.'"

Frankenstein did not answer. Finally he said, "Would that the world had no need of moralizers."

Mary recalled his warning against science from their London meeting. "Come, Mr. Frankenstein. There is no evil in studying God's handiwork."

"A God-fearing Christian might take exception to Professor Darwin's assertion that life began in the sea, no matter how poetically stated." His voice became distant. "Can a living soul be created without the hand of God?"

"It is my feeling that the hand of God is everywhere present." Mary gestured toward the cabinet. "Even in the bones of this stony fish."

"Then you have more faith than I, Miss Bennet—or more innocence."

Mary blushed. She was not used to bantering in this way with a gentleman. In her experience, handsome and accomplished men took no interest in her, and such conversations as she had engaged in offered little of substance other than the weather, clothes, and town gossip. Yet she saw that she had touched Frankenstein, and felt something akin to triumph.

They were interrupted by the appearance of Georgiana and Kitty, entering with Henry Clerval. "There you are!" said Kitty. "You see, Mr. Clerval, I told you we would find Mary poring over these heaps of bones!"

"And it is no surprise to find my friend here as well," said Clerval.

Mary felt quite deflated. The party moved out of the town hall and in splendid sunlight along the North Parade. Kitty proposed, and the visitors acceded to, a stroll on the so-called Lovers' Walk beside the river. As they walked along the gorge, vast ramparts of limestone rock, clothed with yew trees, elms, and limes, rose up on either side of the river. William ran ahead, and Kitty, Georgiana, and Clerval followed, leaving Frankenstein and Mary behind. Eventually they came in sight of the High Tor, a sheer cliff rearing its brow on the east bank of the Derwent. The lower part was covered with small trees and foliage. Massive boulders that had fallen from the cliff broke the riverbed below into foaming rapids. The noise of the waters left Mary and Frankenstein, apart from the others, as isolated as if they had been in a separate room. Frankenstein spent a long time gazing at the scenery. Mary's mind raced, seeking some way to recapture the mood of their conversation in the town hall.

"How this reminds me of my home," he said. "Henry and I would climb such cliffs as this, chase goats around the meadows, and play at pirates. Father would walk me though the woods and name every tree and flower. I once saw a lightning bolt shiver an old oak to splinters."

"Whenever I come here," Mary blurted out, "I realize how small I am, and how great time is. We are here for only seconds, and then we are gone, and these rocks, this river, will long survive us. And through it all we are alone."

Frankenstein turned toward her. "Surely you are not so lonely. You have your family, your sisters. Your mother and father."

"One can be alone in a room of people. Kitty mocks me for my 'heaps of bones.'"

"A person may marry."

"I am twenty-eight years old, sir. I am no man's vision of a lover or wife."

What had come over her, to say this aloud, for the first time in her life? Yet what did it matter what she said to this foreigner? There was no point in letting some hope for sympathy delude her into greater hopes. They had danced a single dance in London, and now they spent an afternoon together; soon he would leave England, marry his cousin, and Mary would never see him again. She deserved Kitty's mockery.

Frankenstein took some time before answering, during which Mary was acutely aware of the sound of the waters, and of the sight of Georgiana, William, and Clerval playing in the grass by the riverbank, while Kitty stood pensive some distance away.

"Miss Bennet, I am sorry if I have made light of your situation. But your fine qualities should be apparent to anyone who took the trouble truly to make your acquaintance. Your knowledge of matters of science only adds to my admiration."

"You needn't flatter me," said Mary. "I am unused to it."

"I do not flatter," Frankenstein replied. "I speak my own mind."

William came running up. "Aunt Mary! This would be an excellent place to fish! We should come here with Father!"

"That's a good idea, Will."

Frankenstein turned to the others. "We must return to the hotel, Henry," he told Clerval. "I need to see that new glassware properly packed before shipping it ahead."

"Very well."

"Glassware?" Georgiana asked.

Clerval chuckled. "Victor has been purchasing equipment at every stop along our tour—glassware, bottles of chemicals, lead and copper disks. The coachmen threaten to leave us behind if he does not ship these things separately."

Kitty argued in vain, but the party walked back to Matlock. The women and William met the carriage to take them back to Pemberley. "I hope I see you again, Miss Bennet," Frankenstein said. Had she been more accustomed to reading the emotions of others she would have ventured that his expression held sincere interest—even longing.

On the way back to Pemberley William prattled with Georgiana. Kitty, subdued for once, leaned back with her eyes closed, while Mary puzzled over every moment of the afternoon. The fundamental sympathy she had felt with Frankenstein in their brief London encounter had been only reinforced. His sudden dark moods, his silences, bespoke some burden he carried. Mary was almost convinced that her mother was right—that Frankenstein did not love his cousin, and that he was here in England fleeing from her. How could this second meeting with him be chance? Fate had brought them together.

At dinner that evening, Kitty told Darcy and Elizabeth about their encounter with the handsome Swiss tourists. Later, Mary took Lizzy aside and asked her to invite Clerval and Frankenstein to dinner.

"This is new!" said Lizzy. "I expected this from Kitty, but not you. You have never before asked to have a young man come to Pemberley."

"I have never met someone quite like Mr. Frankenstein," Mary replied.

"Have you taken the Matlock waters?" Mary asked Clerval, who was seated opposite her at the dinner table. "People in the parish say that a dip in the hot springs could raise the dead."

"I confess that I have not," Clerval said. "Victor does not believe in their healing powers."

Mary turned to Frankenstein, hoping to draw him into discussion of the matter, but the startled expression on his face silenced her.

The table, covered with a blinding white damask tablecloth, glittered with silver and crystal. A large epergne, studded with lit beeswax candles, dominated its center. In addition to the family members, and in order to even the number of guests and balance female with male, Darcy and

Elizabeth had invited the vicar, Mr. Chatsworth. Completing the dinner party were Bingley and Jane, Georgiana, and Kitty.

The footmen brought soup, followed by claret, turbot with lobster and Dutch sauce, oyster pâté, lamb cutlets with asparagus, peas, a fricandeau à l'oseille, venison, stewed beef à la jardinière, with various salads, beetroot, French and English mustard. Two ices, cherry water and pineapple cream, and a chocolate cream with strawberries. Champagne flowed throughout the dinner, and Madeira afterward.

Darcy inquired of Mr. Clerval's business in England, and Clerval told of his meetings with men of business in London, and his interest in India. He had even begun the study of the language, and for their entertainment spoke a few sentences in Hindi. Darcy told of his visit to Geneva a decade ago. Clerval spoke charmingly of the differences in manners between the Swiss and the English, with witty preference for English habits, except, he said, in the matter of boiled meats. Georgiana asked about women's dress on the continent. Elizabeth allowed as how, if they could keep him safe, it would be good for William's education to tour the continent. Kitty, who usually dominated the table with bright talk and jokes, was unusually quiet. The Vicar spoke amusingly of his travels in Italy.

Through all of this, Frankenstein offered little in the way of response or comment. Mary had put such hopes on this dinner, and now she feared she had misread him. His voice warmed but once, when he spoke of his father, a counselor and syndic, renowned for his integrity. Only on inquiry would he speak of his years in Ingolstadt.

"And what did you study in the university?" Bingley asked.

"Matters of no interest," Frankenstein replied.

An uncomfortable silence followed. Clerval gently explained, "My friend devoted himself so single-mindedly to the study of natural philosophy that his health failed. I was fortunately able to bring him back to us, but it was a near thing."

"For which I will ever be grateful to you," Frankenstein mumbled.

Lizzy attempted to change the subject. "Reverend Chatsworth, what news is there of the parish?"

The vicar, unaccustomed to such volume and variety of drink, was in his cups, his face flushed and his voice rising to pulpit volume. "Well, I hope the ladies will not take it amiss," he boomed, "if I tell about a curious incident that occurred last night!"

"Pray do."

"So, then—last night I was troubled with sleeplessness—I think it was the trout I ate for supper, it was not right—Mrs. Croft vowed she had purchased it just that afternoon, but I wonder if perhaps it might have been from the previous day's catch. Be that as it may, lying awake some time after midnight, I thought I heard a scraping out my bedroom window—the weather has been so fine of late that I sleep with my window open. It is my opinion, Mr. Clerval, that nothing aids the lungs more than fresh air, and I believe that is the opinion of the best continental thinkers, is it not? The air is exceedingly fresh in the alpine meadows, I am told?"

"Only in those meadows where the cows have not been feeding."

"The cows? Oh, yes, the cows—ha, ha!—very good! The cows, indeed! So, where was I? Ah, yes. I rose from my bed and looked out the window, and what did I spy but a light in the churchyard. I threw on my robe and slippers and hurried out to see what might be the matter.

"As I approached the churchyard I saw a dark figure wielding a spade. His back was to me, silhouetted by a lamp which rested beside Nancy Brown's grave. Poor Nancy, dead not a week now, so young, only seventeen."

"A man?" said Kitty.

The vicar's round face grew serious. "You may imagine my shock. 'Halloo!' I shouted. At that the man dropped his spade, seized the lantern and dashed round the back of the church. By the time I had reached the corner he was out of sight. Back at the grave I saw that he had been on a fair way to unearthing poor Nancy's coffin!"

"My goodness!" said Jane.

"Defiling a grave?" asked Bingley. "I am astonished."

Darcy said nothing, but his look demonstrated that he was not pleased by the vicar bringing such an uncouth matter to his dinner table. Frankenstein, sitting next to Mary, put down his knife and took a long draught of Madeira.

The vicar lowered his voice. He was clearly enjoying himself. "I can only speculate on what motive this man might have had. Could it have been some lover of hers, overcome with grief?"

"No man is so faithful," Kitty said.

"My dear vicar," said Lizzy. "You have read too many of Mrs. Radcliffe's novels."

Darcy leaned back in his chair. "Gypsies have been seen in the woods about the quarry. It was no doubt their work. They were seeking jewelry."

"Jewelry?" the vicar said. "The Browns had barely enough money to see her decently buried."

"Which proves that whoever did this was not a local man."

Clerval spoke. "At home, fresh graves are sometimes defiled by men providing cadavers to doctors. Was there not a spate of such grave robbings in Ingolstadt, Victor?"

Frankenstein put down his glass. "Yes," he said. "Some anatomists, in seeking knowledge, will abandon all human scruple."

"I do not think that is likely to be the cause in this instance," Darcy observed. "Here there is no university, no medical school. Doctor Phillips, in Lambton, is no transgressor of civilized rules."

"He is scarcely a transgressor of his own threshold," said Lizzy. "One must call him a day in advance to get him to leave his parlor."

"Rest assured, there are such men," said Frankenstein. "I have known them. My illness, as Henry has described to you, was in some way my spirit's rebellion against the understanding that the pursuit of knowledge will lead some men into mortal peril."

Here was Mary's chance to impress Frankenstein. "Surely there is a nobility in risking one's life to advance the claims of one's race. With how many things are we upon the brink of becoming acquainted, if cowardice or carelessness did not restrain our inquiries?"

"Then I thank God for cowardice and carelessness, Miss Bennet," Frankenstein said, "One's life, perhaps, is worth risking, but not one's soul."

"True enough. But I believe that science may demand our relaxing the strictures of common society."

"We have never heard this tone from you, Mary," Jane said.

Darcy interjected, "You are becoming quite modern, sister. What strictures are you prepared to abandon for us tonight?" His voice was full of the gentle condescension with which he treated Mary at all times.

How she wished to surprise them! How she longed to show Darcy and

Lizzy, with their perfect marriage and perfect lives, that she was not the simple old maid they thought her. "Anatomists in London have obtained the court's permission to dissect the bodies of criminals after execution. Is it unjust to use the body of a murderer, who has already forfeited his own life, to save the lives of the innocent?"

"My uncle, who is on the bench, has spoken of such cases," Bingley said.

"Not only that," Mary added. "Have you heard of the experiments of the Italian scientist Aldini? Last summer in London at the Royal College of Surgeons he used a powerful battery to animate portions of the body of a hanged man. According to the *Times*, the spectators genuinely believed that the body was about to come to life!"

"Mary, please!" said Lizzy.

"You need to spend less time on your horrid books," Kitty laughed. "No suitor is going to want to talk with you about dead bodies."

And so Kitty was on their side, too. Her mockery only made Mary more determined to force Frankenstein to speak. "What do you say, sir? Will you come to my defense?"

Frankenstein carefully folded his napkin and set it beside his plate. "Such attempts are not motivated by bravery, or even curiosity, but by ambition. The pursuit of knowledge can become a vice deadly as any of the more common sins. Worse still, because even the most noble of natures are susceptible to such temptations. None but he who has experienced them can conceive of the enticements of science."

The vicar raised his glass. "Mr. Frankenstein, truer words have never been spoken. The man who defiled poor Nancy's grave has placed himself beyond the mercy of a forgiving God."

Mary felt charged with contradictory emotions. "You have experienced such enticements, Mr. Frankenstein?"

"Sadly, I have."

"But surely there is no sin that is beyond the reach of God's mercy? 'To know all is to forgive all.'"

The vicar turned to her. "My child, what know you of sin?"

"Very little, Mr. Chatsworth, except of idleness. Yet I feel that even a wicked person can have the veil lifted from his eyes."

Frankenstein looked at her. "Here I must agree with Miss Bennet. I have to believe that even the most corrupted nature is susceptible to grace. If I did not think this were possible, I could not live."

"Enough of this talk," insisted Darcy. "Vicar, I suggest you mind your parishioners, including those in the churchyard, more carefully. But now I, for one, am eager to hear Miss Georgiana play the pianoforte. And perhaps Miss Mary and Miss Catherine will join her. We must uphold the accomplishments of English maidenhood before our foreign guests."

On Kitty's insistence, the next morning, despite lowering clouds and a chill in the air that spoke more of March than late May, she and Mary took a walk along the river.

They walked along the stream that ran from the estate toward the Derwent. Kitty remained silent. Mary's thoughts turned to the wholly unsatisfying dinner of the previous night. The conversation in the parlor had gone no better than dinner. Mary had played the piano ill, showing herself to poor advantage next to the accomplished Georgiana. Under Jane and Lizzy's gaze she felt the folly of her intemperate speech at the table. Frankenstein said next to nothing to her for the rest of the evening; he almost seemed wary of being in her presence.

She was wondering how he was spending this morning when, suddenly turning her face from Mary, Kitty burst into tears.

Mary touched her arm. "Whatever is the matter, Kitty?"

"Do you believe what you said last night?"

"What did I say?"

"That there is no sin beyond the reach of God's mercy?"

"Of course I do! Why would you ask?"

"Because I have committed such a sin!" She covered her eyes with her hand. "Oh, no, I mustn't speak of it!"

Mary refrained from pointing out that, having made such a provocative admission, Kitty could hardly remain silent—and undoubtedly had no intention of doing so. But Kitty's intentions were not always transparent to Mary.

After some coaxing and a further walk along the stream, Kitty was prepared finally to unburden herself. It seemed that, from the previous summer she had maintained a secret admiration for a local man from

Matlock, Robert Piggot, son of the butcher. Though his family was quite prosperous and he stood to inherit the family business, he was in no way a gentleman, and Kitty had vowed never to let her affections overwhelm her sense.

But, upon their recent return to Pemberley, she had encountered Robert on her first visit to town, and she had been secretly meeting with him when she went into Matlock on the pretext of shopping. Worse still, the couple had allowed their passion to get the better of them, and Kitty had given way to carnal love.

The two sisters sat on a fallen tree in the woods as Kitty poured out her tale. "I want so much to marry him." Her tears flowed readily. "I do not want to be alone, I don't want to die an old maid! And Lydia—Lydia told me about—about the act of love, how wonderful it was, how good Wickham makes her feel. She boasted of it! And I said, why should vain Lydia have this, and me have nothing, to waste my youth in conversation and embroidery, in listening to Mother prattle and Father throw heavy sighs. Father thinks me a fool, unlikely ever to find a husband. And now he's right!" Kitty burst into wailing again. "He's right! No man shall ever have me!" Her tears ended in a fit of coughing.

"Oh, Kitty," Mary said.

"When Darcy spoke of English maidenhood last night, it was all I could do to keep from bursting into tears. You must get Father to agree to let me marry Robert."

"Has he asked you to marry him?"

"He shall. He must. You don't know how fine a man he is. Despite the fact that he is in trade, he has the gentlest manners. I don't care if he is not well born."

Mary embraced Kitty. Kitty alternated between sobs and fits of coughing. Above them the thunder rumbled, and the wind rustled the trees. Mary felt Kitty's shivering body. She needed to calm her, to get her back to the house. How frail, how slender her sister was.

She did not know what to say. Once Mary would have self-righteously condemned Kitty. But much that Kitty said was the content of her own mind, and Kitty's fear of dying alone was her own fear. As she searched for some answer, Mary heard the sound of a torrent of rain hitting the canopy of foliage above them. "You have been foolish," Mary said, holding her.

"But it may not be so bad."

Kitty trembled in her arms, and spoke into Mary's shoulder. "But will you ever care for me again? What if Father should turn me out? What will I do then?"

The rain was falling through now, coming down hard. Mary felt her hair getting soaked. "Calm yourself. Father would do no such thing. I shall never forsake you. Jane would not, nor Lizzy."

"What if I should have a child!"

Mary pulled Kitty's shawl over her head. She looked past Kitty's shoulder to the dark woods. Something moved there. "You shan't have a child."

"You can't know! I may!"

The woods had become dark with the rain. Mary could not make out what lurked there. "Come, let us go back. You must compose yourself. We shall speak with Lizzy and Jane. They will know—"

Just then a flash of lightning lit the forest, and Mary saw, beneath the trees not ten feet from them, the giant figure of a man. The lightning illuminated a face of monstrous ugliness: Long, thick, tangled black hair. Yellow skin the texture of dried leather, black eyes sunken deep beneath heavy brows. Worst of all, an expression hideous in its cold, inexpressible hunger. All glimpsed in a split second; then the light fell to shadow.

Mary gasped, and pulled Kitty toward her. A great peal of thunder rolled across the sky.

Kitty stopped crying. "What is it?"

"We must go. Now." Mary seized Kitty by the arm. The rain pelted down on them, and the forest path was already turning to mud.

Mary pulled her toward the house, Kitty complaining. Mary could hear nothing over the drumming of the rain. But when she looked over her shoulder, she caught a glimpse of the brutish figure, keeping to the trees, but swiftly, silently moving along behind them.

"Why must we run?" Kitty gasped.

"Because we are being followed!"

"By whom?"

"I don't know!"

Behind them, Mary thought she heard the man croak out some words:

"Halt! Bitter!"

They had not reached the edge of the woods when figures appeared ahead of them, coming from Pemberley. "Miss Bennet! Mary! Kitty!"

The figures resolved themselves into Darcy and Mr. Frankenstein. Darcy carried a cloak, which he threw over them. "Are you all right?" Frankenstein asked.

"Thank you!" Mary gasped. "A man. He's there," she pointed, "following us."

Frankenstein took a few steps beyond them down the path. "Who was it?" Darcy asked.

"Some brute. Hideously ugly," Mary said.

Frankenstein came back. "No one is there."

"We saw him!"

Another lighting flash, and crack of thunder. "It is very dark, and we are in a storm," Frankenstein said.

"Come, we must get you back to the house," Darcy said. "You are wet to the bone."

The men helped them back to Pemberley, trying their best to keep the rain off the sisters.

Darcy went off to find Bingley and Clerval, who had taken the opposite direction in their search. Lizzy saw that Mary and Kitty were made dry and warm. Kitty's cough worsened, and Lizzy insisted she must be put to bed. Mary sat with Kitty, whispered a promise to keep her secret, and waited until she slept. Then she went down to meet the others in the parlor.

"This chill shall do her no good," Jane said. She chided Mary for wandering off in such threatening weather. "I thought you had developed more sense, Mary. Mr. Frankenstein insisted he help to find you, when he realized you had gone out into the woods."

"I am sorry," Mary said. "You are right." She was distracted by Kitty's plight, wondering what she might do. If Kitty were indeed with child, there would be no helping her.

Mary recounted her story of the man in the woods. Darcy said he had seen no one, but allowed that someone might have been there. Frankenstein, rather than engage in the speculation, stood at the tall windows staring across the lawn through the rain toward the tree line.

"This intruder was some local poacher, or perhaps one of those gypsies," said Darcy. "When the rain ends I shall have Mr. Mowbray take some men to check the grounds. We shall also inform the constable."

"I hope this foul weather will induce you to stay with us a few more days, Mr. Frankenstein," Lizzy ventured. "You have no pressing business in Matlock, do you?"

"No. But we were to travel north by the end of this week."

"Surely we might stay a while longer, Victor," said Clerval. "Your research can wait for you in Scotland."

Frankenstein struggled with his answer. "I don't think we should prevail on these good people any more."

"Nonsense," said Darcy. "We are fortunate for your company."

"Thank you," Frankenstein said uncertainly. But when the conversation moved elsewhere, Mary noticed him once again staring out the window. She moved to sit beside him. On an impulse, she said to him, sotto voce, "Did you know this man we came upon in the woods?"

"I saw no one. Even if someone was there, how should I know some English vagabond?"

"I do not think he was English. When he called after us, it was in German. Was this one of your countrymen?"

A look of impatience crossed Frankenstein's face, and he lowered his eyes. "Miss Bennet, I do not wish to contradict you, but you are mistaken. I saw no one in the woods."

Kitty developed a fever, and did not leave her bed for the rest of the day. Mary sat with her, trying, without bringing up the subject of Robert Piggot, to quiet her.

It was still raining when Mary retired, to a separate bedroom from the one she normally shared with Kitty. Late that night, Mary was wakened by the opening of her bedroom door. She thought it might be Lizzy to tell her something about Kitty. But it was not Lizzy.

Rather than call out, she watched silently as a dark figure entered and closed the door behind. The remains of her fire threw faint light on the man as he approached her. "Miss Bennet," he called softly.

Her heart was in her throat. "Yes, Mr. Frankenstein."

"Please do not take alarm. I must speak with you." He took two sudden steps toward her bed. His handsome face was agitated. No man, in any circumstances remotely resembling these, had ever broached her bedside. Yet the racing of her heart was not entirely a matter of fear.

"This, sir, is hardly the place for polite conversation," she said. "Following on your denial of what I saw this afternoon, you are fortunate that I do not wake the servants and have you thrown out of Pemberley."

"You are right to chide me. My conscience chides me more than you ever could, and should I be thrown from your family's gracious company it would be less than I deserve. And I am afraid that nothing I have to say to you tonight shall qualify as polite conversation." His manner was greatly changed; there was a sound of desperation in his whisper. He wanted something from her, and he wanted it a great deal.

Curious, despite herself, Mary drew on her robe and lit a candle. She made him sit in one of the chairs by the fire and poked the coals into life. When she had settled herself in the other, she said, "Go on."

"Miss Bennet, please do not toy with me. You know why I am here."

"Know, sir? What do I know?"

He leaned forward, earnestly, hands clasped and elbows on his knees. "I come to beg you to keep silent. The gravest consequences would follow your revealing my secret."

"Silent?"

"About—about the man you saw."

"You *do* know him!"

"Your mockery at dinner convinced me that, after hearing the vicar's story, you suspected. Raising the dead, you said to Clerval—and then your tale of Professor Aldini. Do not deny it."

"I don't pretend to know what you are talking about."

Frankenstein stood from his chair and began to pace the floor before the hearth. "Please! I saw the look of reproach in your eyes when we found you in the forest. I am trying to make right what I put wrong. But I will never be able to do so if you tell." To Mary's astonishment, she saw, in the firelight, that his eyes glistened with tears.

"Tell me what you did."

And with that the story burst out of him. He told her how, after his mother's death, he longed to conquer death itself, how he had studied chemistry at the university, how he had uncovered the secret of life. How, emboldened and driven on by his solitary obsession, he had created a man from the corpses he had stolen from graveyards and purchased from resurrection men. How he had succeeded, through his science, in bestowing it with life.

Mary did not know what to say to this astonishing tale. It was the raving of a lunatic—but there was the man she had seen in the woods. And the earnestness with which Frankenstein spoke, his tears and desperate whispers, gave every proof that, at least in his mind, he had done these things. He told of his revulsion at his accomplishment, how he had abandoned the creature, hoping it would die, and how the creature had, in revenge, killed his brother William and caused his family's ward Justine to be blamed for the crime.

"But why did you not intervene in Justine's trial?"

"No one should have believed me."

"Yet I am to believe you now?"

Frankenstein's voice was choked. "You have seen the brute. You know that these things are possible. Lives are at stake. I come to you in remorse and penitence, asking only that you keep this secret." He fell to his knees, threw his head into her lap, and clutched at the sides of her gown.

Frankenstein was wholly mistaken in what she knew; he was a man who did not see things clearly. Yet if his story were true, it was no wonder that his judgment was disordered. And here he lay, trembling against her, a boy seeking forgiveness. No man had ever come to her in such need.

She tried to keep her senses. "Certainly the creature I saw was frightening, but to my eyes he appeared more wretched than menacing."

Frankenstein lifted his head. "Here I must warn you—his wretchedness is mere mask. Do not let your sympathy for him cause you ever to trust his nature. He is the vilest creature that has ever walked this earth. He has no soul."

"Why then not invoke the authorities, catch him, and bring him to justice?"

"He cannot be so easily caught. He is inhumanly strong, resourceful, and intelligent. If you should ever be so unlucky as to speak with him, I warn you not to listen to what he says, for he is immensely articulate and satanically persuasive."

"All the more reason to see him apprehended!"

"I am convinced that he can be dealt with only by myself."

Frankenstein's eyes pleaded with her. "Miss Bennet—Mary—you must understand. He is in some ways my son. I gave him life. His mind is fixed on me."

"And, it seems, yours on him."

Frankenstein looked surprised. "Do you wonder that is so?"

"Why does he follow you? Does he intend you harm?"

"He has vowed to glut the maw of death with my remaining loved ones, unless I make him happy." He rested his head again in her lap.

Mary was touched, scandalized, and in some obscure way aroused. She felt his trembling body, instinct with life. Tentatively, she rested her hand on his head. She stroked his hair. He was weeping. She realized that he was a physical being, a living animal, that would eventually, too soon, die. And all that was true of him was true of herself. How strange, frightening, and sad. Yet in this moment she felt herself wonderfully alive.

"I'll keep your secret," she said.

He hugged her skirts. In the candle's light, she noted the way his thick, dark hair curled away from his brow.

"I cannot tell you," he said softly, "what a relief it is to share my burden with another soul, and to have her accept me. I have been so completely alone. I cannot thank you enough."

He rose, kissed her forehead, and was gone.

Mary paced her room, trying to grasp what had just happened. A man who had conquered death? A monster created from corpses? Such things did not happen, certainly not in her world, not even in the world of the novels she read. She climbed into bed and tried to sleep, but could not. The creature had vowed to kill all whom Frankenstein loved. Mary remembered the weight of his head upon her lap.

The room felt stiflingly hot. She got up, stripped off her nightgown, and climbed back between the sheets, where she lay naked, listening to the rain on the window.

Kitty's fever worsened in the night, and before dawn Darcy sent to Lambton for the doctor. Lizzy dispatched an urgent letter to Mr. and Mrs. Bennet, and the sisters sat by Kitty's bedside through the morning, changing cold compresses from her brow while Kitty labored to breathe.

When Mary left the sick room, Frankenstein approached her. His desperation of the previous night was gone. "How fares your sister?"

"I fear she is gravely ill."

"She is in some danger?"

Mary could only nod.

He touched her shoulder, lowered his voice. "I will pray for her, Miss Bennet. I cannot thank you enough for the sympathy you showed me last night. I have never told anyone—"

Just then Clerval approached them. He greeted Mary, inquired after Kitty's condition, then suggested to Frankenstein that they return to their hotel in Matlock rather than add any burden to the household and family. Frankenstein agreed. Before Mary could say another word to him in private, the visitors were gone.

Doctor Phillips arrived soon after Clerval and Frankenstein left. He measured Kitty's pulse, felt her forehead, examined her urine. He administered some medicines, and came away shaking his head. Should the fever continue, he said, they must bleed her.

Given how much thought she had spent on Frankenstein through the night, and how little she had devoted to Kitty, Mary's conscience tormented her. She spent the day in her sister's room. That night, after Jane had retired and Lizzy fallen asleep in her chair, she still sat up, holding Kitty's fevered hand. She had matters to consider. Was Kitty indeed with child, and if so, should she tell the doctor? Yet even as she sat by Kitty's bedside, Mary's mind cast back to the feeling of Frankenstein's lips on her forehead.

In the middle of the night, Kitty woke, bringing Mary from her doze. Kitty tried to lift her head from the pillow, but could not. "Mary," she whispered. "You must send for Robert. We must be married immediately."

Mary looked across the room at Lizzy. She was still asleep.

"Promise me," Kitty said. Her eyes were large and dark.

"I promise," Mary said.

"Prepare my wedding dress," Kitty said. "But don't tell Lizzy."

Lizzy awoke then. She came to the bedside and felt Kitty's forehead. "She's burning up. Get Dr. Phillips."

Mary sought out the doctor, and then, while he went to Kitty's room, pondered what to do. Kitty clearly was not in her right mind. Her request

ran contrary to both sense and propriety. If Mary sent one of the footmen
to Matlock for Robert, even if she swore her messenger to silence, the
matter would soon be the talk of the servants, and probably the town.

It was the sort of dilemma that Mary would have had no trouble
settling, to everyone's moral edification, when she was sixteen. She hurried
to her room and took out paper and pen:

> *I write to inform you that one you love, residing at Pemberley House,
> is gravely ill. She urgently requests your presence. Simple human
> kindness, which from her description of you I do not doubt you
> possess, let alone the duty incumbent upon you owing to the compact
> that you have made with her through your actions, assure me that we
> shall see you here before the night is through.*
>
> Miss Mary Bennet

She sealed the letter and sought out one of the footmen, whom she
dispatched immediately with the instruction to put the letter into the
hand of Robert Piggot, son of the Matlock butcher.

Dr. Phillips bled Kitty, with no improvement. She did not regain
consciousness through the night. Mary waited. The footman returned,
alone, at six in the morning. He assured Mary that he had ridden to the
Piggot home and given the letter directly to Robert. Mary thanked him.

Robert did not come. At eight in the morning Darcy sent for the
priest. At nine-thirty Kitty died.

On the evening of the day of Kitty's passing, Mr. and Mrs. Bennet
arrived, and a day later Lydia and Wickham—it was the first time Darcy
had allowed Wickham to cross the threshold of Pemberley since they had
become brothers by marriage. In the midst of her mourning family, Mary
felt lost. Jane and Lizzy supported each other in their grief. Darcy and
Bingley exchanged quiet, sober conversation. Wickham and Lydia, who
had grown fat with her three children, could not pass a word between
them without sniping, but in their folly they were completely united.

Mrs. Bennet was beyond consoling, and the volume and intensity of
her mourning was exceeded only by the degree to which she sought to
control every detail of Kitty's funeral. There ensued a long debate over

where Kitty should be buried. When it was pointed out that their cousin Mr. Collins would eventually inherit the house back in Hertfordshire, Mrs. Bennet fell into despair: who, when she was gone, would tend to her poor Kitty's grave? Mr. Bennet suggested that Kitty be laid to rest in the churchyard at Lambton, a short distance from Pemberley, where she might also be visited by Jane and Bingley. But when Mr. Darcy offered the family vault at Pemberley, the matter was quickly settled to the satisfaction of both tender hearts and vanity.

Though it was no surprise to Mary, it was still a burden for her to witness that even in the gravest passage of their lives, her sisters and parents showed themselves to be exactly what they were. And yet, paradoxically, this did not harden her heart toward them. The family was together as they had not been for many years, and she realized that they should never be in the future except on the occasion of further losses. Her father was grayer and quieter than she had ever seen him, and on the day of the funeral even her mother put aside her sobbing and exclamations long enough to show a face of profound grief, and a burden of age that Mary had never before noticed.

The night after Kitty was laid to rest, Mary sat up late with Jane and Lizzy and Lydia. They drank Madeira and Lydia told many silly stories of the days she and Kitty had spent in flirtations with the regiment. Mary climbed into her bed late that night, her head swimming with wine, laughter, and tears. She lay awake, the moonlight shining on the counterpane through the opened window, air carrying the smell of fresh earth and the rustle of trees above the lake. She drifted into a dreamless sleep. At some point in the night she was half awakened by the barking of the dogs in the kennel. But consciousness soon faded and she fell away.

In the morning it was discovered that the vault had been broken into and Kitty's body stolen from her grave.

Mary told the stablemaster that Mrs. Bennet had asked her to go to the apothecary in Lambton, and had him prepare the gig for her. Then, while the house was in turmoil and Mrs. Bennet being attended by the rest of the family, she drove off to Matlock. The master had given her the best horse in Darcy's stable; the creature was equable and quick, and despite her inexperience driving, Mary was able to reach Matlock in an hour.

All the time, despite the splendid summer morning and the picturesque
prospects which the valley of the Derwent continually unfolded before
her, she could not keep her mind from whirling through a series of
distressing images—among them the sight of Frankenstein's creature as
she had seen him in the woods.

When she reached Matlock she hurried to the Old Bath Hotel and
inquired after Frankenstein. The concierge told her that he had not seen
Mr. Frankenstein since dinner the previous evening, but that Mr. Clerval
had told him that morning that the gentlemen would leave Matlock later
that day. She left a note asking Frankenstein, should he return, to meet
her at the inn, then went to the butcher shop.

Mary had been there once before, with Lizzy, some years earlier. The
shop was busy with servants purchasing joints of mutton and ham for
the evening meal. Behind the counter, Mr. Piggot senior was busy at his
cutting board, but helping one of the women with a package was a tall
young man with thick brown curls and green eyes. He flirted with the
house servant as he shouldered her purchase, wrapped in brown paper,
onto her cart.

On the way back into the shop, he spotted Mary standing unattended.
He studied her for a moment before approaching. "May I help you,
miss?"

"I believe you knew my sister."

His grin vanished. "You are Miss Mary Bennet."

"I am."

The young man studied his boots. "I am so sorry what happened to
Miss Catherine."

Not so sorry as to bring you to her bedside before she died, Mary
thought. She bit back a reproach and said, "We did not see you at the
service. I thought perhaps the nature of your relationship might have
encouraged you to grieve in private, at her graveside. Have you been
there?"

He looked even more uncomfortable. "No. I had to work. My
father—"

Mary had seen enough already to measure his depth. He was not a
man to defile a grave, in grief or otherwise. The distance between this
small-town lothario—handsome, careless, insensitive—and the hero

Kitty had praised, only deepened Mary's compassion for her lost sister. How desperate she must have been. How pathetic.

As Robert Piggot continued to stumble through his explanation, Mary turned and departed.

She went back to the inn where she had left the gig. The barkeep led her into a small ladies' parlor separated from the taproom by a glass partition. She ordered tea, and through a latticed window watched the people come and go in the street and courtyard, the draymen with their percherons and carts, the passengers waiting for the next van to Manchester, and inside, the idlers sitting at tables with pints of ale. In the sunlit street a young bootblack accosted travelers, most of whom ignored him. All of these people alive, completely unaware of Mary or her lost sister. Mary ought to be back with their mother, though the thought turned her heart cold. How could Kitty have left her alone? She felt herself near despair.

She was watching through the window as two draymen struggled to load a large square trunk onto their cart when the man directing them came from around the team of horses, and she saw it was Frankenstein. She rose immediately and went out into the inn yard. She was at his shoulder before he noticed her. "Miss Bennet!"

"Mr. Frankenstein. I am so glad that I found you. I feared that you had already left Matlock. May we speak somewhere in private?"

He looked momentarily discommoded. "Yes, of course," he said. To the draymen he said, "When you've finished loading my equipment, wait here."

"This is not a good place to converse," Frankenstein told her. "I saw a churchyard nearby. Let us retire there."

He walked Mary down the street to the St. Giles Churchyard. They walked through the rectory garden. In the distance, beams of afternoon sunlight shone through a cathedral of clouds above the Heights of Abraham. "Do you know what has happened?" she asked.

"I have heard reports, quite awful, of the death of your sister. I intended to write you, conveying my condolences, at my earliest opportunity. You have my deepest sympathies."

"Your creature! That monster you created—"

"I asked you to keep him a secret."

"I have kept my promise—so far. But it has stolen Kitty's body."

He stood there, hands behind his back, clear eyes fixed on her. "You find me astonished. What draws you to this extraordinary conclusion?"

She was hurt by his diffidence. Was this the same man who had wept in her bedroom? "Who else might do such a thing?"

"But why? This creature's enmity is reserved for me alone. Others feel its ire only to the extent that they are dear to me."

"You came to plead with me that night because you feared I knew he was responsible for defiling that town girl's grave. Why was he watching Kitty and me in the forest? Surely this is no coincidence."

"If, indeed, the creature has stolen your sister's body, it can be for no reason I can fathom, or that any God-fearing person ought to pursue. You know I am determined to see this monster banished from the world of men. You may rest assured that I will not cease until I have seen this accomplished. It is best for you and your family to turn your thoughts to other matters." He touched a strand of ivy growing up the side of the garden wall, and plucked off a green leaf, which he twirled in his fingers.

She could not understand him. She knew him to be a man of sensibility, to have a heart capable of feeling. His denials opened a possibility that she had tried to keep herself from considering. "Sir, I am not satisfied. It seems to me that you are keeping something from me. You told me of the great grief you felt at the loss of your mother, how it moved you to your researches. If, as you say, you have uncovered the secret of life, might you—have you taken it upon yourself to restore Kitty? Perhaps a fear of failure, or of the horror that many would feel at your trespassing against God's will, underlies your secrecy. If so, please do not keep the truth from me. I am not a girl."

He let the leaf fall from his fingers. He took her shoulders, and looked directly into her eyes. "I am sorry, Mary. To restore your sister is not in my power. The soulless creature I brought to life bears no relation to the man from whose body I fashioned him. Your sister has gone on to her reward. Nothing—nothing I can do would bring her back."

"So you know nothing about the theft of her corpse?"

"On that score, I can offer no consolation to you or your family."

"My mother, my father—they are inconsolable."

"Then they must content themselves with memories of your sister as she lived. As I must do with my dear, lost brother William, and the traduced and dishonored Justine. Come, let us go back to the inn."

Mary burst into tears. He held her to him and she wept on his breast. Eventually she gathered herself and allowed him to take her arm, and they slowly walked back down to the main street of Matlock and the inn. She knew that when they reached it, Frankenstein would go. The warmth of his hand on hers almost made her beg him to stay, or better still, to take her with him.

They came to the busy courtyard. The dray stood off to the side, and Mary saw the cartmen were in the taproom. Frankenstein, agitated, upbraided them. "I thought I told you to keep those trunks out of the sun."

The older of the two men put down his pint and stood, "Sorry, Gov'nor. We'll see to it directly."

"Do so now."

As Frankenstein spoke the evening coach drew up before the inn and prepared for departure. "You and Mr. Clerval leave today?" Mary asked.

"Yes. As soon Henry arrives from the Old Bath, we take the coach to the Lake District. And thence to Scotland."

"They say it is very beautiful there."

"I am afraid that its beauty will be lost on me. I carry the burden of my great crime, not to be laid down until I have made things right."

She felt that she would burst if she did not speak her heart to him. "Victor. Will I ever see you again?"

He avoided her gaze. "I am afraid, Miss Bennet, that this is unlikely. My mind is set on banishing that vile creature from the world of men. Only then can I hope to return home and marry my betrothed Elizabeth."

Mary looked away from him. A young mother was adjusting her son's collar before putting him on the coach. "Ah, yes. You are affianced. I had almost forgotten."

Frankenstein pressed her hand. "Miss Bennet, you must forgive me the liberties I have taken with you. You have given me more of friendship than I deserve. I wish you to find the companion you seek, and to live your days in happiness. But now, I must go."

"God be with you, Mr. Frankenstein." She twisted her gloved fingers into a knot.

He bowed deeply, and hurried to have a few more words with the draymen. Henry Clerval arrived just as the men climbed to their cart and drove the baggage away. Clerval, surprised at seeing Mary, greeted her warmly. He expressed his great sorrow at the loss of her sister, and begged her to convey his condolences to the rest of her family. Ten minutes later the two men climbed aboard the coach and it left the inn, disappearing down the Matlock high street.

Mary stood in the inn yard. She did not feel she could bear to go back to Pemberley and face her family, the histrionics of her mother. Instead she reentered the inn and made the barkeep seat her in the ladies' parlor and bring her a bottle of port.

The sun declined and shadows stretched over the inn yard. The evening papers arrived from Nottingham. The yard boy lit the lamps. Still, Mary would not leave. Outside on the pavements, the bootblack sat in the growing darkness with his arms draped over his knees and head on his breast. She listened to the hoofs of the occasional horse striking the cobbles. The innkeeper was solicitous. When she asked for a second bottle, he hesitated, and wondered if he might send for someone from her family to take her home.

"You do not know my family," she said.

"Yes, miss. I only thought—"

"Another port. Then leave me alone."

"Yes, miss." He went away. She was determined to become intoxicated. How many times had she piously warned against young women behaving as she did now? *Virtue is its own reward.* She had an apothegm for every occasion, and had tediously produced them in place of thought. *Show me a liar, and I'll show thee a thief. Marry in haste, repent at leisure. Men should be what they seem.*

She did not fool herself into thinking that her current misbehavior would make any difference. Perhaps Bingley or Darcy had been dispatched to find her in Lambton. But within an hour or two she would return to Pemberley, where her mother would scold her for giving them an anxious evening, and Lizzy would caution her about the risk to her reputation. Lydia might even ask her, not believing it possible, if she had an assignation with some man. The loss of Kitty would overshadow Mary's indiscretion, pitiful as it had been. Soon all would be as it had been, except Mary would be alive and Kitty dead. But even that would fade. The shadow of Kitty's death would hang over the family for some time, but she doubted that anything of significance would change.

As she lingered over her glass, she looked up and noticed, in the now empty taproom, a man sitting at the table farthest from the lamps. A huge man, wearing rough clothes, his face hooded and in shadow. On the table in front of him was a tankard of ale and a few coppers. Mary rose, left the parlor for the taproom, and crossed toward him.

He looked up, and the faint light from the ceiling lamp caught his black eyes, sunken beneath heavy brows. He was hideously ugly. "May I sit with you?" she asked. She felt slightly dizzy.

"You may sit where you wish." The voice was deep, but swallowed, unable to project. It was almost a whisper.

Trembling only slightly, she sat. His wrists and hands, resting on the table, stuck out past the ragged sleeves of his coat. His skin was yellowish brown, and the fingernails livid white. He did not move. "You have some business with me?"

"I have the most appalling business." Mary tried to look him in the eyes, but her gaze kept slipping. "I want to know why you defiled my sister's grave, why you have stolen her body, and what you have done with her."

"Better you should ask Victor. Did he not explain all to you?"

"Mr. Frankenstein explained who—what—you are. He did not know what had become of my sister."

The thin lips twitched in a sardonic smile. "Poor Victor. He has got things all topsy-turvy. Victor does not know what I am. He is incapable of knowing, no matter the labors I have undertaken to school him. But he does know what became, and is to become, of your sister." The creature tucked the thick black hair behind his ear, a sudden unconscious gesture that made him seem completely human for the first time. He pulled the hood further forward to hide his face.

"So tell me."

"Which answer do you want? Who I am, or what happened to your sister?"

"First, tell me what happened to—to Kitty."

"Victor broke into the vault and stole her away. He took the utmost care not to damage her. He washed her fair body in diluted carbolic acid, and replaced her blood with a chemical admixture of his own devising. Folded up, she fit neatly within a cedar trunk sealed with pitch, and is at present being shipped to Scotland. You witnessed her departure from this courtyard an hour ago."

Mary's senses rebelled. She covered her face with her hands. The creature sat silent. Finally, without raising her head, she managed, "Victor warned me that you were a liar. Why should I believe you?"

"You have no reason to believe me."

"*You* took her!"

"Though I would not have scrupled to do so, I did not. Miss Bennet, I do not deny I have an interest in this matter. Victor did as I have told you at my bidding."

"At your bidding? Why?"

"Kitty—or not so much Kitty, as her remains—is to become my wife."

"Your wife! This is insupportable! Monstrous!"

"Monstrous." Suddenly, with preternatural quickness, his hand flashed out and grabbed Mary's wrist.

Mary thought to call for help, but the bar was empty and she had driven the innkeeper away. Yet his grip was not harsh. His hand was warm, instinct with life. "Look at me," he said. With his other hand he pushed back his hood.

She took a deep breath. She looked.

His noble forehead, high cheekbones, strong chin, and wide-set eyes might have made him handsome, despite the scars and dry yellow skin, were it not for his expression. His ugliness was not a matter of lack of proportion—or rather, the lack of proportion was not in his features. Like his swallowed voice, his face was submerged, as if everything was hidden, revealed only in the eyes, the twitch of a cheek or lip. Every minute motion showed extraordinary animation. Hectic sickliness, but energy. This was a creature who had never learned to associate with civilized company, who had been thrust into adulthood with the passions of a wounded boy. Fear, self-disgust, anger. Desire.

The force of longing and rage in that face made her shrink. "Let me go," she whispered.

He let go her wrist. With bitter satisfaction, he said, "You see. If what I demand is insupportable, that is only because your kind has done nothing to support me. Once, I falsely hoped to meet with beings who, pardoning my outward form, would love me for the excellent qualities which I was capable of bringing forth. Now I am completely alone. More than any starving man on a deserted isle, I am cast away. I have no brother, sister, parents. I have only Victor, who, like so many fathers, recoiled from me the moment I first drew breath. And so, I have commanded him to make of your sister my wife, or he and all he loves will die at my hand."

"No. I cannot believe he would commit this abomination."

"He has no choice. He is my slave."

"His conscience could not support it, even at the cost of his life."

"You give him too much credit. You all do. He does not think. I have not seen him act other than according to impulse for the last three years. That is all I see in any of you."

Mary drew back, trying to make some sense of this horror. Her sister, to be brought to life, only to be given to this fiend. But would it be her sister, or another agitated, hungry thing like this?

She still retained some scraps of skepticism. The creature's manner did not bespeak the isolation which he claimed. "I am astonished at your grasp of language," Mary said. "You could not know so much without teachers."

"Oh, I have had many teachers." The creature's mutter was rueful. "You might say that, since first my eyes opened, mankind has been all my study. I have much yet to learn. There are certain words whose meaning has never been proved to me by experience. For example: *Happy.* Victor is to make me happy. Do you think he can do it?"

Mary thought of Frankenstein. Could he satisfy this creature? "I do not think it is in the power of any other person to make one happy."

"You jest with me. Every creature has its mate, save me. I have none."

She recoiled at his self-pity. Her fear faded. "You put too much upon having a mate."

"Why? You know nothing of what I have endured."

"You think that having a female of your own kind will ensure that she will accept you?" Mary laughed. "Wait until you are rejected, for the most trivial of reasons, by one you are sure has been made for you."

A shadow crossed the creature's face. "That will not happen."

"It happens more often than not."

"The female that Victor creates shall find no other mate than me."

"That has never prevented rejection. Or if you should be accepted, then you may truly begin to learn."

"Learn what?"

"You will learn to ask a new question: Which is worse, to be alone, or to be wretchedly mismatched?" Like Lydia and Wickham, Mary thought. Like Collins and his poor wife Charlotte. Like her parents.

The creature's face spasmed with conflicting emotions. His voice gained volume. "Do not sport with me. I am not your toy."

"No. You only seek a toy of your own."

The creature was not, apparently, accustomed to mockery. "You must not say these things!" He lurched upward, awkwardly, so suddenly that he upended the table. The tankard of beer skidded across the top and spilled on Mary, and she fell back.

At that moment the innkeeper entered the bar room with two other men. They saw the tableau and rushed forward. "Here! Let her be!" he shouted. One of the other men grabbed the creature by the arm. With a roar the creature flung him aside like an old coat. His hood fell back. The men stared in horror at his face. The creature's eyes met Mary's, and with inhuman speed he whirled and ran out the door.

The men gathered themselves together. The one whom the creature had thrown aside had a broken arm. The innkeeper helped Mary to her feet. "Are you all right, miss?"

Mary felt dizzy. Was she all right? What did that mean?

"I believe so," she said.

When Mary returned to Pemberley, late that night, she found the house in an uproar over her absence. Bingley and Darcy both had been to Lambton, and had searched the road and the woods along it throughout the afternoon and evening. Mrs. Bennet had taken to bed with the conviction that she had lost two daughters in a single week. Wickham condemned Mary's poor judgment, Lydia sprang to Mary's defense, and this soon became a row over Wickham's lack of an income and Lydia's mismanagement of their children. Mr. Bennett closed himself up in the library.

Mary told them only that she had been to Matlock. She offered no explanation, no apology. Around the town the story of her conflict with the strange giant in the inn was spoken of for some time, along with rumors of Robert Piggot the butcher's son, and the mystery of Kitty's defiled grave—but as Mary was not a local, and nothing of consequence followed, the talk soon passed away.

That winter, Mary came upon the following story in the Nottingham newspaper.

Ghastly Events in Scotland

Our northern correspondent files the following report. In early November, the body of a young foreigner, Mr. Henry Clerval of Geneva, Switzerland, was found upon the beach near the far northern town of Thurso. The body, still warm, bore marks of strangulation. A second foreigner, Mr. Victor Frankstone, was taken into custody, charged with the murder, and held for two months. Upon investigation, the magistrate Mr. Kirwan determined that Mr. Frankstone was in the Orkney Islands at the time of the killing. The accused was released in the custody of his father, and is assumed to have returned to his home on the continent.

A month after the disposition of these matters, a basket, weighted with stones and containing the body of a young woman, washed up in the estuary of the River Thurso. The identity of the woman is unknown, and her murderer undiscovered, but it is speculated that the unfortunate may have died at the hands of the same person or persons who murdered Mr. Clerval. The woman was given Christian burial in the Thurso Presbyterian churchyard.

The village has been shaken by these events, and prays God to deliver it from evil.

Oh, Victor, Mary thought. She remembered the pressure of his hand, through her dressing gown, upon her thigh. Now he had returned to Switzerland, there, presumably, to marry his Elizabeth. She hoped that he would be more honest with his wife than he had been with her, but the fate of Clerval did not bode well. And the creature still had no mate.

She clipped the newspaper report and slipped it into the drawer of her writing table, where she kept her copy of Samuel Galton's *The Natural History of Birds, Intended for the Amusement and Instruction of Children*, and the *Juvenile Anecdotes* of Priscilla Wakefield, and a Dudley locust made of stone, and a paper fan from the first ball she had ever attended, and a dried wreath of flowers that had been thrown to her, when she was nine years old, from the top of a tree by one of the town boys playing near Meryton common.

After the death of her parents, Mary lived with Lizzy and Darcy at Pemberley for the remainder of her days. Under a pen name, she pursued a career as a writer of philosophical speculations, and sent many letters to the London newspapers. Aunt Mary, as she was called at home, was known for her kindness to William, and to his wife and children. The children teased Mary for her nearsightedness, her books, and her piano. But for a woman whose experience of the world was so slender, and whose soul it seemed had never been touched by any passion, she came at last to be respected for her understanding, her self-possession, and her wise counsel on matters of the heart.

John Kessel co-directs the creative writing program at North Carolina State University in Raleigh. A winner of the Nebula Award, the Theodore Sturgeon Award, the Locus Poll, and the James Tiptree, Jr. Award, his books include *Good News from Outer Space*, *Corrupting Dr. Nice*, and *The Pure Product*. His story collection, *Meeting in Infinity*, was named a notable book of 1992 by the *New York Times Book Review*. Writer Kim Stanley Robinson has called *Corrupting Dr. Nice* "the best time travel novel ever written."

Kessel recently coedited two anthologies with James Patrick Kelly, *Feeling Very Strange: The Slipstream Anthology* and *Rewired: The Post-Cyberpunk Anthology*. Kessel lives with his family in Raleigh, North Carolina.